D1452947

Sweatshops on Wheels

Sweatshops on Wheels

Winners and Losers
in Trucking Deregulation

Michael H. Belzer

OXFORD
UNIVERSITY PRESS

2000

OXFORD
UNIVERSITY PRESS

Oxford New York
Athens Auckland Bangkok Bogatá Buenos Aires Calcutta
Cape Town Chennai Dar es Salaam Delhi Florence Hong Kong Istanbul
Karachi Kuala Lumpar Madrid Melbourne Mexico City Mumbai
Nairobi Paris São Paulo Singapore Taipei Tokyo Toronto Warsaw

and associated companies in
Berlin Ibadan

Copyright © 2000 by Oxford University Press

Published by Oxford University Press, Inc.
198 Madison Avenue, New York, New York 10016

Oxford is a registered trademark of Oxford University Press

Library of Congress Cataloging-in-Publication Data
Belzer, Michael H.
Sweatshops on wheels : winners and losers in
trucking deregulation / Michael H. Belzer
p. cm.
Includes bibliographical references.
ISBN 0-19-512886-9
1. Trucking—Deregulation—United States.   I. Title.
HE5623 .B43 2000
388.3'24'0973—dc21   00-035970

Have a question or a comment about *Sweatshops on Wheels*?
Do you have a story to tell about your experience as a truck driver?
Send a message to the author at:
www.ilir.umich.edu/SweatshopsOnWheels
or e-mail to: SweatshopsOnWheels@umich.edu.

1 3 5 7 9 8 6 4 2

Printed in the United States of America
on acid-free paper

To Charlotte and Kyle,
for their infinite patience and support

Preface

What would the world be like if we all worked like truck drivers? Imagine a world in which there is no effective minimum wage and no 40-hour workweek or time-and-one-half for overtime.

Imagine a world in which most people work more than 60 hours per week—not to get "ahead" but just to make ends meet.

Imagine a world in which most of us compete to offer our services at the lowest possible price but which is so competitive that we get what we want—and end up working longer hours just to earn enough to subsist.

Imagine a world in which people work like this with no regular schedule—irregular days and irregular hours, switching from day to night and back again with little predictability.

Imagine a world in which production workers' wages stop abruptly with every hiccup in the assembly line.

Imagine a world in which employers decide which work to pay you for and which you have to perform for free—and that work comprises 25% of your work day!

Imagine no further, because that is the life of the truck driver today in the hyper-competitive trucking industry. This book documents how truck drivers' work has changed over the last two decades of deregulation. Truck drivers work longer hours for lower real pay than they earned decades ago. They suffer the indignity of being forced to wait for hours to get loaded or unloaded while people whose time is more highly valued are taken care of first. Their work and pay structure often calls for them to forego compensation for their time in trade for the opportunity to put in extra hours to run extra miles every week, often keeping them away from home for weeks at a time.

Does this picture fit the model of the nineteenth-century sweat-shop? Long hours, low wages, and unsafe conditions characterized sweatshops a hundred years ago. Haven't we banished them to the dustbin of history? As we recently have learned, this economic environment can coexist in the modern world with our gleaming cities, prosperous stock market, and high-tech occupations. Workers in the service sector, just beneath the façade of our prosperity, labor to clean our hotels and office buildings, grow and cook our food, and deliver our freight. In today's market economy, while that work retains its inherent dignity, it no longer retains its pay.

How does this affect each one of us? Truck drivers, like others in the service sector, know the competitive forces in our economy very well. Construction workers too have seen wages and conditions fall over the past two or three decades, with low-wage workers and the practice of subcontracting increasingly threatening their standard of living. Other "blue-collar" workers throughout the manufacturing sector—especially those old enough to remember the 1980s—have experienced belt-tightening wage cuts, downsizing, and subcontracting over the past decades.

Recently, high-tech workers and professionals have begun to experience this same downward pressure. Many highly skilled workers, including those in the high-flying computer software industry, find themselves working extremely long hours in an effort to climb their career ladders, only to find themselves burned out early and replaced by a new group of energetic, ambitious, youthful professionals. During the late 1990s news stories began appearing with increasing frequency announcing union organizing efforts by computer programmers, doctors, and other professionals. Many professionals, especially creative ones, have found their industries transformed by economic forces they may dimly perceive but which have forced them to become independent contractors themselves, taking on multiple jobs and clients to patch together a career, while struggling to provide themselves with health and retirement benefits.

Who—or what—is the culprit? The simplistic answer blames employers for this state of affairs. After all, it is easy to see who apparently holds the power in this personal dynamic. A closer look, however, suggests that the individual competitiveness embedded in our economic institutions has a dark side: competition breeds winners and losers, and the market, by itself, does not care how they are distributed. It does not matter if competition makes a few winners extremely wealthy while a large number of losers become relatively poor, as long as average wealth increases.

The trucking industry gives us a powerful lens through which to view the effects of economic competitiveness. Since deregulation in 1980, trucking has become extremely competitive, with both good and bad effects. Distribution and logistics power our world economy, and the trucking industry today is more innovative and sophisticated than ever, providing tremendous value at a low cost. Indeed, trucking is the key link in the production and distribution chain, and the foundation on which our prosperity is built.

This book shows us the dark side of that competition. While economists build explanatory models based on perfect competition in which economic profits tend toward zero, with destructive competition profits may decline below zero. Trucking may be an industry on roller skates in which competition is so fierce that profits are below those needed to cover the opportunity cost of owners' equity and wages tend toward subsistence.

Low wages and long hours may actually be the mortar that holds together the foundations of distribution and trade, and those conditions characterize both labor and management in trucking. *Sweatshops on Wheels* documents the extent to which those who have drawn the short straw subsidize our prosperity and suggests the limits to which competition may push the losers. It also shows us that motor carriers are price-takers in this competitive world. That is, they do not have the power to raise wages substantially because they are caught in a race to the bottom. Trucking is a labor-intensive industry and transportation service is a commodity, subject to intense competitive pressure.

The problem therefore is more complex than a simple struggle between management and labor. The problem lies with public policy that supports unbridled competition in every sphere as a blanket solution to our social and economic problems. In our effort to replace government regulation with market institutions we may have thrown the baby out with the bath water. Since the market itself is a regulatory framework, we merely have replaced institutional regulation with market regulation. In the process, we may have created a raging bull that can do a lot of damage to civil society. Make no mistake: a democratic society cannot long coexist with the kind of deep social and economic stratification that we are developing today.

I wish to thank the following individuals for their help reading previous versions of the manuscript and giving me feedback and conceptual advice: Harry Katz, Susan Christopherson, and Vernon Briggs of Cornell; Stephen Herzenberg of the Keystone Research Center; Mark Junod, Paul Boldin, and Norman Weintraub from the Teamsters; Russell Capelle (formerly of the American Trucking Associations and now with the Bureau of Transportation Statistics); Jack Fiorito, Thomas Corsi (who provided key usable data sets), Stephen Burks (who also provided some research assistance), Eileen Appelbaum, Paula Voos, Lawrence Root, Greg Saltzman, and David Wazeter; and research assistant Andrew Lewis. To Professor Katz I credit the original inspiration for the book, to answer the fundamental question: "What if the rest of the work world looked like trucking?" I would like to give special thanks to Dale Belman, my colleague in the University of Michigan Trucking Industry Program who, with help from Kristen Monaco, directed the driver survey discussed in the book and was co-author of one of the articles from which this book was drawn. I wish also to thank Scott Cooper of Cooper Communications Consulting for extensive help assembling and editing this manuscript in preparation for publication.

I would also like to thank the following organizations for institutional support. My work has been in part sponsored by the Sloan Foundation, through its support of the University of Michigan Trucking Industry Program. During earlier phases of this research I also received support from the New York State School of Industrial and Labor Relations at Cornell University, the Institute of Collective Bargaining (also of Cornell), the Economic Policy Institute, and the late Office of Technology Assessment (formerly an agency of the Congress of the United States). Most recently I have received support from the University of Michigan Institute of Labor and Industrial Relations and the University of Michigan Trucking Industry Program. I received data from the American Trucking Associations and the International Brotherhood of Teamsters.

Some of the research in this book has previously appeared in the *Industrial and Labor Relations Review*, the *1995 Proceedings of the Industrial Relations Research Association, Contemporary Collective Bargaining in the Private Sector* and *Government Regulation of the Employment Relationship* (published by the Industrial Relations Research Association and edited by Paula Voos), and in *Paying the Toll*, a policy monograph for the Economic Policy Institute. A summary of this work also appeared in a much-edited and specialized form in *Dollars and Sense*.

I am grateful to my wife, Charlotte, and children, Erin, Neal, and Kyle, for their patience and support. For how many years have they listened to me wrestle with these issues?

Finally, I owe a great debt to the late Bennett Harrison, a professor of political economy, from whose work I have drawn inspiration and guidance. He has been missed.

Ann Arbor, Michigan   M. H. B.
January 2000

Contents

Sweatshops on Wheels

1 A New Look at Competitive Forces

Government regulation was one of the hallmarks of the first three quarters of the twentieth century in the United States. Whether to improve social or environmental conditions, ensure that those who create negative competitive externalities pay for them, assure fair business practices, or control prices, regulations have become a familiar part of the American economic landscape. Anyone who uses electricity, drives a car, talks on the telephone, or pays taxes is familiar with government regulation. Since the Ten Commandments, regulations have reached into every area of our social and economic relationships.

Public policy has undergone a veritable revolution during the last generation, however. Since the 1970s, and with particular earnest since 1980, government policy has been to dismantle regulation in favor of market competition, wherever possible. Deregulation has become an American mantra, appealing to values that are intrinsic to what often is referred to as the American psyche: liberty over control, individualism over community.

The industries that have been deregulated are myriad: long-distance telecommunications, airlines, trucking, construction, banking, and many others. Battles rage in state after state over how best to replace the regulated monopolized electric utility industry with an institutional framework that allows market forces to regulate the competition needed to lower prices and amplify service offerings.

The principal proponents of deregulation hold sway at the major international financial institutions such as the International Monetary Fund and the World Bank. They dominate the debate over trade and negotiate free trade policies. They prescribe a simple policy in country after country, industry after industry: unfettered competition is the best way to allocate national resources. In many instances, market proponents call for the elimination of all regulation. Those who disagree often are branded as hidebound conservatives, opposed to change and risk.

But unfettered competition often comes with considerable social and economic costs. Recognizing these costs and raising concerns about them is a far cry from abandoning market regulation or policies that support competition. Rather, full balancing of the benefits and costs of competition suggests a need to review the role of markets and institutions in public policy. Perhaps government policy should view competition as a force to be harnessed for economic and social purposes, rather than as a goal in itself. Government regulation is one tool we can use to channel competition to promote both efficiency and equity.

Just as we need to think carefully every time we consider establishing new regulations, we should examine free market policies empirically each time we consider stepping away from institutional regulation and toward market regulation. Unfortunately, though, we normally ask but two questions: does the policy lower prices and improve services, and is that a benefit to consumers?

I would like to suggest some other questions:

- How does the policy affect wages? How does it influence hours and working conditions? Does it increase the gap between winners and losers in the economic contest, or structurally alter the terms of competition to favor one group over another?
- Does the policy promote or undermine institutions that provide training and maintain standards? Does it encourage or discourage long-term investment in skills? Does it promote the high road or the low road to economic growth?
- How does the policy affect safety and health? Does competition create an unhealthy work environment and put workers at greater risk of occupational illness or injury? Especially important for trucking, does the policy make our highways safer or more dangerous? What is the potential risk to other motorists? Who pays the cost for added risk?

- If this policy is implemented, will we eventually need new regulations and incur additional costs to ensure the public welfare? Do the market incentives that promote efficiency for private goods encourage an optimal allocation of public goods?

This book about the trucking industry illustrates how deregulation—intense market competition—has affected one important segment of American industry. It shows in microcosm what deregulation has meant for many workers and may portend for workers in other extremely competitive industries. I decided to look at the trucking industry because I know it—I worked as an over-the-road truck driver for ten years—and because trucking deregulation clearly has transformed the lives of drivers, companies, and consumers. Using the trucking industry as a case study, my goal—to use the language of literary scholars—is to deconstruct deregulation, to tear it apart conceptually and gain an understanding in order to explore its ramifications and determine whether we need other policies to balance efficiency with equity.

Why Sweatshops?

Some readers may take issue with my use of the term "sweatshop" in the title. Sweatshops conjure up images of cramped, poorly illuminated, poorly ventilated chambers in which workers toil away at piecework, making a starvation wage by competing with one another to produce more product even as their employers cut rates in an unceasing struggle to compete based on price.

The literature on the "sweating system" extends back into the nineteenth century. Originally the term referred to a pre-industrial subcontracting system. Goods producers subcontracted routine work—the production of ready-made mass produced goods ("bespoke work" as opposed to custom goods)—to middlemen, called "sweaters," who made their profit from the margin between the money they earned for the contracted goods produced and the price they paid to their employees or subcontractors. The physical conditions under which the goods were made gave rise to the term "sweatshop," and the profit was made off the sweat of the workers.

By the late nineteenth and early twentieth century, the concept of sweatshop broadened to include employed as well as subcontracted workers. Observers recognized that sweating did not require subcontracting (indeed, some of the best paid workers were in the building trades, traditionally characterized by subcontracting). The key underlying conditions, however, remained unchanged.

Three general conditions characterized sweatshops.[1] First, the wages were so low that they were below subsistence. That is, they were so low that workers would be unable to support their families well enough to maintain the family's current class position and skill level and reproduce that level in succeeding generations. Wages this low were considered socially inefficient, as they would not entice less skilled workers to enhance their human capital enough to enter the trade, thus producing a vicious downward cycle of labor shortages in skilled trades and a surplus of low skilled workers. The evils of child labor developed as a consequence of this system. Low wages forced everyone in the family to go to work, and lack of nutrition left parents and children hungry and chronically ill. Since children were pressed into work (particularly at home or in small shops) at an early age they did not learn how to read and write and did not learn a skill, condemning them to follow in their parents' footsteps and adding to the undifferentiated low-skilled labor pool.

Wages were also characteristically based on piecework. Workers were paid based on their output, rather than based on the number of hours worked. The more goods one produced, the greater the income. The emphasis on quantity contributed to the growth of child labor, as everyone in the family pitched in. After all, since much of this "outwork" was done at home, it was a simple matter for wives and children to pitch in whenever their other tasks were complete. The piecework basis of pay naturally led to greater competition in the market place, further driving down wages and increasing hours of work.

The second necessary condition was overwork, a natural extension of low wage rates. As compensation rates declined during periods of the nineteenth century, workers extended their hours to make ends meet. Just as the sweating system drew in whole families, it encouraged workers to extend their work day and extend their work week. During the very period in which some workers were fighting for the ten and eight hour day, the mechanization of production and the development of the sweating system caused many workers' hours to increase. Records are sketchy on hours of work, since pay was by the piece, but it appears that the 12- to 14-hour day became commonplace and many workers put in six or seven days of work per week. One source devotes an entire chapter to nineteenth-century "traffic workers," men who drove wagons and omnibuses. Drivers averaged 15 hours a day and worked 13 days out of every two weeks.[2] Drivers who worked on long-haul "flying waggons" worked 60 to 70 hours per week in 24 hour shifts.[3]

Third, sweating involved unhealthy conditions of work. As technology made it possible to subdivide production into small workshops and homes (particularly with the invention of the sewing machine), workers crammed into small, poorly lit and ventilated rooms, creating the image we have in our minds today. Beyond lighting and ventilation, workers were exposed to high levels of poisonous chemicals, dangerous machinery, and the debilitating effects of fatigue and monotony.

So what does this have to do with trucking in the late twentieth century? This book will show that these three conditions of work—low wages, long hours, and unsafe and unsanitary working conditions—have returned to trucking since economic decontrol. While these conditions are not universal (and they were not universal during the nineteenth century either), they have become sufficiently widespread to produce the same problems: low wages, long hours, unsanitary conditions, fatigue, labor market churning, and skilled labor shortages.

It is critical to understand, however, that the presence of sweatshop-like conditions does not mean that evil, money-grubbing bosses just choose to exploit workers; that caricature would be a cartoon. If this were the problem it would hardly be a policy concern. Just as nineteenth-century sweaters did not get rich, today's trucking companies are not earning above normal profits. Unfettered competition drives the conditions of work in the trucking industry, as elsewhere—just as it did during the nineteenth century.

Most over-the-road truck drivers are paid according to a piecework standard: they earn their pay by the mile or as a percentage of freight revenue. Their incentives may be completely aligned with those of the firm. To augment their earnings, they "sweat" their labor—they increase the intensity of their work and extend their hours. Between 1977 and 1987 truck drivers' real mileage wage rates declined by 44%.[4] As effective hourly wages have declined, the only option left for individual drivers who are trying to maintain their standard of living is to increase earnings by driving faster and working more hours.

This seems like an unfair image for the trucking industry to shoulder, but economic deregulation has produced the kind of business competition that forces many trucking employers in some sectors to drive workers in a similarly intensive way. Where competition keeps freight rates low, and where few institutional limits act to keep a lid on labor market competition, drivers in some segments of the trucking industry increase the number of miles they drive and the hours they work to turn subsistence wages into enough earnings to maintain their families' living standards. Collective bargaining no longer appears to be a possibility for these workers, as their dispersion makes organization extremely difficult and ineffectual labor laws give employers wide leeway to fight unionization. Laws designed to protect individual labor standards do not help either, as hours-of-service regulations conflict with underlying competitive forces and are very difficult to enforce, with half of all over-the-road drivers exceeding legal limits.[5] Institutional restraints provided by the Fair Labor Standards Act (which mandates the 40-hour workweek and minimum wage for most workers) also do not apply fully in the trucking industry, further exacerbating the labor market competition. Loose regulation and uneven enforcement make trucking's labor market one of the nation's most unregulated.

Is the "sweatshop" analogy apt? Several similarities come to mind, as do several differences. While many low-wage drivers operate old and unsafe equipment, many others drive chrome-laden beauties with all the amenities a driver could desire. The most important similarity, however, is the fact that labor earns its pay by increasing its intensity—by working harder, not smarter. The labor and product markets are so competitive that the only way a driver can earn a living is by extending his hours. The only brake on work hours comes from fear of enforcement action, though enforcement is sufficiently spotty so that many drivers consider the threat remote enough that they can minimize it by prudent evasive action. This kind of labor market competition encourages drivers to reduce their rates to get the work and offset low wages by working longer and longer hours.

Workers in successful sweatshops may collaborate in the sweating process, and this condition holds for trucking. The work process in trucking is so decentralized that drivers sweat themselves. Perhaps most interesting, hundreds of thousands of owner operators (drivers who own and operate their own trucks and rent themselves and their trucks to carriers and shippers) commingle their labor and equipment revenue, providing a deep motivation for self-sweating. Many such drivers, hard for government agencies to monitor and easily slipping between the regulatory cracks, arguably do not understand their own cost of operation and willingly sweat their own labor to pay for their equipment as well as their labor, yet earn less than their employee-driver counterparts. While small businesses historically have depended on their owners' willingness to work long hours, the broad expansion of the use of owner operators in the trucking industry (like subcontracting in other industries) has opened a Pandora's box that contributes to the broad expansion of sweatshop conditions.

Before we explore trucking in depth, though, let us take a brief look at the history of deregulation.

The Deregulation Debate

Deregulation is a political term. Any economic system is regulated, at least by the market itself. In fact, our free market system has a slew of laws that define the limited liability corporation, fair and unfair business practices, and fraud and the limits of deception, along with a host of agencies entrusted with enforcement of laws and regulations designed to ensure that competition is effective and fair. The Securities and Exchange Commission must police Wall Street, for example, and prevent securities fraud and insider trading. Bankruptcy laws explicitly define the rules under which corporations may protect themselves from creditors and define the order in which creditors line up to claim the assets of firms in which they have an interest. An elaborate code of labor conduct defines the rules under which workers may enforce collective bargaining rights and also circumscribes discrimination on the basis of gender, race, and religion.

As this brief typology suggests, we can divide the concept of regulation into two broad categories: economic regulation and social regulation. While all rules have economic consequences, some are aimed at limiting social practices (such as discrimination), while others are aimed explicitly at defining the economic rules of engagement. Many social regulations deal with externalities created by the market (external effects of competitive processes, such as pollution, that the market does not regulate by itself). Economic regulations directly affect the market by regulating prices and market structure. Historically, utilities such as electric and gas, cable television, and telephone have been regulated monopolies because we did not want every potential competitor to string up its own wires or cables in an overlapping and duplicative network. We legislated licensed monopoly franchises that traded their monopoly market position for tight regulation of service and price.

During the last two decades, technological and political changes have encouraged the "deregulation" of many of these markets. The conceptual arguments in favor of replacing institutional regulation with market regulation have dominated the debate, feeding off the public's frustration with cumbersome, rigid, and sometimes unresponsive regulatory agencies and monopolies. Those defending the need for institutional regulation have been on the defensive, having lost sight of the rationale that spurred regulation originally. Our legislators continue to enact certain types of ground rules, primarily in the form of social regulation designed to restrict social and personal behavior (restrictions on abortion, drug use, and the like). They also have passed laws affecting the workplace, such as the Americans with Disabilities Act and the Family and Medical Leave Act, which circumscribe undesirable practices or encourage desirable ones.

The primary economic effort of legislators in the last two decades, however, has been to increase competition by lifting many of the economic regulations that have long governed U.S. industry. As markets operate more freely, much of the institutional framework governing them has withered away and competition has become more intense. Chapter 3 will provide a more detailed explanation distinguishing economic and social regulation, but the general trend has been to reduce economic regulation and allow markets to allocate resources and determine winners and losers, while using social regulation more broadly to limit the consequences of the ensuing negative externalities.

Price mechanisms increasingly regulate markets, including those in the core transportation industries of airlines, trucking, and railroads, as well as in telecommunications, banking, electric and gas, and others. Meanwhile, government has sharply curtailed its regulation of the economic activities of labor markets, bringing greater competition among employees for scarce employment opportunities and widening the gap between skilled and unskilled workers. Since the 1970s federal and state policymakers have loosened, repealed, and reinterpreted a wide variety of laws that have traditionally governed employment relations. Laws relating to area or "prevailing" wage standards, minimum wages, working at home, eligibility requirements for unemployment insurance, and disability standards under workers' compensation all have come under attack as part of the move toward unfettered labor market competition.

Increasing competition within the labor market has emboldened employers' labor relations practices. As labor market competition has increased within the United States and between workers in the United States and the rest of the world, the U.S. government has been less inclined to support free collective bargaining as a primary wage-setting tool. Although U.S. labor law prescribes collective bargaining by unionized workers as the nation's primary method of private sector wage-setting, continuing reinterpretation of the National Labor Relations Act by the National Labor Relations Board and by the courts (a reinterpretation tacitly endorsed by Congressional inaction) has severely limited employees' rights to organize and represent themselves collectively.[6] Unions today are hard to organize, and, once organized, workers find it extremely hard to negotiate first contracts. Even successive contracts have become difficult to negotiate as employers' relatively easy use of temporary and permanent replacement workers (along with intense competitive pressures) has reduced the national strike rate to historically low levels.

At the same time we have experienced a dramatic growth in the number of U.S. workers employed as subcontractors or temporaries, encouraged by judicial reinterpretations of labor law. The subcontracting process exposes an even greater portion of the labor force to the perils of an unconstrained market, because these workers enjoy virtually no protections—even compared to nonunion workers. Social regulations that have remained on the books to protect full-time workers rarely are extended to this growing number of nonstandard employees.

Finally, the free trade treaties sought by trade negotiators, embodied by the North American Free Trade Agreement (NAFTA) and the General Agreement on Tariffs and Trades (GATT; now known as the World Trade Organization), also have enhanced market competitiveness. These agreements, arguably constituting a deregulation of international trade, have made international labor markets extremely competitive, especially as international labor standards agreements lag behind the development of trade agreements.

The bottom line is that many workers now compete with one another on the basis of wages and working conditions in ways we have not seen since the early twentieth century, well before the Great Depression and the growth of unions internationally. To find such a competitive environment, we may have to go back as far as the second half of the nineteenth century, during which time workers fought unsuccessfully for regulations supporting the eight- or ten-hour day and for the right to be represented by trade unions. The future promises more of the same, as both state and federal legislators continue to push new rules encouraging market regulation in place of institutional regulation.

The political question, however, is not whether or not we allow the market to regulate economic affairs. The question is how best to organize and regulate markets. Should we leave economic processes completely unrestrained, or is the well-being of individuals and society better served if we harness the market processes through regulation and institutionalization? This book attempts to answer this question by examining the consequences of economic deregulation in the trucking industry.

Trucking: A Case Study of Market Competition

The deregulation of the trucking industry provides an example of the effects on labor of ending economic regulation of product markets. For nearly two decades, the trucking industry has functioned in a largely unregulated economic world. The goal of trucking deregulation was to get the government out of the industry and to let the market do its job. Deregulation's proponents argued that unregulated trucking is a competitive industry, and monopoly market power is impossible. Unlike government regulation of monopolies, regulation of trucking was designed to prevent overly intense competition. While it may have been necessary in the early days of trucking to protect the industry by limiting competition, this rationale has long since become obsolete. Competition should allocate capital and labor optimally, and everyone will be better off.

But some of the outcomes many analysts predicted have not come to pass. Trucking is indeed inherently competitive, with strong tendencies toward under-pricing and destructive competition. Many in the trucking industry, including employees and employers, have suffered serious losses and dislocations. Competitive forces have broken the industry into many competitive segments. Wages have declined considerably, and working conditions have deteriorated. Despite industry recognition of substandard wages, market forces have failed to keep driver earnings at the standard expected by similarly skilled workers in other industries, producing a widely recognized labor shortage.

Further, it appears as if the role of the Teamsters Union in protecting workers—and in doing so, perhaps the industry itself—has taken on a new and heightened significance. This book shows, more precisely and in a more nuanced way than previous studies, the union effect on wages and conditions in an extremely competitive economic environment.

Other studies of the effects of deregulation have shown a similar pattern of industry segmentation and wage dispersion. Airlines, the example most similar to trucking, concentrated following an initial period of new competition. As the airline industry shifted structurally, carriers developed a hub-and-spoke system similar to the hub-and-spoke system in trucking. Retreating behind these fortress hubs, airlines developed strong market power within their regions and near monopoly power at their hubs. Ownership consolidated into a few big airlines with identifiable regional concentration. The airlines' regional concentration is similar to that in trucking. Unlike trucking, however, regulation limiting the allocation of terminal gates allowed the hub-and-spoke system to become a fortress for the airlines creating market power.

Patterns of industrial relations in the airline industry also are similar to those in trucking, though the labor law framework is quite different. Union density declined somewhat, in part owing to outright union-busting such as at Continental Airlines; union settlements declined; and wage patterns differentiated among markets. The airline industry's original effort produced two-tier wage scales, but those contracts generally provided for low-wage new hires to catch up eventually with their senior co-workers. More recently, the airline industry has advocated successfully for the development of regional airlines, subsidiaries of the majors, that pay dramatically lower salaries and require more onerous work schedules and conditions. The recent dispute and strike at American Airlines resulted in part from the airline's move to expand a two-tier system in which fewer airline employees remain in the high-wage "national" sector and the airline shifts more work and employees into the low-wage "regional" sector. The same issue lies behind the recent conflict between USAirways and its employees. While the original two-tier wage system failed to bring wages down permanently, the two-tier systems envisioned by airlines today will produce a low-wage industry segment that eventually may overwhelm its high-wage parent.

Economists and private-sector manufacturing and distribution interests pushed hard for economic deregulation in trucking. Economists claimed regulation created a cartel from which the industry and its employees gained premium returns (called "rents") from unearned market power. Some economists explicitly sought the reduction of union bargaining power. At the very least, policymakers expected economic deregulation to increase competition and reduce rates charged by carriers.

"Economic regulation" affected the structure of the trucking industry. Before regulation, the industry suffered from very low rates of return and high levels of turnover among firms. The extremity of price competition, particularly when raiding less-than-carload freight from the railroads, kept labor costs low. While the system of regulation established under the Motor Carrier Act of 1935 created inefficiencies, it did stabilize the industry, addressing the problems of truckers, of shippers, and of the public, and provided a basis for resolving labor issues. While regulation did not raise wage rates directly, rate regulation provided the foundation for improving truckers' wages and working conditions, and the Teamsters Union became the vehicle for that improvement.

Deregulation abruptly replaced the rules of the old Interstate Commerce Commission (ICC) with the rules of the market, compelling carriers to redesign their business strategies quickly. Competition divided general commodity trucking into two segments, less-than-truckload (LTL) and truckload (TL). Less-than-truckload carriers maintained and even extended their terminal network structure, which was needed to sort and re-ship their small cargo (averaging perhaps 1,200 pounds). Truckload carriers got rid of any existing terminal structure and focused on large shipments (more than 10,000 pounds) that they picked up from shippers and delivered directly to consignees (see Glossary for definitions).

Most of the surviving carriers in the general freight segment of the trucking industry became LTL carriers, though some repositioned themselves in the TL market. New entry carriers, who gravitated almost exclusively to truckload, were not contractually obligated to maintain union-scale wages, health insurance, or pensions and were not burdened by the extensive capital investment in terminals implicitly required by earlier ICC regulations. By specializing, they could skim truckload freight from the general freight market—while removing the effects of collective bargaining as well. This truckload freight initially commanded relatively high tariffs, but soon competition in TL drove down rates, which carried wages down with them.

Industry restructuring drove down revenues and earnings, as trucking costs declined modestly as a percentage of gross national product. Lower prices emerged, caused in part by a more efficient use of resources—truckload carriers did not need the expensive terminal structure used by existing common carriers, for example—but lower prices also can be attributed to substantially lower wages and reduced profits. Both carriers and their employees lost as a result of deregulation as the average return on equity for general freight carriers eroded and hourly wages dropped substantially. Pension coverage has also declined, as most of the new entrants have not provided much in the way of deferred earnings as part of their compensation packages. With wages already low and competition intense, retirement earnings took second place to immediate family survival.

As I will discuss in later chapters, the public policy of deregulation and deinstitutionalization has strongly influenced the structure and health of the trucking industry. Regulatory decisions, made administratively or legislatively, have affected management, labor, and stockholders. Indeed, the trucking industry has lost a great deal as a result of regulatory reform and risks greater losses from continuing institutional instability. Bankruptcies among a wide range of trucking carriers continue. Despite the promises of deregulation's supporters, the overall investment rate in the industry continues to be modest over the long term.[7]

Deregulation of trucking can be associated with increased income inequality both within the industry and between the industry and its labor market competitors. Low wages and poor working conditions have had serious consequences for the industry, for employees, and for the public. It converted middle-class jobs with reasonable benefits and retirement possibilities into low-wage jobs unlikely to provide career employment and carrying no retirement benefits. And economic deregulation has had one effect its proponents never imagined: it has actually compelled the government to enact extensive and intrusive new regulations—social regulations—which create a complex new regulatory structure that places substantial burdens on trucking firms and enforcement agencies. Paradoxically, economic deregulation led to increased social regulation, as policymakers sought to cope with negative externalities created by intense competition.

Deconstructing Deregulation

Despite all of these changes, our economy will always be regulated. To a significant extent, the last 25 years have taken us not from regulation to deregulation, but from institutional regulation to market regulation. Yes, the market itself is a form of regulation—albeit it one without the institutions, governmental and otherwise, that Americans have come to expect to protect their interests.

To deconstruct the meaning of the term "deregulation," one must recognize that we have merely exchanged one form of regulation for another. It is an exchange by no means complete: direct and indirect economic regulations remain core governing structures in our economy. But public policy has taken a decided shift in support of the market, as evidenced by the trucking experience and that of many other industries. While there has been a considerable expansion of social regulation, many of our economic relationships have been deinstitutionalized.

Why does all of this matter? If we do not look beyond our own homes, it might not make any difference. It does matter, however, from a societal perspective. We are individuals in pursuit of personal material goods and a society in pursuit of broader goals that require collective maintenance of both individual and community rights.

Consider competitiveness and competition. We hear about it all of the time. The Clinton Administration appointed a blue-ribbon panel, the Dunlop Commission, to study our current labor law in the context of both labor rights and industrial competitiveness. The Commerce Department commissioned a study by economists to determine whether we can afford environmental regulation when we need to ensure competitiveness. A national debate surrounded the labor side accord to the North American Free Trade Agreement (NAFTA) and free trade advocates worried that U.S. labor standards might obstruct our competitive position. Labor and environmental side agreements to NAFTA ensure maintenance of national regulatory standards though they do not harmonize those standards among signatories to the agreement. An index of competitiveness has become a regular part of the economic information we receive.

Although increased competition has produced benefits, particularly for consumers, theory and experience indicate that such benefits often entail costs for some individuals. Market structures and economic conditions exist under which increased competition simply is detrimental to employees, to consumers, to firms, or to society at large. Should goods produced by prison or child labor, or even by slavery or indentured servitude, be exempted from free trade provisions? Should we be concerned?

Expanded trade with developing countries, a product of deregulation writ large, reduced employment in the manufacturing sector by 1.2 million net jobs between 1978 and 1990. Why? Because this trade often is founded on differences in compensation and working conditions as well as on differences in environmental protection. Developing countries are more "competitive" because workers there earn less and work under worse conditions and because environmental regulations are lax. Continued expansion of this trade threatens greater losses to workers and the environment.[8] Does this matter? Is competition a policy goal or a mechanism to reach a higher standard of living in tandem with some standard of fairness? Is competition a means to an end or the end in itself?

As I have already suggested, the trucking industry provides an ideal case study with which we can analyze the consequences of a nearly unlimited free market, and particularly the consequences of an unregulated labor market. As I will show, public policy has created extremely competitive labor and product markets in which government regulations serve only to ameliorate the consequences of competition, acting as an inadequate effort to close the barn door after the cows are out. Trucking thus becomes an ideal case study of the pros and cons of deregulation and deinstitutionalization. In the next chapters, I will describe the precipitous downward slide—in terms of wages, benefits, and working conditions—on which truckers have found themselves, and on which their employers have all too often found themselves as well.

About This Book

This book will tell the story of the trucking industry after economic deregulation. The gloves are off in an industry in which the market may be as perfect as any. What does this market get us? What does it mean for employees? Does it create good jobs or bad jobs? Does it lead to the high road, inducing the development of highly-valued skilled work, including high-value services? Alternatively, does it lead to a low road of low-valued undifferentiated labor, producing a low standard of living?

Chapter 1 has introduced the reader to the paradoxical problems created by the transformation of the regulatory regime from institutions to markets. Chapter 2 examines the declines truck drivers and others in the trucking industry have experienced since deregulation began in 1977. Employment is up while wages are down, and drivers put on more miles than ever. Chapter 3 covers the history of the political conflict over deregulation, detailing the long battle to reintroduce market forces into the trucking industry. Chapter 4 describes an industry transformed by those market forces, showing the changes in the structure of the industry, employment effects, changes in collective bargaining, and changes in workers' wages and working conditions. Chapter 5 shows how the union has remained an important player in the trucking industry market. Although union density has declined broadly for all drivers, in certain important sectors of the trucking industry the union still determines wages and regulates the limits of competition. Chapter 6 shows how the changes in competitive forces, and the changes in union representation, have shifted risk from employers to employees, especially drivers. Research shows that non-union drivers generally pay the cost of inefficient operations and even assume much of the risk for equipment failure and shippers' and receivers' failure to be ready to load or unload on time. Finally, chapter 7 summarizes the impact of intense economic competition on drivers and suggests some routes we might use to ameliorate the negative impact of competition while retaining its benefits.

The implications of deregulation for the U.S. economy and for our values as a society are substantial. The trucking story is an allegory, telling us a cautionary tale of unfettered competition, creating a social dilemma that, extended to other industries, could have significant consequences for the American way of life.

2 Two Decades of Decline

American truck drivers have ridden a roller coaster over the last few decades. Unfortunately, since the peak in 1973, the overall movement has been down. While unions—mainly the Teamsters—represented about 60% of all truck drivers twenty years ago, today they represent less than 25% of all drivers. Truckers' wages, once among the highest in American industry, have plummeted, particularly among non-union drivers.

Although employment in the trucking industry increased 3.9% per year since the early 1980s, average real annual earnings dropped 30% between 1977 and 1995. In 1997 dollars, the average driver earned $11,793 less in 1995 than he would have, had his current wages been at the same level as his 1977 wages—a 30% earnings drop. While average blue-collar wages declined throughout this period, the decline for truckers is almost four times the average annual earnings decline among all manufacturing production workers, whose annual earnings were $2,881, or 8%, below those of 1977. Had real wages remained constant for truckers during this period, the average worker in the trucking industry would have earned a total of $140,658 more than he did between 1977 and 1996, making him and his family much wealthier than they currently are.[1]

This decline reversed an earlier trend toward better wages and conditions. Trucking employees had improved their lot steadily during the 1950s and 1960s. Although prior to 1958 truckers earned wages comparable to most manufacturing workers, successful unionization and the collective bargaining efforts of early Teamster leaders moved their wages into the range of auto and steel workers, typically the highest paid American manufacturing workers. Although they lagged substantially behind construction workers, whose wages skyrocketed during the broad construction boom of the 1950s and 1960s, truck drivers had reached the kind of wage plateau that made the job attractive to a broad spectrum of the work force.

The Evolution of Trucking: Regulation and Unionization

The trucking industry, which evolved from the teaming industry, has its origins in the precolonial period. Teamsters (also called cartmen, draymen, and hackmen) usually owned their own carts and horses, and larger municipalities licensed them as public utilities. In 1792 New York City teamsters formed the Cartmen's Society to provide mutual support and relief. This association existed to support tradesmen and represent them to public rate-setting agencies, much like associations created by craftsmen in other trades.

As industrialization and commerce expanded, the demand for drayage increased: teamsters hauled goods among ports, canals, and rail lines, and between factories and consumers. By the end of the nineteenth century, drayage employed more than 1.6% of all U.S. workers.[2] With the 1896 introduction of the motorized truck, the industry began to develop its modern character. Although horse teams remained on American streets for decades afterward, motor trucking stimulated a demand for better highways and more extensive service.

Initially developed as an adjunct to railroads, the trucking industry began to expand to intercity work during World War I and grew even further as the system of hard surfaced roads expanded to satisfy the demands of the automobile.[3] Trucking became a dominant player in the U.S. transportation system after the 1950s with the development of the National System of Defense and Interstate Highways (referred to subsequently as the Interstate Highway System).

Unionization came at the end of the nineteenth century. The American Federation of Labor (AFL) chartered the Team Drivers International Union (TDIU) in 1899. Team drivers then typically worked 80 to 100 hours per week for between $10 and $14 (which translates to between $158 and $221 weekly in 1997 dollars).[4] They would feed, groom, and harness their horses and bring them to an early-morning shapeup. If work was not available, they would return their horses and unharness, feed, and groom them again—earning no pay at all.

There was turmoil from the beginning over the issue of "owner operators." The TDIU allowed drivers who owned up to five teams to belong to the union. Chicago teamsters objected, arguing that this provision allowed employers undue influence, and split to form the Teamsters National Union in 1902. In 1903 the groups uneasily reunited under the new AFL–chartered International Brotherhood of Teamsters (IBT). The new rules represented a compromise but favored the position of the Chicago teamsters: they allowed only employed drivers and drivers with one team to join.

The 1907 election of Bostonian Daniel J. Tobin to the Teamsters presidency led to the union's stabilization. Tobin, a fiscally conservative, traditional craft unionist,[5] led the Teamsters for the next 45 years—walking a fine line between centralized organization and localized power. He fought to keep over-the-road general freight drivers out of the Teamsters because he considered them unskilled, compared with local draymen and drivers delivering coal, beer, laundry, bread, and other items used by businesses and consumers. But Tobin's was a losing battle: intercity trucking continued to grow, taking an increasing share of the railroads' market.

Two important developments in the union paralleled the industry's growth. First, Dave Beck, a Teamster leader from Seattle, began to extend Teamster organizing into road operations during the early 1920s. With the Depression and the passage of the National Industrial Recovery Act of 1934, Beck and others intensified their drive to organize the western region and tie truckload truckers—those whose shipments are so large that a single shipment fills a truck, and who pick up their load at one shipper and deliver it to one consignee—and other over-the-road drivers into the union.

The second development flowed from a series of successful strikes in 1934 to organize truckers in Minneapolis.[6] Militant Teamster leaders, aligned with a small Trotskyist organization, led a series of strikes, starting with coal delivery drivers and spreading to drivers and non-driving employees of trucking and other companies throughout Minneapolis.

These strikes led to explosive growth in the Teamsters' membership in Minneapolis, but their success also led them to realize the extent to which truckers' unionization could not succeed in one place alone. After succeeding in their original goal of "making Minneapolis a union town," the Teamsters set their sights on the entire Midwest.

With the development of a sophisticated "leap-frog" approach to organizing the region, the Teamsters' organizing efforts culminated in an 11-state over-the-road agreement in 1938, creating the first regionwide, multistate unified contract. The leap-frog method combined road driver outreach with the secondary strike, or boycott. Road drivers carried their message from city to city, telling dockworkers and drivers regionwide that unionization could bring them far better wages and conditions than they had experienced to date. Once terminals in these cities organized, they began to refuse to load or unload non-union drivers' trucks, leveraging their local success into regional organization borne on the power of the secondary boycott. Both local and regional organizing drives succeeded, as the Teamsters perfected the use of the secondary boycott for organizing purposes. Both drives also led to the formation of large regional organizations within the Teamsters, later institutionalized as conferences.[7]

These drives also revolutionized the Teamsters internally. Although the Teamsters Union remained a member of the craft-based AFL, members flooded in on an industrial basis. The newly activist Teamsters organized firms "wall-to-wall," including everyone from drivers and dockworkers to mechanics and office personnel, in part because of the strategic advantage of complete unionization and in part because workers broadly demanded representation. To this extent the Teamsters, like the rest of the labor movement, followed this social movement rather than led it. This expansion not only extended the breadth and power of the union, but it blunted the attempt by the AFL's rival, the Congress of Industrial Organizations (CIO), to create an alternative to the Teamsters.

Meanwhile Congress, concerned about regulating the patchwork of both legitimate and fly-by-night motor carriers, enacted the Motor Carrier Act of 1935 (MCA of 1935), which required trucking companies to operate within a framework determined explicitly by the Interstate Commerce Commission (ICC). The MCA of 1935 was consistent with the goals inherent in the National Industrial Recovery Act and, more important, with states' demands that the federal government take responsibility for regulating intense interstate competition that had led to broad-based safety concerns on state and federal highways. Courts had repeatedly ruled states' efforts to regulate truck safety an unconstitutional obstruction of interstate commerce, making congressional action necessary. Rather than merely regulating safety practices, however, Congress decided to try to get at the source of the problem by regulating the underlying competitive marketplace.

The ICC restricted entry to prevent "destructive competition" in each market, which meant that new service providers rarely entered any new markets. The ICC–sanctioned rate bureaus, within which carriers met to set rates, required public service carriers (called "common carriers") to accept any shipment for which they had operating authority; regulated the transfer of interregional freight and revenue between small regional carriers (national carriers did not exist); and prohibited discrimination in favor of large shippers. The ICC also made carriers responsible for the value of the freight they hauled (to discourage collusion between truckers and thieves, historically a problem in the transportation industry, especially teaming). Further, they disallowed discount rates that did not cover costs, making it impossible for carriers to encroach on each other's business using cutthroat rates designed to lure business at a loss. This regulatory regime brought order to the industry and discouraged carriers from using unsafe practices to cut costs.

Under this system, competition was limited mainly to quality of service. Eventually legislation explicitly exempted motor carriers, acting under the authority of rate bureaus, from antitrust laws. Not that competition was absent altogether. Shippers generally had several carriers from which to choose. While price did not vary widely, carriers could file exceptions to the bureau's tariffs. Service varied as well. Since no motor carriers had blanket national coverage and they had strong local and regional roots, rate bureau tariff rules created a basis on which carriers could share freight and freight charges. Interline shipments, or shipments traveling on more than one carrier, required cooperation between or among carriers that shared the revenue and the liability proportionate to their role in moving the shipment.

It is worth noting here that many critics of regulation have claimed that collective rate-making as established in the MCA of 1935, coupled with a strong union and strong collective bargaining, created a "cost plus" environment in trucking. According to this argument, carriers had no incentive to resist union demands for higher wages because they could simply pass along the cost of wage hikes to the victimized consumer. This later became one of the arguments for deregulation.

The historical evidence, however, suggests that industrial relations were notoriously conflictual throughout the regulated period. Early attempts to organize the industry met with fierce company resistance. Teaming—along with longshoring, logging, and mining—characteristically has always been conflictual.[8] If it had been so easy to pass along costs to captive consumers, it seems reasonable that conflict would have been much more limited.

Motor carriers viewed their greatest competition as coming from outside their industry: from railroaders, not other truckers. Trucking industry leaders, and Teamster leaders as well, very carefully managed the elasticity of demand for trucking so that their industry remained competitive with railroads in spite of the price differential. They sought a market position that would allow trucking to take market share from the railroads based on a combination of price and service while maintaining a high standard of wages, benefits, and working conditions. Regulation, however, limited that competition, particularly among truckers themselves, and limited motor carriers' ability to respond to the market in innovative ways.

Still, the trucking industry flourished, as did the Teamsters Union, which continued to grow throughout the post–World War II period. The most dramatic period of growth began in 1934 and continued, at a rapid but more or less steady rate, through the early 1970s. James R. "Jimmy" Hoffa rose to power during the 1950s and unified bargaining with general freight carriers by the mid-1960s, solidifying the Teamsters Union's influence throughout the nation in his drive to transform pattern bargaining into centralized bargaining.

Hoffa—unconstrained following the Teamsters' expulsion from the AFL-CIO in 1957 for corruption—sought to expand Teamster influence and membership throughout transportation and other industrial sectors. He widened the Teamsters' organizing efforts to include all workers and made a special, albeit unsuccessful, effort to unify all transportation unions under one roof.

The backdrop to this expansion and growth, however, was the corruption of local union leadership and local ties to organized crime. Tobin managed to keep the International Union[9] above reproach during his 45-year tenure, but he had been unable to root out corruption at the local level. However, four out of the next five IBT general presidents were either charged with or convicted of various crimes, including jury tampering, bribery, extortion, and misappropriation of union funds. Most recently, reformer Ron Carey was expelled from the union under a cloud, as several of his lieutenants were charged with and convicted of more "modern" crimes relating to improper election fundraising and contributions. Although evidence against Carey himself was undeveloped, and there was never any evidence he either took money or used union funds for his own personal benefit, authorities decided he had breached his fiduciary responsibility by not instituting procedures that would have made such embezzlement impossible.

The steady rise in wages for truck drivers and workers on the loading docks began in the 1930s and continued as the union consolidated bargaining power during the first two decades following the Second World War, reaching a plateau in 1964, when the international union negotiated its first National Master Freight Agreement (NMFA).[10] While many people contributed to the development of this bargaining power, Hoffa himself set the strategic preconditions and personally worked to centralize bargaining. He held wage increases down in some areas, such as the East, where wages already were high, and he brought wages up in other areas, such as the mountain states and the South, where wages had been notoriously low. This wage convergence, or "solidarity wage," produced higher average wages, as employers could not play one terminal, city, or region against another. Hoffa did not need social science to tell him how pattern bargaining worked. Indeed, he reveled in showing social scientists how it was done.[11]

Real wages remained stable until 1970, when labor unrest rocked the nation. Hoffa had gone to jail in 1967, and Teamster leaders, jockeying to fill the power vacuum, promised better contracts to the members who voted to elect them. By 1973 competition among these leaders had produced a 20% real wage increase.

Shifting Public Policy: The Deregulation Movement

The wage increases of the early 1970s came at a time of increasing concern over inflation and economic stagnation in the nation, factors that combined to stir political support for a new approach to trucking industry regulation. Many economists argued that wage increases were fueling inflation and that the only restraint would come from reducing economic regulation governing industries, while deregulating and deinstitutionalizing the labor market directly. In other words, advocates of deregulation were arguing that the institutional environment should be changed to make it more difficult to unionize new operations or to maintain unionization in existing ones. So, while economic deregulation promised new flexibility for both truckers and their customers, the deregulation movement also could be interpreted as a thinly veiled attack on collective bargaining itself.

The pro-deregulation argument ultimately prevailed. In 1977 the ICC began to loosen the regulations that tightly defined each carrier's market and pricing policy, beginning a process that eventually dismantled the institutional and regulatory environment governing the economics of the interstate trucking industry. Trucking workers felt the change quickly, as the weakest trucking companies began to fail. Some carriers, recognizing the significance of the regulatory change and the potential impact to their business strategy, began to change early and implemented policies designed to create a focused market strategy. Those carriers that identified their future niche as truckload specialty haulers began to put intense pressure on unionized employees to cut their wages and conditions sharply. Common carriers remaining in the less-than-truckload market responded to the new competition likewise, demanding that their employees cut their wages too.

Congress affirmed administrative deregulation when it passed the Motor Carrier Act of 1980 (MCA of 1980), formally beginning the era of economic deregulation. The new rules allowed free entry into the market, eliminated indirect routings designed to protect carriers from competition, sharply limited collective rate-making (formerly encouraged by the ICC to stabilize rates), and allowed carriers to charge discriminatory prices (discount pricing to high-volume customers). For the first time, compensatory rates—rates that would cover the cost of the service—were not required; rates could be lower than the fully distributed cost of hauling the freight.

Immediately after Congress passed the MCA of 1980, carriers began to demand contract re-openers and sought major givebacks. Specialized carriers, already in the truckload business, sought a significant amount of the general TL freight previously hauled by the general commodity common carriers. New TL carriers formed and went after that freight also. Most of these carriers were non-union, so they were able to pay much lower wages and little or no benefits, and underbid the rates of the established general freight carriers, taking the freight from them. The competition became so intense in truckload that employees either agreed to drop their wage under the pressure of "forcing" strategies or the carriers shifted to "avoidance" strategies, breaking the union's hold entirely.[12]

Less-than-truckload carriers took a similar approach in response to the challenge from TL carriers and the intense competition for freight among remaining common carriers, and the surviving LTL carriers successfully forced the union to make concessions in wages and working conditions. The Teamsters, laboring under the corrupt regimes of Roy Williams and Jackie Presser, appeared to have no strategy other than concessions, so the influence of the union waned.

During the 1980s the Teamsters Union allowed major changes in work practices, such as flexible starting times and flexible workweeks, that ended the Monday-through-Friday workweek and the regular morning starting time. Many contracts also froze wages, diverted automatic cost-of-living adjustment wage increases to benefit plans, created a lower wage for new hires, and used Employee Stock Ownership Plans (ESOPs) and profit sharing plans to hide wage cuts.[13]

Meanwhile, the market took over the regulatory function. Economic deregulation opened up every market to free entry, withdrew price regulatory authority from rate bureaus, effectively required carriers to discriminate by accepting and rejecting freight according to their particular business strategy and by charging much higher rates to small shippers, and allowed carriers to set whatever rates the market would bear. Since traditionally everyone's primary haul is someone else's secondary haul, and since many carriers would gladly earn just enough on the secondary haul to cover their fuel (and perhaps labor), carriers began to cut each other's throats by discounting rates broadly.

Deregulation and Union Reform

Concessions wrought by severe competition, along with longstanding allegations of corruption, began to influence change within the Teamsters Union as well. Through the first decade of deregulation, charges of corruption and abuse of power continued to shadow the union. However, a national reform movement that began in 1972 with the founding of PROD (the "Professional Drivers' Council for Safety and Health") and built up a head of steam after merging with Teamsters for a Democratic Union (TDU) in 1979 (retaining the TDU name) began to mobilize sucessfully rank-and-file Teamsters to fight corruption and abuse, as well as the concessionary contracts that characterized the deregulatory era. TDU's efforts helped to produce the groundswell that eventually led to a big change in the Teamsters.

Although TDU has never been very large relative to the size of the Teamsters, it crystallized the conflict between increasingly unresponsive and frequently corrupt union officials and workers' declining living and working standards. Constantly under attack, politically and physically, its members tenaciously and unceasingly kept on the offensive, pressuring Teamster incumbents at all levels.[14]

The success of TDU stemmed from the fact that its membership and leadership focused their attention on issues of equity and democracy simultaneously. In addition, they maintained national and local pressure on contract bargaining and enforcement as well as democracy. As a result, they avoided the crucial pitfall of preaching, rather than doing, particularly around rather abstract issues of representational democracy. Finally, they persistently devoted a considerable proportion of their budget and effort to training and educating members. TDU dedicates much of each annual convention to education on steward training, organization building, and legal self-defense and education.

The Teamster reform movement had several crucial victories during the 1980s that suggested there might be big cracks in the incumbents' apparent monolith. TDU leaders and sympathizers won offices in union locals in many parts of the nation. Although most of these victories were short-lived, they demonstrated the breadth of the disaffection and the potential for the democratic "reform" solution.[15]

The United Parcel Service (UPS) and National Master Freight Agreements in 1984 and 1985 passed by relatively narrow margins, owing in large part to TDU's efforts to publicize contract terms and oppose ratification. TDU also challenged in court the Teamsters' NMFA voting procedure, which excluded casuals (part-time, irregular employees). In an out-of-court settlement, TDU agreed not to challenge the outcome of the 1985 contract vote in exchange for an important union concession. Faced with clear irregularities in defining regular and casual employees, the union agreed to allow casual Teamsters with at least 90 days of work the previous calendar year to vote in contract referenda.[16] Finally, drivers rejected the 1985 carhaul contract by more than 80%, and a three-week strike resulted in the passage of an improved contract.[17] TDU's struggle to define itself as both reformer and concession-fighter had begun to bear fruit.

The reform movement's success in fighting concessions turned a crack into a chasm. In 1987 and 1988 members rejected the UPS and NMFA contracts by 51 and 64% margins, respectively.[18] Teamster presidents Jackie Presser and Weldon Mathis[19] incurred the ire of the membership when they invoked the "two-thirds rule" in each case, signing the contract even though the majority had rejected it. Drivers also rejected the 1988 carhaul contract, but this time it was by a 72.1% margin, forcing the new president, William McCarthy, to renegotiate for better terms. TDU not only was in touch with the members' bread-and-butter dissatisfaction, but now it had the organization to defeat top level union officials. The reform movement also finally challenged the Teamsters' "two-thirds rule" in court. Five TDU members filed a lawsuit against the International Union, three days before the May 29 imposition of the 1988 NMFA.[20] The Teamsters' constitution allowed the local union executive board, at its discretion, to declare an employer's offer a final offer and require a two-thirds vote to reject. The General Executive Board, faced with unprecedented resistance to its negotiated contracts, decided to interpret national contract ratifications the same way. Although it was ambiguous, the use of this provision exposed the declining power of the Teamsters' International General Executive Board.

The TDU suit distinguished between the two-thirds vote required for a strike and a majority vote required for acceptance. It further alleged that the union did not poll all eligible members in the 1988 NMFA contract ratification vote, which potentially would have been enough votes to push the actual rejection rate above two-thirds. Using its extensive grass-roots support, TDU built an overwhelming mountain of evidence to support its allegations. On October 17, 1988, the General Executive Board agreed to an out-of-court settlement that changed the constitution, dropping the two-thirds rule except in situations when fewer than half of covered members voted.[21]

Campaigning for delegate positions at the 1986 International Brotherhood of Teamsters convention, TDU members stepped up their demand for the right to vote for top union officers. While supporting Sam Theodus, president of Cleveland general freight Local 407, TDU collected 100,000 signatures on a National Right to Vote Petition, demonstrating significant support for reform. Although only 24 of more than 2,000 delegates voted for Theodus, 100 delegates actually signed an open letter supporting democratic elections.[22] While symbolic, the extent of floor dissent in a Teamster convention was large enough to expose the leadership's continuing weakness.

The federal government's long investigation of Teamster corruption and on-and-off enforcement efforts took a new and perhaps decisive turn in 1988 with the use of anti-racketeering laws. The Justice Department filed a civil suit against the Teamsters under the Racketeer Influenced and Corrupt Organizations (RICO) provisions of the 1970 Organized Crime Control Act, charging that the Teamsters were mob-dominated. In 1989 the Teamsters, facing a certain date in court, at the last moment before the trial began negotiated a consent decree with the Justice Department, agreeing to settle racketeering charges out of court in exchange for the union's agreement to governance by a court-appointed administrator, investigations officer, and elections officer. This triumvirate had extensive power to administer the union and investigate and discipline corrupt officials, as well as to conduct a "one person—one vote" election of national officers. After extensive talks with Teamster officials, TDU, and others, including the independent watchdog group Association for Union Democracy (AUD), the court agreed to structure a plebiscite in which each member could vote for international-level union officers. The consent decree also provided that the court would retain oversight after the election, including the right to administer at least one subsequent election and continue oversight through an Independent Review Board (IRB), with the authority to investigate and recommend discipline for corrupt officials. The consent decree required the Teamsters to pay for all of the activities of the three court-appointed agents, including their oversight of the 1991 election. The agreement allowed the government to supervise subsequent elections, but at its own expense. In all of these processes, the federal court retained considerable oversight authority.

Ron Carey entered the national scene in the 1991 supervised election. The son of a UPS worker, Carey went to work for UPS in 1955 after a tour of duty in the Marine Corps. In 1967 he was elected president of Teamsters Local 804, a large local representing UPS workers on Long Island, New York. Long a thorn in the side of the "Old Guard"—those who had run the Teamsters during the years the union developed its corrupt reputation—Carey now challenged them for control of the International Union by running for the Teamster presidency.

Carey had developed a reputation as a tough and honest unionist. As Local 804 president, he established a routine of visiting his constituents' workplaces daily, keeping in close touch with his members' concerns.[23] He withstood a lot of pressure from UPS, and from IBT International Union leaders as well. When the Teamsters sought to develop a national UPS contract that Carey believed would take away his autonomy and authority to negotiate for his members—and one that he had good reason to believe would be inferior to his own contract—he fought and won the right to stay independent. This lasted until the mid-1980s, when he was forced into a national contract.

Securing the support of TDU, Carey mounted a challenge to the "Old Guard," running for president in 1991. The Old Guard split, running two slates, one headed by R. V. Durham (with the blessing of the incumbent General Executive Board) and the other led by Walter Shea (representing a minority of Executive Board members and other leaders). Relying heavily on TDU's extensive nationwide network of rank-and-file organizers and leaders, Carey and his whole slate swept in with a strong plurality against split "Old Guard" forces, receiving just shy of a majority of all votes cast.

After Carey's election, the Teamsters Union took a hard line on contract negotiations, resulting in high-profile strikes such as the relatively unsuccessful one over the NMFA during the spring of 1994 and the very successful strike against UPS in the summer of 1997. While bargaining results may be uneven, a broad cross-section of trucking employees got the message that the Teamsters were once again a tough labor organization.

Ron Carey's reelection effort in 1996, however, ran into trouble. Carey decided to continue his policy of strategic compromise with middle-ground forces in his union and avoided bruising campaigns for delegates to the 1996 Teamsters convention. Although he came into the election claiming majority support from delegates, Carey lost a vote testing his strength on the first day. While the vote was close, it was also unambiguous: his opponents had a slim but solid majority support of delegates. After a week of the most conflictual sort of wrangling, Carey held on to power, the forces that opposed him failing to take control of the convention. While Carey had won the battle, he had yet to win the war. Many local leaders left the convention very angry at Carey's tactics, and Carey's opponents got a windfall political issue.

A significant proportion of traditional trade unionist forces in the union, dissatisfied with many of Carey's more aggressive policies (particularly internal policies such as the dissolution of the area conferences two years before), had rallied behind James P. Hoffa, son of the former president. Rejecting the pleas of many activists, Carey dragged his feet and failed to mobilize an organization, sticking with strategic compromises and avoiding grass roots mobilizing even after the disaster at the convention. He then failed to campaign actively during the election, leaving his supporters to create their own campaign. Carey's slate won the ensuing election by the skin of its teeth.

More setbacks came in the following year. About the time of Carey's second inauguration, information began to surface suggesting key Carey operatives had employed classical political fundraising techniques to line their own pockets while raising funds for his campaign. Even as Carey and his bargaining team were facing down UPS in the summer of 1997, the court-appointed elections officer was preparing a report charging that these key individuals had used union funds (spent in the general election of 1996) to leverage donations to Carey's campaign. Within a week after the end of the UPS strike, the elections officer overturned Carey's reelection and ordered a new election. Though she did not find at the time that Carey knew of the embezzlement, soon afterward she resigned because of conflict of interest: she had a personal relationship with Citizen Action, one of the organizations named in the probe as a recipient of union political donations.

The court appointed a new "special master" to investigate the election in her stead, and in November 1997 he issued a report sharply critical of Carey. The report banned him from the ballot because investigators had found that he either knew of the transactions or should have known. Six months of disarray ensued, including a period during which Carey's anointed successor, Ken Hall, announced for General President and then withdrew (though with no public announcement), unable to pull together a slate. Carey's supporters simply did not believe the charges, so trusting were they of the man who had led the first democratically-elected General Executive Board. By the summer of 1998 the Independent Review Board had banned Ron Carey, the disgraced failed former reformer, for life.

The mantle of reform was picked up by Tom Leedham, the director of the union's 400,000-member Warehouse Division. Leedham, the new standard-bearer for "bottom up" unionism, entered the race at the end of May when Ken Hall faded away. Supported by TDU's organization of activists, Leedham ran an energetic but uphill campaign over the next six months, eventually earning nearly 40% of the vote. The "reform" vote was split, however, as a third candidate, John Metz, also entered the race (he received 6% of the vote). James Hoffa received the remainder, 55% of the vote in an election in which about 30% of the eligible members voted by mail ballot.

As of this writing, the future of the union hangs in the balance. Hoffa has been elected and installed as General President, although some possible problems remain. The Independent Review Board charged one of his vice presidential candidates just as ballots were being counted. The candidate, Tom O'Donnell, accused of "bringing disrepute on the union" by filing a false financial report during Hoffa's 1996 election (which Hoffa signed), could be barred from the union just as he is on the verge of installation as International Vice President. The financial report had falsely indicated that the campaign was paying the wife of an individual—a convicted felon—it had hired as an organizer. The campaign paid the wife of the organizer, rather than the organizer himself, to hide the fact that they had hired a felon.

Soon afterward, the IRB charged another of Hoffa's running mates, J. D. Potter, with making illegal contributions to the Hoffa campaign. These accusations, along with other possible charges that might result from Hoffa's own false reporting in the 1996 election, could well destabilize Teamster politics again in the near future.[24]

Deregulation's Dénouement

Neither the revitalized Teamsters Union nor the lobbying efforts of the trucking industry by their American Trucking Associations (ATA), however, were able to buck the trend toward further deregulation. Effective January 1995, Congress ordered the states to stop regulating intrastate trucking businesses, unleashing competition among carriers that specialize in transporting goods within state borders. This federal mandate for intrastate economic deregulation completed the process of shifting the regulatory burden from government agencies to the market. As a result, the aggressive competition and the shakeout that characterized interstate carriage during the 1980s came to intrastate trucking. Smaller carriers, unable to offer the kind of blanket freight service provided by large national and regional carriers, were threatened with extinction as another shakeout began. Intrastate carriers that possessed the capability expanded into regional markets to blunt the competitive threat of interstate carriers that now targeted intrastate markets. Intrastate carriers without those human and capital resources, or those already burdened with debt, exited the industry by sale or bankruptcy.

Deregulation's Effect on Wages and Working Conditions

As the trucking industry became more competitive following interstate deregulation in 1980, wages began to slide. Real wages have never returned to pre-deregulation levels, and intrastate deregulation in 1995 continued the decrease, though to a more moderate extent. Wages are the variable cost easiest to cut. Widespread rate-cutting and competition among carriers, especially in the intensely competitive truckload (TL) sector, produced strong downward pressure on wages. Today, average real wages in trucking are no better than they were in the late 1950s. For the TL sector, average wages hover around the minimum wage.

As wages declined, they also diverged, following disparate product and labor markets. The Teamsters' decades-long campaign to equalize wages for truck drivers, regardless of region or product hauled, came apart at the seams under relentless economic pressure compounded by its own corrupt leadership. Now, while drivers for unionized national less-than-truckload (LTL) motor carriers earn top dollar, most non-union drivers for long-haul TL carriers work extremely long hours for very low wages. A survey conducted in 1997 by the University of Michigan Trucking Industry Program (UMTIP) shows that while the median non-union long-haul truckload driver earns $10.75 per hour for all hours worked at straight time rates

(31.2¢ per mile while driving), he also works 65 hours per week.[25] Considering that the legal limit is 60 hours per week, the study suggests an extensive effort by firms and drivers themselves to sweat their labor to reach target earnings levels.

Large differences between carriers and among labor markets make it easy for employers to move employment domiciles to low-wage areas and to subcontract union work to low-wage non-union employees and operations. Since the long-haul truckload carriers need not constrain themselves to domiciles from which they haul or to which they deliver loads, many carriers have chosen to hire workers from low-wage rural areas in order to keep wages very low. Unfortunately, this approach has produced long-term harm to the industry, as a labor market paradox has developed. At the same time that motor carriers complain about a severe labor shortage, they continue to hire the lowest wage workers they can find from wherever they can find them, which drives wages down further throughout the labor market and exacerbates the skilled driver shortage.

This wide variance in wages and conditions also puts unionized employees on the defensive. Any strike by Teamster drivers runs the risk of attracting low-paid, non-union drivers—"replacement workers"— who might have no compunction about taking jobs at a fraction of the union wage. While the union has held up to this pressure so far, double-breasting by unionized carriers (the development of non-union subsidiaries doing virtually the same work as their unionized parents) has given the carriers tremendous leverage. The overall effect has been to crank wages down tighter, paradoxically making the job less desirable than the carriers wish it to be. In effect, an unfettered market for labor produces a continuous and destructive slide that threatens the industry itself.

This is the environment wrought by deregulation and deinstitutionalization. Wages have declined over the long term, as have working conditions. There has been a notable decline in collective bargaining in the industry, and with that a decline in the protections truck drivers have enjoyed in recent years. Intense competition has demeaned the former "knights of the road," threatening the professional driver and his occupation.

Not surprisingly, the competition produced by deregulation has resulted in some undesirable side effects, or externalities, that have attracted the ire of the public and the attention of legislators. These negative externalities have demanded and received legislative redress, creating and extending a new regulatory imperative—what political scientists call "social" regulation[26] (more about this in the next chapter). Since 1980 social regulation of trucking industry operations has expanded in direct response to economic deregulation, affecting both the industry's costs and its functions. Highway safety, in particular, has become a major policy issue. While crashes per mile have remained relatively stable, truck traffic has increased dramatically over the past two decades, increasing the public's exposure to truck wrecks. While assessments vary, the U.S. Department of Transportation (DOT) has recently estimated that 15% of all truck-related crashes are due to fatigue.

Who Benefits from Deregulation?

The switch from institutional to market regulation of trucking created two distinct sectors within the industry. The LTL sector has suffered the greatest carrier shakeout and the greatest job losses, though the growth of the largest carriers (including UPS) has compensated for much of the decline. The TL sector has registered the greatest wage losses and the greatest employment gains.

These outcomes result from the specific operational characteristics of each sector. The TL market is composed of common and contract carriers, as well as specialized carriers, that elect to focus on the large-shipment direct pickup and delivery market. Truckload shipments require only a single truck and trailer to deliver a load and require no complex pickup and delivery network. Each driver accomplishes his work independently of other drivers. Because little or no cooperation among drivers is needed to get the work done, it is relatively easy for companies to play drivers against each other. Intense wage competition among drivers results, keeping wages low.[27]

The LTL market is built out of the industry's original common carrier base. The smaller shipments in the LTL sector—where the truck's contents come from different shippers and is delivered to multiple consignees—require an elaborate network of pickup and delivery drivers, dockworkers, and road drivers. Each LTL shipment demands the coordination and cooperation of many employees, and each employee depends on others to deliver the goods successfully. While all LTL carriers are not unionized, this interdependence of employees encourages the kind of solidarity that keeps wage levels high in general and makes unions successful in particular. It is in the company's interest that its employees work together, and they are a source of mutual support when negotiating wages.

Because of the unique complexity of handling these small shipments, LTL firms also face less competition within their own markets than TL firms. Technically, anyone with a truck can handle a truckload shipment. While large TL carriers operate sophisticated networks connected to a control base by direct communication via satellite, anyone willing to work for less can make a low bid and take the freight. This pressure keeps rates low and limits the ability of these carriers to raise wages even if they wanted. Many TL carrier executives wring their hands over the trap in which they see themselves, unable to raise wages to the level needed to attract the kind of drivers they want.

We might expect that trucking company owners benefit from labor's pains, but the truth is much more complicated. Just as drivers' wages took a nose-dive, trucking company revenues have had an uncertain record of keeping pace with expenses. Following economic deregulation, motor carriers initially came under extreme financial pressures. While thousands of carriers entered the industry after 1980, most were very small, and many served mainly to put cost pressures on everyone else. Operating ratios (the ratio of total carrier operating expenses to total carrier operating revenues) for the larger interstate haulers have been stable, on average, since economic deregulation. Return on equity remained flat for the first decade, fell in the late 1980s, then increased in the boom years from 1992 to 1995, only to decline again when Congress mandated intrastate deregulation in 1995. For Class I and Class II carriers (carriers with more than $1 million in revenue; see Glossary), average operating ratios have eroded steadily since 1970, registering an average 0.07% annual increase between 1970 and 1990. Historically, their best year was 1971, when they earned nearly six cents on the dollar from operations. Taking the long-term view, this does not look like a monopoly industry taking rents.

The industry experienced a massive shakeout after decontrol, with some big winners and many big losers. The Teamsters report that, between passage of the Motor Carrier Act of 1980 and the summer of 1993, about half of the Class I and Class II general freight carriers that existed when deregulation began had gone bankrupt (most expired in the early 1980s). These large and small carriers—close to 150 of them—accounted for half of the revenue in the intercity general freight industry and employed more than 175,000 workers.

The bankruptcies easily have cost investors millions of dollars. The industrial restructuring engendered by deregulation also has directly dislocated more than half of all employees in the general freight industry. While many of these employees found jobs elsewhere in the trucking industry, those who found their way into the TL sector of the industry found themselves making around half the wages and working much longer hours. Many others found jobs in other industries or retired, greatly reducing the available human capital.

Most important, deregulation has forced carriers to specialize either in TL or LTL shipments. Truckload and less-than-truckload carriers are very different types of businesses. The average LTL shipment weighs about 1,200 pounds, and a single load of LTL shipments may include 30 shipments. A TL shipment weighs at least 10,000 pounds, with an average of about 26,000 pounds, filling up an entire truck. In addition, while an LTL firm must maintain an extensive network of pickup and delivery drivers and terminals, along with a staff of dockworkers, a TL firm needs only a truck and a telephone, as all of its pickups and deliveries directly connect shippers and consignees.

Deregulation's proponents insisted that competition would mean more carriers competing for business. Again, actual experience is more complicated. The new LTL general freight industry, built around the core operations of general freight common carriers, became very concentrated as the majority of general freight carriers went out of business. While the gross number of carriers registered with the DOT increased greatly, the ICC–regulated general freight trucking business concentrated about five-fold during the first ten years after the passage of the MCA of 1980. The four largest LTL carriers that existed before deregulation doubled their share of the revenue. UPS alone earned $1.8 billion in profits in 1998 on nearly $25 billion in revenue.

The rest of the business went to a virtually new industry that deregulation created—one composed exclusively of truckload carriers. Before economic deregulation, general freight common carriers hauled a mix of TL and LTL freight. These "mixed" carriers vastly outnumbered the relatively small TL-only carriers.

The new TL general freight industry, built around both the peripheral truckload haulers in the original common carrier group and a comparatively small group of truckload contract and special commodity carriers, exploded in the years immediately following deregulation. While the TL industry shows signs of economies of density that favor large carriers, the industry still is highly competitive and does not show substantial concentration.[28]

As this new TL business grew rapidly out of the relatively small, historically non-union specialized freight and contract carrier sectors, it stripped existing common carriers of their TL shipments. The new industry also developed during an era extremely hostile to unions— the Reagan Administration. Since Reagan-era interpretations of labor law made it nearly impossible to organize the long-haul TL business, it remains almost entirely non-union. Workers displaced from other declining industries during the 1980s and 1990s have drifted into long-haul TL trucking, only to find onerous conditions that many find untenable. Non-union long-haul drivers work long hours, typically stay on the road for three weeks at a time, and earn low wages, producing a high turnover rate.

Just how low are wages? Definitive data are not available, as the federal government does not collect very much information on the industry. But a recent survey conducted by the University of Michigan indicates that the median long-haul driver works 65 hours per week and drives 117,000 miles per year. Since this figure is a median, we know that more than half of all drivers exceed the 60-hour legal limit set by the Department of Transportation, and many work 80 to 100 hours per week, far in excess of the legal limit: the driver at the

75th percentile works 80 hours per week and the driver at the 90th percentile works 95 hours per week. Since the Fair Labor Standards Act (FLSA) exempts employees of interstate trucking companies from the 40-hour workweek (and time-and-one-half for more than 40 hours of work), many drivers find that they effectively do not earn much more than minimum wage while working the equivalent of two or three full-time jobs. With no penalty for assigning drivers long hours of work, there is no disincentive to discourage use of these employees to the maximum extent allowed by law or human endurance. The low-wage rate, furthermore, encourages drivers to become complicit in this regime, sweating their labor to reach their desired earnings threshold. In addition, with hundreds of thousands of mostly small firms, the maximum hours rules are nearly unenforceable.

These low wages and harsh conditions in some sectors of the industry have made trucking an occupation of last resort. Turnover in unionized carriers remains very low, but turnover in non-union, long-haul carriers typically runs around 100%. Turnover is so high that some companies may need to hire two or three drivers yearly just to keep one truck on the road. During the recent economic expansion that began in 1992, many long-haul trucking companies have had to refuse work, leaving trucks in their yards because they could not find enough drivers. Even in the recession of the late 1980s and early 1990s, these companies complained of a driver shortage. They simply could not recruit, hire, train, and retain drivers who could both do the job and pass stringent drug and other screenings required by law—especially at the wages the companies were willing and able to pay. And what about the public itself? Several studies have claimed that regulatory restructuring caused a net social gain, thanks to a decline in overall national distribution costs. However, regulatory reform may merely have transferred wealth from carriers to shippers, with uncertain net gain to consumers. The public, meanwhile, likely bears costs associated with reduced safety and healthcare and pension coverage.

Let us not forget that the millions of people who work in the trucking industry are also part of this public. How have these policy changes affected them, and has the net result been to impoverish or enrich the nation? If the new economic order limits job creation in the trucking industry to low-wage jobs with insecure careers, are we, as a nation, better off?

Bargaining Power: Individual or Collective?

The Teamsters Union continues to represent a significant fraction of unionized trucking industry employees—even though a large section of the Teamsters' core industry, general freight, has undergone a wrenching restructuring. Teamster employees rarely have voted the union out.[29] But the development of a large non-union truckload industry, along with the growth of the specialized trucking and logistics industries, has diluted the Teamsters' strength. Bargaining has become much more difficult in trucking, as it has in other deunionized industries.

Census data indicate truckers' overall union membership has declined from about 60% to 25% over the last quarter century. In the general freight sector of the trucking industry, the growth of large unionized LTL and package carriers—Consolidated Freightways, Yellow Freight System, Roadway Express, ABF, and UPS—has helped offset the loss of union jobs caused by the massive shakeout that deregulation produced. Most LTL carriers, especially national ones, have long traditions of collective bargaining. While data are somewhat fragmentary, it appears that overall unionization among interstate general freight carriers, including package delivery, has only dropped to about 65%.

Should the general public even care whether unions represent truckers? Unionization means collective bargaining, and collective bargaining may be one way to ensure that the market can regulate effectively, in lieu of the elaborate regulatory environment that once prevailed in trucking. With no social institutions acting as backstops, labor market competition now threatens to create an underclass of low-paid but fully-employed workers, and the truckload driver may represent just the first wave of sweated labor in America. This low road, while leaving college educated workers untouched for now, might well become a cancer within the American political system, prompting a backlash that could produce antidemocratic consequences. Absent the "regulation" that collective bargaining can establish, intense price competition can have serious repercussions for workers. Since wages are both the largest component of trucking operations and the easiest one to affect, unfettered competition might drive workers' wages into the ground.

Collective bargaining, endorsed by Section 7 of the National Labor Relations Act, is a form of private regulation designed to allow labor and management to establish wages, hours, and work rules that are both equitable and efficient because they require minimal government interference. If this private regulatory regime fails to function, legislators eventually may be inclined to extend direct public regulation to trucking's labor market, putting the industry under the Fair Labor Standards Act (FLSA). While this would bring trucking in line with the rest of the private sector, it may require trading efficiency for equity, an alternative less palatable to the industry.

What Lessons Can We Learn from Trucking?

The new trucking industry clearly has driven a great deal of cost out of the system. Many analysts have shown how the consumer has benefited from deregulation. Shippers' rates have declined, and manufacturers and distributors have profited from deep discounting.

Competition allows—even forces—carriers to discriminate in favor of shippers tendering a large volume of freight. While before 1980 regulations required rates and service to be nondiscriminatory, carriers since deregulation commonly offer discounts greater than 60% and have discounted even further when necessary to secure the freight. With such widespread discounting, economists assume savings have made their way to end consumers as well. Regardless, the savings bred by the restructuring of the distribution industry make every producer cost-conscious. Nobody pays "retail" except the smallest shipper, such as the individual who ships packages via UPS.

Scholars of industrial relations might ask how much of these savings come from increased efficiencies and how much come from reduced wages to employees. While such calculations remain educated guesses, during the first decade of deregulation perhaps 80% of the savings to consumers came from reduced employee wages.

What lessons does this teach us as a society? Even though consumers benefit from low prices, they may do so at the expense of other consumers, skewing the distribution of the gain. With welfare reform putting all able-bodied individuals into the work force, workers compete with one another for jobs, driving wages ever lower. As wages drop, it becomes irrational for individual workers, such as those in trucking, to invest in their human capital—what they have built up in skills and marketability over years working in the industry. This further devalues their labor and ends up attracting to the industry those workers with the fewest employment alternatives. What if this happened in all industries?

Much has been made of the uniqueness of the transportation industry and the trucking industry in particular. Governed by a complex set of regulations and requiring a language distinct from that used to describe other service and manufacturing industries, trucking industry analysis has remained insulated from and resistant to investigation by scholars in the industrial relations field.

But suppose the trucking industry is no different from other industries. Suppose the rest of American industry lived under trucking's rules—without the full benefit of the Fair Labor Standards Act. Suppose the rest of American industry lived in a world of unfettered competition, particularly in the labor market.

Since the FLSA does not fully apply to trucking, trucking companies are free to sweat drivers for greater production without paying overtime. The legal workweek in the trucking industry is 60 hours, yet road drivers average 65.7 hours per week. For unionized LTL drivers, long hours provide the pay for which they are legendary. In 1997 the average unionized road driver earned $43,165, according to the driver survey. The survey also showed that the average union road driver worked 60 hours per week, earning an hourly rate of $13.97 at straight time rates (60 hours per week multiplied by 50 weeks per year and 2.25 weeks of vacations and holidays at 8 hours per day). If he were in any other industry and earned time-and-one-half for overtime, he would have earned $12.02 per hour for the same work (40 hours per week at straight time plus 20 hours of overtime per week, plus the same vacation and paid holiday time).[30] This is as good as it gets.

For non-union truckload drivers, pay is lower and hours are longer. While the legal workweek is 60 hours, the average workweek is 70 hours. According to our survey, the average non-union road driver earned $35,551 in 1996. We asked drivers to report to us all of the hours they worked, not just those for which they were paid. The survey showed the average driver worked well over the legal maximum, giving him an average hourly rate of $9.88 at straight time (calculated at 50.25 weeks at 70 hours per week plus 2 weeks at 8 hours per day). If he were in any other industry and earned a premium wage for overtime, we could recalculate this rate to $8.17 (again, accounting for the yearly average of five vacation days and three holidays they averaged, plus time-and-one-half for overtime). These figures substantiate calculations I have made elsewhere based on motor carrier financial and operating statistics formerly reported to the ICC and now reported to the Bureau of Transportation Statistics and are 30% higher than calculations based on the Current Population survey.[31]

What causes this large segment of the trucking industry to pay such low wages for work performed under difficult conditions? The trucking industry has become extremely competitive, particularly in certain sectors, since deregulation. For potential employees, relative ease of entry (at least until the Commercial Drivers License, or CDL, became a requirement) and modest minimum skills made it easy for workers displaced from other industries to take up truck driving as an alternative occupation. Farmers displaced by the deep farm recession in the early 1980s easily shifted to trucking, using their equipment-operating skills. Factory workers, displaced by the deep general recession of the early 1980s, by the dislocation produced by runaway shops, and by the downsizing produced by lean manufacturing, have taken up truck driving as an alternative occupation.

The recent broadening of employment cutbacks into the white-collar sector eventually will force more workers from other occupations and industries into trucking as a fall-back opportunity. As the trucking industry grows yet sustains its chronic high turnover rates of more than 100%, its churning labor market favors persistence of this pattern of low wages and tough working conditions. Everyone thinks he can at least drive, and that if he can drive a truck—and if he likes driving and taking trips—he can become a truck driver. The fallacy is that not everyone can tolerate the work and the pressure, the irregular hours, as well as the long hours away from home. But as long as the market for manual labor remains unstable, someone will take that low-wage trucking job—if only on a temporary basis.

Other institutions do their part to create this difficult situation. The deregulation of industrial relations—the significant weakening of regulations that protect the rights of employees to seek collective representation—affects the trucking industry with particular salience. While it is exceedingly difficult to organize any enterprise and successfully negotiate a first contract, it is even more difficult to do so in trucking. There is plenty of evidence that employers can and do take extreme actions to break union drives. In the extreme, such actions include terminal closure and relocation, and even business termination and reorganization.

For an industry riding on roller skates, such actions are routine. National truckload carriers especially can locate anywhere in the country with a favorable industrial relations environment—such as open shop or "right-to-work" states in which it is difficult to organize and maintain unions—and operate from there, and regional TL carriers have similar opportunities. Their employees, dispersed over hundreds or thousands of miles, face tremendous challenges if they seek to develop the kind of contact and coordination needed to secure their rights through bargaining. In sum, the union faces a daunting—perhaps impossible—task when it tries to organize these companies. If drivers successfully organize themselves, the lax regulation provided by the nation's labor laws makes it simple for a carrier to refuse to bargain a first contract. Even if the employees and their union succeed in climbing these impossible mountains, the continual infusion of new employees into the industry, however temporary, can break any picket line; workers would be permanently replaced with drivers from far-flung communities, willing to work for less.

The trucking industry, then, may represent the nearest thing available to the ideal competitive model. The industry is hypercompetitive. It is constantly changing and almost infinitely mobile. It has a seemingly inexhaustible well of employees, even if it grinds them up and spits them out at a fearful rate. Where competition is the greatest, profits are lowest. The competitive ideal, in which profits are eliminated, comes very close to realization.

3 The Road from Institutional to Market Regulation

Since the 1950s academics and practitioners, including trucking industry management and the people who once handled cases before the Interstate Commerce Commission, have debated the relative costs and benefits of transportation regulation. Some economists argue that economic regulation benefits regulated industries at the expense of consumers, while others contend that regulation benefits consumers by ensuring stable, high-quality distribution. Some maintain that regulation stifles industry competition and thereby innovation, encouraging inefficiency. Others argue that it prevents transportation industries from engaging in destructive competitive practices that would undermine the industry's ability to make "normal profits"—the minimum amount of profit a firm must earn in order to induce reinvestment. Still others argue that transportation is a utility that benefits everyone, and the government interest in preventing monopolistic practices, including rate gouging and restricted service output, as well as in preventing discrimination in service and price, justifies the cost of somewhat inefficient allocation. These supporters of economic regulation claim it provides a framework within which to base competitive business strategies that promote investment in new service capability.

The rationale for economic deregulation has been taken, in large part, from economic theory. Conventional wisdom holds that most government intervention cannot improve on the outcomes of a free market. The proponents of deregulation insist that the reduction or elimination of government control over markets will improve economic efficiency. Although these proponents acknowledge that particular groups may be disadvantaged by deregulation, they believe competition makes society as a whole better off.

The problem, though, is that unfettered competition may not assure efficient, let alone equitable, outcomes. The debate shifts, then, to the degree to which competition itself is regulated.

A major restructuring of trucking's regulatory regime occurred between 1977 and 1980. In effect, the policy of "deregulation" replaced one regulatory structure with another—like a dramatic social experiment. Today we can examine the results. Who were the winners and who were the losers? Are consumers better off? How has the transportation industry fared? What happened to the wages, employment security, and the safety of truck drivers? How did regulatory change affect industrial relations in general and the Teamsters Union in particular?

While the regulatory regime that existed for some 50 years allowed competition, it regulated that competition within what policymakers at the time thought were socially desirable bounds. Admittedly, the agency responsible for that regulation, the ICC, interpreted its authority very narrowly and structured competition so tightly that it became a parody of bureaucratic intervention. Today, though, economic regulation is so slight that it provides few bounds on competition. The trucking industry experiment thus shows both the benefits and the limits of that nearly unlimited competition.

What Is Regulation?

Regulation is a broad term for institutional rules governing mixed-market economies. Governments in these economies intervene to modify the market, seeking socially desirable ends. The variations are infinite—intervention may range from simple information-gathering to complete control of products and profits. In all cases, thorough and effective policy analysis requires policymakers to weigh each regulation's benefits against its political, social, and economic costs. How do the results of the restructuring of trucking industry regulation stack up?

All markets are regulated in some way. In the most extreme interventions, government may step in to regulate price, quantity, or quality. At a minimum, rules are established governing the structure and responsibilities of the corporation, as well as what ought to happen should a corporation become insolvent. Even in a relatively unregulated economy, government may outlaw price-fixing conspiracies, define business practices that unlawfully restrain free trade, and forbid extortion and usury. Thus, the clamor to deregulate various markets really is nothing more than a demand to alter the existing form of regulation and replace it with another.[1]

Understanding regulation's consequences requires evaluation along several dimensions. One regulatory scheme might protect the environment from a specific industrial depredation while unintentionally creating some other environmental hazard or risk that outweighs the original peril. Another might ensure nondiscriminatory employment practices but be awkwardly written, making compliance so difficult that only lawyers may benefit. A third set of regulations might produce an efficient economic solution that destabilizes political forces and creates a threat to democratic civil society. For instance, it may be economically efficient that the rich get richer and the poor get poorer in the new competitive global economy. Excessive compensation rates for CEOs have been given high-visibility coverage in the media for years, and some argue that these executives are getting what they deserve. But what if those feeling the pinch decide to revolt?

There are potential problems with any type of regulation. The rules governing bankruptcy, for example, protect viable companies while they restructure debt and protect the property of creditors. The same regulations, however, may allow insolvent companies to compete unfairly against solvent companies, distorting the market to the detriment of more efficient operators. Rights of copyright and patent provide exclusive use of a concept or a product for some period of time but restrict competition based on those concepts as well. Patented medicines, for example, provide exclusive marketing rights that inflate prices to consumers. While the pharmaceutical company needs this protection to encourage investment in research and development, the regulation remains restrictive nonetheless.

Regulation falls into two broad categories. Economic regulation defines the market environment within which industries operate and often establishes governmental agencies that authorize particular business operations. This category of regulation generally deals with such issues as price, entry, and rate of return. Social regulation bounds the market, establishes limits to competition, and provides social accountability for economic externalities created by the forces of private competition. Social regulation also encompasses attempts by political interest groups to achieve non-economic goals through the imposition of controls on private enterprise.[2]

No regulation is entirely benign. Both types of regulation—economic and social—produce winners and losers. Licensing of medical professionals may create higher quality health care, for instance, but it limits the market by specifying what constitutes a bona fide medical service. Professional teacher certification may raise teacher effectiveness and standardize teacher qualifications, but it closes the market to those who may know their subjects well but have not accepted the regimentation of educational methodology propagated in education certification programs. Further, it creates a sizable interest group that benefits from more educational regulation.

The same effects can be seen in trucking. The national Commercial Drivers License may raise and unify licensing standards for truck drivers, but it limits the labor market to those who can read and write well enough to pass the written test and have general test competency, to those who have access to commercial vehicles to use for the road test (such as those with current driving jobs), and to those with current jobs who can get a medical certification. Universal pre-hire, random, and for-cause drug testing may reduce drug use among transportation personnel, but it limits the labor market to those who accept this invasion of privacy.

Once set, regulations seem to develop lives of their own, becoming resistant to modification or elimination. Eventually, we may even take them for granted and forget there was ever a time they did not exist.

Both types of regulation have political origins and consequences. Typically, policymakers have cited the public interest as justification for these regulations. More than 200 years ago, New York City licensed operators of local for-hire horse teams, called "cartmen," fixing cart size, speed, noise and safety rules, entry and rates, and industry structure.[3] City officials enacted these regulations to protect commerce from the extortive potential of organized cartmen and to safeguard the public from individual competitive actions. In a more recent example, Congress enacted the law requiring mandatory drug testing of truck drivers. The context was public hysteria over drug use in the 1980s, inflamed for political reasons by the Reagan/Bush "war on drugs."

This type of regulation is not atypical. Legislators and agencies often take regulatory action after the public has become aroused by some abuse or catastrophe, and the arousal creates pressure for legislation or regulation (or more cynically, a grandstanding opportunity for politicians). The Federal Aviation Administration is a good example. It was established to promote air travel as well as oversee air safety after two planes collided over the Grand Canyon in the mid-1950s.

Even the definition of the public interest is inherently political, though. Congress passed the Interstate Commerce Act of 1887 in response to agrarian populist agitation for public controls over the monopolistic practices of railroads and, paradoxically, in response to the established railroads' support of the same regulation to eliminate competitive threats from smaller upstarts. Originally supported by railroads threatened by trucker competition, the Motor Carrier Act of 1935 eventually won the endorsement of most economists as an appropriate public response to the destructive competition that appeared to plague the trucking industry, producing low profits and wages as well as inadequate and irregular service. The Federal Coordinator of Transportation produced a report in 1934 recommending social and economic regulation of both common and contract motor carriers.[4] In the context of the Great Depression, which many believed resulted from unfettered and often speculative market behavior, this regulatory effort made sense.

The states also actively supported regulation, viewing unregulated trucking as bad for local business and dangerous to the public. State governments agitated for federal legislation after the Supreme Court blocked state regulation of motor carriers engaged in interstate commerce.[5] Opposed at first by truckers, the Motor Carrier Act of 1935 eventually became the institutional foundation upon which industry structure and profitability rested.

From the Pure Food and Drug Act of 1906 to the Clean Air Act of 1990, political forces have spawned social regulation to cope with the externalities of the competitive process. Private production creates public goods that individual actions can devalue. An individual entrepreneur can make money on a defective product only until his reputation catches up with him; if he is clever, he will take the money and run. If such practices become widespread, though, they can shake public confidence in an industry's products or services, harming the industry's reputation. In this instance, the individual's defective goods impose a negative externality on the marketplace, diminishing the value of the goods made by legitimate producers. Markets can be fragile, and the recent cases of e-coli–contaminated meat and parasite-contaminated produce reminds us that in an economy dependent on multiple private transactions, quality standards create a public good— in this case, trust in the safety of the food supply.

Highway safety provides another example. Safety is a public good consumed by all highway users, and irresponsible individual operators who violate safety rules in pursuit of private gain create a negative externality. Safety and health regulations, originally implemented by the ICC and later transferred to the DOT, aim to preserve a level playing field in transportation, so self-seeking individuals harm neither the industry nor public safety. Without regulations, individual operators might drive 1,000 miles per day and work around the clock, creating market imperatives that destroy the personal health of drivers and endanger the safety of the public. In other words, the market can transfer the risk to an innocent, uninvolved party. In fact, before regulation, individuals and carriers drove themselves without limitation, at enormous risk to themselves and others.[6] Social regulations, such as those limiting hours of service, affect the economic well-being of the trucking industry and therefore are part of the fabric that we must consider as we weigh regulation's costs and benefits.

Trucking is a "derived demand" industry, meaning that the demand for trucking is derived from the demand for goods. The shippers of goods directly consume trucking services; end purchasers of goods consume trucking services only indirectly. In fact, logistics and distribution, whether purchased or not, are integral to the production process.

Therefore, the relative efficiency of the distribution process, and the costs added to the production of goods, have a significant effect on product marketability. Efficient regulation may enhance the economic distribution of goods, while inefficient regulation may add unnecessary costs.

The Regulation Debate

The debate over regulative restructuring has been cast rather starkly as one between "good guys" and "bad guys."[7] Here, the good guys are those who support free enterprise and the unregulated market—"procompetitive deregulation"—and the bad guys are "special interests" who appropriate the political process for their own private ends. These critics argue that virtually all regulation is anticompetitive.[8] But the issue is far more complicated than that.

The primary supporters of a reduction in economic regulation have been two obvious special interests: the nation's largest shippers of goods and their trade associations, and the customers of those shippers. For shippers, deregulation means lower prices, more choices among transport modalities, and a greater ability to compete globally. Besides across-the-board declines in rates, large manufacturers expected that regulatory reduction would allow them to use the additional economic leverage of large-scale purchase of transportation services to drive down their particular cost structures and gain advantage over their competitors, many of which are small businesses.

The nation's owner operators (variously estimated between 200,000 and 400,000 strong) and their associations also supported this position. Owner-drivers eyed high trucking rates and wanted some of the largesse. Believing they had lower cost structures than their potential competitors—who had to carry union-scale wages and benefits as well as costly investments in terminals, warehouses, and support staff—these owner operators expected to reap a bonanza of new business opportunities. As individuals, however, they did not consider what it would mean if all of them entered the market without rate and entry control. Further, they did not anticipate the growth in social regulation designed to curb abuses and redistribute externalities, as many of the burdens of social regulation fall disproportionately on small operators.

Most microeconomists, who adhere to a theory of market economics that regards regulatory institutions with skepticism, offered their support for regulatory restructuring. But even Ann Friedlaender, a supporter of economic deregulation with a background in transportation economics, cautioned in 1969—rather prophetically—that the elimination of governmental regulation could seriously harm some sectors of the transportation industry (particularly trucking companies) and might cause the industry to concentrate and create multimodal transportation empires, potentially restricting competition in the long run.[9] Others were more certain that the elimination of most economic regulation would be an unmitigated success.[10]

As expected, the opponents of regulatory restructuring had a stake in the existing system. Trucking companies, with a collective $3 to $4 billion investment in operating authority required by the existing system of regulation,[11] generally opposed economic deregulation. Carriers understood that with a stroke of the pen these rights would become worthless. By 1980, however, some of these companies had adjusted successfully to administrative deregulation and figured they might ultimately benefit. In addition, since the Motor Carrier Act of 1980 primarily codified the administrative deregulation enacted by the ICC over the previous three years,[12] the American Trucking Associations (ATA) came out in support of the Act, reasoning that it might shut the door on further economic deregulation.

Many economists reasoned that the Teamsters were the main beneficiaries of regulation, siphoning off economic rents for the workers they represent.[13] To many free market adherents, unions themselves inherently represent a restraint of trade and are anticompetitive organizations of special interests (employees).[14] Organized labor, therefore, became one of the main targets of the proponents of regulatory restructuring.

The Teamsters recognized that reduction of controls on rate and entry would mean thousands of new non-union competitors and would greatly complicate collective bargaining in the trucking industry. Since the union already was beset with problems caused by the pernicious inflation of the 1970s, combined with economic stagnation that had reduced tonnage, the Teamsters expected disastrous consequences from entry and rate decontrol.

Many transportation economists also opposed wholesale reduction of regulatory oversight, rejecting the argument that the un-regulated market would be a panacea. These economists predicted correctly that regulatory restructuring would produce market concentration.

Some transportation economists believed destructive competition would result from deregulation. They reasoned that the peculiar structure of the transportation industry would create a market in persistent crisis, driving profits too low to support reinvestment and driving wages too low to support recruiting.[15] Such destructive competition might also encourage concentration, as only a small number of carriers would survive such a shakeout.

The policy debate, then, ended up being framed as a choice between regulation and deregulation. In practice, however, concerns over public interest and the public good following economic deregulation led to the enactment of a patchwork of social regulation that replaced one regulatory framework with another. The choice should have been between economic and social regulation, between market and institutional regulation. Government makes tradeoffs between these two options, not between institutional regulation and no regulation at all.

Evaluating the effectiveness of these regulatory frameworks requires an overview of the regulations that comprised each of them. Let us take them one by one.

Economic Regulation before 1977

Intense competition among truckers developed during the 1920s and intensified during the Great Depression. This unbridled competition produced low rates and irregular service. Policymakers considered irregular service a threat to interstate commerce, as well as to the budding motor trucking industry. Low rates also threatened the railroads, as intercity truck transport invaded the railroads' less-than-carload market.[16]

Congress passed the Motor Carrier Act of 1935 after ten years of agitation by state regulatory agencies, the ICC, business, and labor.[17] Later incorporated as Part II of the Interstate Commerce Act of 1940, the MCA of 1935 followed the pattern set by the Interstate Commerce Act of 1877, regulating interstate trucking for the benefit of both the industry and the public good.

This federal regulation did not arise in a vacuum. While the Commerce Clause of the U.S. Constitution prohibited states from establishing regulations that affected interstate commerce, most states required carriers to obtain intrastate operating certificates based on a convenience and necessity standard. They also regulated carrier safety based on their ordinary police powers. As motor carriers of freight and passengers sought to extend their business to adjoining states, they were hampered by inconsistent state regulation and certification.[18]

Regulation, as administered by the ICC, closed the trucking industry to most new entrants. Existing carriers of most commodities had to apply to the ICC for certification, and new carriers had to establish, to the ICC's satisfaction, that there was a need for service that existing carriers could not meet. Carriers also had to prove that they were capable of meeting the demand for service specified by their certificates and had to certify insurance coverage. Common carriers and contract carriers differed in these fitness standards: the former had to be available to serve the public based on publicly filed rates, while the latter limited themselves to serving individual shippers under rates determined by private contract. Finally, the law established value-of-service pricing as the legal standard, and rates had to be compensatory.[19]

The MCA of 1935 created a legal and structural taxonomy that remains the foundation for motor carrier industry structure today (although the competitive imperatives in the absence of regulations defining responsibility continually break down these distinctions). The Act split for-hire trucking among three types of carriage: contract, common, and exempt. Common carriers hauled a wide range of commodities according to published tariffs filed with the ICC. They set tariffs collectively, using rate bureaus, or filed rates independently.[20] Common carriers made their services available to the public over regular or irregular routes on a scheduled or unscheduled basis. The MCA of 1935 made common carriers liable for the full value of the freight they hauled, and their rates reflected that liability. We can find precedent for this liability in English Common Law, as English authorities created this legal structure to discourage collusion between "waggon" carriers and highwaymen.[21]

The MCA of 1935 allowed for-hire contract carriers to haul a similar range of goods, but they were governed by private contracts between the shipper and the trucker specifying rates and services, generally for truckload shipments. Although contract carriers filed their rates with the ICC, they did not make their services available to the public through a posted tariff. Unlike common carriers and depending on the private contract between shipper and carrier, contract carriers ordinarily were not liable for the value of freight.

Following the MCA of 1935, the Interstate Commerce Commission sought to draw a clear line between common and contract carriage. While the ICC required common carriers to meet strict standards of "convenience and necessity," availability, nondiscrimination, and load liability, it required contract carriers to serve a narrow niche. Contract carriers were subject to a rather arbitrary Rule of Eight: carriers could be contracted (and dedicated) to a maximum of eight shippers. While common carriers set rates collectively and filed them with the ICC, contract carriers set rates within a private contract framework between shipper and trucker.

Exempt carriers hauled commodities, including raw agricultural goods, newspapers, and several other specific products, that were free of federal regulation. Carriers that operated within designated urban commercial zones remained unregulated. Finally, the MCA of 1935 exempted intrastate and local cartage and shipments that were part of continuous air freight movements. Private carriers, which exist primarily for the transportation of goods or services produced or sold by non-transportation firms, also were exempt.

The 1977–1980 Transition

Everything started to change in 1977, when deregulation of the trucking industry began in earnest. Between 1977 and 1980, with the active bipartisan support of both the Carter Administration and Congress, the ICC used its administrative discretion to reduce its economic control incrementally.[22] Annual operating authority applications dramatically increased as ICC approval rates[23] rose to 98% in 1979. The Commission also allowed some carriers to transfer dormant authority even though it harmed protesting carriers. The ICC eliminated gateways, cities through which regular route carriers had to haul their freight between origin and destination. This assured the ICC that the carrier would be available to serve shippers along specified freight lanes.

To further open the market, the ICC allowed carriers to hold both contract and common carrier authority for the first time and stopped enforcing the Rule of Eight.[24] The ICC even departed from the "convenience and necessity" standard that had applied to common carriers for at least 100 years. It permitted private carriers to act as for-hire carriers on the backhaul, ostensibly to facilitate energy savings. Private carriers also set up separate transportation divisions to engage in "compensated intercorporate transportation," transporting freight for the entire corporation and its related entities.[25] Perhaps most important, the ICC began to reduce the power of the rate bureaus.[26]

This last move went to the heart of transportation regulation—the issue of price. The natural and regulated origins of price long have been a source of controversy. Should we base transportation rates on the cost of the service provided by the transporter, or on the value to the shipper of the service demanded? Those who argue that the cost of service should determine rates claim that regulated value-of-service rates distort the market and cause allocative inefficiency.[27] Economist Alfred Kahn, an important proponent of deregulation, claims that truck common carriers merely matched rail value-of-service rates and took the cream off the market: "Once the trucking alternative was available, defining value of service (or demand inelasticity) in terms of the value of the commodities being shipped became highly illogical."[28] According to the cost-of-service argument, unregulated competition will ensure that carriers base freight rates on the actual marginal cost of transportation.

Others argue that value-of-service pricing is a logical approach to the pricing of transportation services and that it is inherently efficient, since the demand for service determines the rate people will pay to move the freight. Philip Locklin, perhaps the most venerable of transportation economists, cites F. W. Taussig: "Ability to stand the transportation charge is the test of the utility of the carriage."[29] Value-of-service theory contends that transportation market efficiency will cause transporters to set rates according to the relative value to the shipper of moving the freight at the optimum speed appropriate to the carrying cost and time sensitivity of the freight. The law of supply and demand will force those with inelastic demand to pay higher rates and fully allocated costs, or more. Conversely, those with elastic demand will hold their goods and more likely pay the marginal cost of transportation, or less.[30]

According to this argument, value-of-service pricing is consistent with Marshall's Law for a derived demand: competition will ensure that truckers base freight rates on the value to the shipper of moving any particular shipment of goods at a specified level of service, and that value will relate directly to inventory cost.[31] The elasticity of demand thus corresponds directly to the value of the goods transported. If value-of-service theory explains price, and the value of the service corresponds with the inventory cost, then the value of goods may be a reasonable proxy with which to define freight rates.

In fact, cost-of-service pricing may not exist in the competitive market. The logistics strategies of shippers and the business strategies of carriers may tend to replicate "value-of-service" pricing even without regulation. For example, recent empirical research shows that value-of-service pricing determines rates in the produce-hauling market, which has never been regulated.[32]

While regulatory restructuring in trucking began as an incremental process, the Motor Carrier Act of 1980 gave legislative sanction to the administrative actions of the late 1970s transitional period.[33] However, this legislative regulatory restructuring did not extend significantly beyond the administrative deregulation already carried out by the Carter-era ICC and arguably provided a fallback position, albeit a deep one, for the industry.[34] Thus, it was the Carter Administration, and not the Reagan Administration—as some scholars attribute[35]—that was largely responsible for the change.

Economic Regulation after 1980

And what should we call that change? Again, the trucking industry has not been deregulated, strictly speaking, although the change commonly is described as deregulation. More accurately, legislation restructured regulation along several dimensions, increasing restrictions on some activities and decreasing restrictions on others. On the economic side, the critical changes involved relaxation of industry and market entry rules and of controls over rates. On the other hand, the entry and rate filing structures remained until 1994, and intrastate economic regulation remained until 1995. Carriers still had to obtain authority and common carriers still had to file rates, although the ICC's lack of enthusiasm for rate filing led to chaotic procedures and inconsistent law enforcement.[36]

The MCA of 1980 set the following key rules:

- Individuals or businesses seeking to enter the interstate trucking business "need only prove a 'useful public purpose' rather than public convenience and necessity." Carriers must apply for and receive operating authority, demonstrate they are able to provide the service they plan to offer, and prove insurance coverage.
- The new regulations eliminated gateways and indirect routings through the cities for which carriers had authority, allowing carriers to take the most direct route. The new rules supported ICC grants of blanket round-trip authority and struck "unreasonable and excessively narrow territorial limitations."
- A "zone of rate freedom" authorized carriers' rates to vary within a specified range, without requiring the carrier to file a new tariff. New rules allowed released value rates, relieving common carriers of liability for the value of freight if the tariff specified it.
- New regulations limited rate bureau authority. The ICC phased out bureaus' single-line rates (the rate for a shipment on a single

carrier) after January 1984 and eliminated the antitrust immu-
nity that had allowed carriers to meet under the rubric of the rate
bureau to devise rates and frameworks within which to share
revenue and liability for shipments requiring the services of two
or more carriers. Rate bureaus still functioned after 1984 in a
research and advisory capacity, and in limited collective rate-
making. In the confusing environment that resulted, carriers
collectively raised tariffs beyond the rate of inflation and then
deeply discounted those rates on an individual, shipper-by-
shipper basis, producing sharp discrimination between large and
small shippers. However, carriers still filed rates with the ICC.[37]

- The new rules formally eliminated the Rule of Eight, allowing
contract carriers to haul for a wider range of shippers and to hold
both contract and common authority. Private carriers gained
expanded hauling rights, and other rules were loosened.[38]

In spite of economic deregulation of ICC-regulated carriers, most
interstate carriers still had some filing and reporting requirements. By
1990, however, approximately 58% of all intercity ton-miles were completely exempt from federal economic regulation, and exempt trucking accounted for 54% of all truck freight revenue. Exempt carriers'
share of tonnage increased 1.62% during the 1980s, though their share
of revenue dropped 1.48% over the same period.[39] While the extent of
economic regulation diminished throughout this era for the regulated
carriers, common carriers still had to apply for certification and operate within its limits, provide proof of insurance, file tariffs,[40] charge
according to filed tariffs, and keep and file specified financial and operating reports.[41]

All of these practices came to a grinding halt in January 1995. Congress, in a rider to an airport funding bill, mandated intrastate economic deregulation. This final coup de grace developed out of a dispute between competitors UPS and Federal Express that came to a head
in California. FedEx originally was an "air taxi" and "air express" carrier
using trucks and small planes. As the company transformed itself into
a general freight carrier, it maintained this special status, never having
been covered by the Motor Carrier Act. UPS, originally a local store delivery carrier from the Seattle area, was classified by the ICC as a motor
carrier from the beginning. In the confusing semiregulated environ-

ment, UPS and FedEx thus found themselves competing under very different rules in California. With its classification, FedEx was free to change intrastate rates as it pleased, because the state of California had no authority over rail and air carriers. As a motor carrier, UPS was regulated by the state public utilities commission and had to apply to it for rate changes. This gave FedEx a dramatic competitive advantage.

The dispute landed in the courts, of course, and the court favored FedEx. This proved to be the last straw. Politicians from many regulated states complained that unregulated states had an unfair advantage, and politicians from unregulated states complained that regulated states prevented the free flow of commerce. Caught in the crosshairs, economic regulation of trucking was dead in its tracks. The ICC died along with it; Congress "sunsetted" the agency, and the doors closed for good in January 1996. The ICC's remaining responsibilities were distributed among other agencies.

As argued elsewhere in this book, deregulation does not mean the end of regulation. It does not mean the end of "big government" either. In fact, with a rider to an airport funding act Congress centralized regulation by mandating that states conform to a national standard under which markets regulate motor carriers. Congress took away the states' right to choose regulatory forms, with dramatic consequences for carriers, employees, and consumers. Although economic regulation ceased after January 1995, social regulation remained significant.

In the case of FedEx and UPS, in particular, the difference in regulatory regimes spells an ominous conflict in policy that recently has had serious consequences. UPS, classified as a motor carrier by the now defunct ICC, is covered by the National Labor Relations Act (NLRA, as amended), the labor regulation that covers the rest of private industry, with few exceptions. Two of those exceptions are the airline and rail industries.

Airlines and railroads, including "express" carrier FedEx, are covered by the Railway Labor Act (RLA).[42] Under the RLA, unions must be elected by a majority of all employees nationwide, not by a majority of voting employees or a majority of employees voting in a single production unit. This makes it difficult for the Teamsters to organize

FedEx. The RLA also has an elaborate set of negotiation and mediation requirements, including built-in political interference, that makes rail and air labor negotiations drag on for years after every contract expires and that gives politicians great leeway to interfere once a strike or lockout has commenced. As a result, FedEx operates under a completely different labor-management regulation regime. Since UPS's air freight operation has been classified as an air carrier, UPS's pilots are covered by the RLA. The difference in outcomes is notable, as UPS successfully used the RLA to insulate itself from a potential pilots' strike in 1997. In contrast, the NLRA allowed the Teamsters to successfully strike UPS's ground operations the same year, incidentally shutting off the supply of air freight. The NLRA narrowly limited the president's authority to intervene in the latter case, as only a national emergency can justify intervention under the NLRA. Under the RLA, by contrast, intervention by the National Mediation Board is routine and the threshold for intervention at the presidential level is much lower generally.

Social Regulation of the Trucking Industry

The restructuring of economic regulation reduced government economic controls but left social regulation intact. In fact, regulation of working conditions, and especially of highway safety, increased during the 1980s. Arguably, this made the trucking industry more regulated than ever.[43]

Safety

We turn first to safety regulation, which originated from state police powers.[44] Forty-four states have established intrastate transportation regulatory agencies, and 23 states have their own departments of transportation.[45]

As the trucking industry expanded beyond local cartage into interstate commerce, single-state regulation became less effective, and the federal government stepped in to set national safety standards. The Motor Carrier Act of 1935 established economic and safety regulation on a national basis, giving enforcement authority to the Interstate Commerce Commission. The ICC issued its first set of safety standards in 1940, applicable to common, contract, and private carriers.[46] Authority for safety supervision further centralized following the establishment of the Highway Trust Fund in 1956, the same year that the federal government first standardized size and weight limits. States that did not conform to the new national standards risked losing federal highway aid. After 1956 this use of federal funds to leverage states' compliance with federally established standards became routine.

The Highway Safety Act of 1966 directed the secretary of commerce to set new standards for "driver education and licensing; vehicle registration, operations, and inspections; accident investigations and reporting; traffic control; and highway design and maintenance."[47] The National Traffic and Motor Vehicle Safety Act, passed the same year, created the National Traffic Safety Agency to develop new safety and performance standards. Later in 1966 Congress transferred safety regulation from the Commerce Department and the ICC to the newly created Department of Transportation (DOT).

Within the DOT, several agencies are responsible for various aspects of trucking safety. The Federal Highway Administration (FHWA) took over administration of employee qualification, hours of service, operations, and truck safety.[48] The Federal Motor Carrier Safety Administration (known until 1999 as the FHWA's Office of Motor Carriers or OMC[49]) administers motor carrier safety programs. The National Highway Traffic Safety Administration (NHTSA), created by the Federal-Aid Highway Act of 1970, has broader responsibility for highway, vehicle, driver, passenger, and pedestrian safety, with most of its focus on automobiles. The National Transportation Safety Board (NTSB), created by the Department of Transportation Act of 1966, is an independent agency responsible for investigating transportation accidents and developing proposals designed to promote transportation safety.[50]

The nation's concern with high accident and fatality rates on the highways motivated much of the federal regulation of the 1960s and 1970s. To enforce these new regulations, Congress and the president enhanced the power of the purse. Between the 1950s and the 1970s the tax and program burdens shifted to the federal government, forcing states to comply with the new federal standards or risk losing valuable federal funds.[51] By the 1970s dependence on the federal government was complete, enabling President Richard Nixon to force states to adopt the 55-mile-per-hour speed limit—despite great opposition—under the threat of losing federal highway funds.

While regulatory restructuring in the late 1970s and early 1980s may have reduced economic regulation, social regulation slowed only briefly. It was not long before redoubled efforts to protect public safety in the wake of economic deregulation led to an intensification of regulation.

Initially, the Carter Administration attempted to combine economic deregulation with modernized regulations regarding hours-of-service. These were designed to limit competition based on overwork, or the sweating of labor. Extensive studies of the nature of driver fatigue, including its causes and potential solutions, led the DOT to propose several possible changes in hours-of-service rules in 1978. But these new rules failed to win full enactment during the Carter Administration. Armed with a cost-benefit analysis prepared by consultants from Booz-Allen & Hamilton that claimed the costs outweighed the benefits, the Reagan Administration threw the rules out soon afterward.[52]

Despite the failure to revise these 40-year-old rules on hours-of-service—first issued in 1937 and 1938—the federal government continued to pair highway funding and safety legislation. The government sometimes combined highway and safety funding with productivity enhancements for the industry that many safety advocates claimed posed safety risks. The Surface Transportation Assistance Act (STAA) of 1982, for example, raised highway taxes while establishing uniform minimum size and weight limits on interstate highways and other interstate-quality highways that were part of the FHWA's "designated highway system" for STAA vehicles. This mandate forced states with lower maximum weights and shorter maximum lengths to allow larger trucks on the interstates. Again, states that did not comply risked losing federal highway funds. The STAA also established the Motor Carrier Safety Assistance Program (MCSAP), designed to help states develop programs that intensified enforcement of safety and hazardous materials regulations, including training of roadside inspectors, audits of interstate carriers' terminals, and increased enforcement of the

55-mile-per-hour speed limit. These programs also provided special funding to help states develop programs to enforce federal motor carrier standards, including state standards that are at least as rigorous as the federal ones.[53]

The STAA established protections for drivers and other trucking employees from discipline or discharge for reporting a safety problem or for refusing to violate safety laws. However, the law charges the Occupational Safety and Health Administration (OSHA) with enforcement of this whistle-blower protection, and critics such as Teamsters for a Democratic Union charge OSHA with failure to enforce the law.[54] Indeed, truckdriver safety seems to have fallen between the cracks as critics charge that neither DOT nor OSHA has taken clear responsibility for truck driver safety and health.

Still concerned about safety, Congress passed the Motor Carrier Safety Act of 1984. This Act gave the states five years to meet federal safety standards or risk federal preemption of state laws. Directing the DOT to establish minimum vehicular and operational standards, the Act increased fines and enforced regulations administratively, thereby avoiding the need to win criminal convictions in federal courts. The Motor Carrier Safety Act of 1984 also required states to conduct equipment inspections at least annually. The Tandem Truck Safety Act of 1984, part of the Motor Carrier Safety Act, allowed governors to ask the DOT to prohibit larger trucks and doubles, generally permitted by the STAA of 1982, from specified highways, while it forced the states to permit STAA-allowed truck combinations "reasonable" access from interstate highways to truck terminals.[55]

Driver licensing has long been an issue for safety proponents. Truck drivers in some states could get a license simply by passing a written chauffeur's test—the same test that covers all commercial drivers, from taxi drivers to tractor-trailer drivers. Record keeping was an issue as well: while some states kept detailed driving records for a long time, drivers with suspended or revoked licenses could easily obtain licences from certain other states. In 1986 Congress passed another Motor Carrier Safety Act, requiring commercial drivers to acquire a national driver's license and establishing nationwide certification and record keeping. On April 1, 1992, all commercial drivers were required to have a Commercial Driver's License (CDL), a special license appropriate to the equipment they drive and the loads they haul.

Congress has modified the foregoing laws repeatedly, further tightening the rules under which motor carriers operate. For example, the Motor Carrier Safety Act of 1990 specified civil and criminal penalties for failure to maintain records required by the Motor Carrier Safety Act of 1984[56] and prohibited the operations of carriers that receive unsatisfactory safety ratings. The Motor Carrier Act of 1991 forced the states to conform with national and international fuel tax and registration standards,[57] granted further funds to the states to develop motor carrier safety programs, and gave the secretary of transportation authority to approve states' safety programs. The Act attempts to ensure states' participation in the Commercial Vehicle Safety Alliance (CVSA) and SAFETYNET,[58] encourages private sector development of training programs for entry-level drivers, and directs the transportation secretary to require states to set up mandatory alcohol and drug testing programs. The Act funds up to 80% reimbursement for states' costs to implement these new federally mandated standards, while providing that states that do not set up the mandated programs according to federal standards will have funds withheld.[59] Again, a federal mandate intensified regulation, even as the states struggled to retain their ability to regulate the underlying market process that undermines their ability to control the operations of motor carriers.

Since January 1, 1992, DOT regulations have required all motor carriers to do preemployment, reasonable cause, and random periodic drug testing of all employees. The DOT estimates that the regulation affects more than 200,000 trucking operations, employing approximately 3 million drivers, and the FHWA estimates that it will cost government and industry $1.6 billion to implement these regulations. The DOT requires that enough testing take place to ensure that 50% of all employees will be spot-tested during any single year.[60] Further, new DOT rules resulting from the 1991 Omnibus Transportation Employee Testing Act required alcohol breath-testing (including random testing of 25% of all employees annually) of 6.6 million truck and bus drivers, at a cost of $200 million per year.[61] Initial implementation of the rule required carriers with a failure rate of 1% or greater to test 50% of employees randomly, while carriers with a failure rate of .05% annually were required to test only 10% of employees.[62] Alcohol violations were low enough that the FHWA reduced the testing rate to 10% on January 1, 1998, for all carriers.

In sum, if the 1980s brought less economic regulation, intensified social regulation made trucking operations even more complicated and expensive. And while the trucking industry has worried about highway safety for many years, the intensely competitive environment associated with reduced economic regulation may have exacerbated the problem.

Since economic deregulation, hundreds of thousands of owner operators and drivers working for small, unregulated carriers have become harder to locate, supervise, train, and monitor, compared with drivers working for certificated, regulated carriers. In addition, the highly competitive market fostered by regulatory restructuring provides a daily incentive to violate rules designed to encourage safe operations.[63] Thus, economic deregulation may have compromised public safety even as social regulation made it more costly and complicated for carriers to comply with safety rules.

Carriers that now are exempt from economic regulation still must comply with DOT safety regulations and come under the jurisdiction of these safety agencies. Control over these carriers, however, has become tenuous. In addition, the federal government constructed a mandate maze through which states must navigate to get their tax money returned to them in the form of programs. The result, say many carrier executives, is a monumentally difficult business environment.

Working Conditions

Safety is only one part of the social regulation picture. There is also the matter of regulation of working conditions.

Unlike most other private-sector workers, employees of motor carriers subject to the Motor Carrier Acts of 1935 and 1980 are not subject to the maximum hour (overtime) provisions of the Fair Labor Standards Act of 1938 (FLSA). The law exempts more than 1.3 million employees of these MCA–regulated carriers, whether they are city or road drivers, helpers, platform workers, or mechanics. Congress created the exemption ostensibly to prevent jurisdictional conflict between the ICC[64] and the Department of Labor (DOL) because of the public service nature of the industry.[65] Now that the ICC has been abolished, such reasoning has become obsolete. The DOL, however, still has not extended its authority, and trucking employees remain only partially covered by the law and subject to extremely long hours of work.

In 1981 the Minimum Wage Study Commission (MWSC)[66] decided this exemption was acceptable because union contracts covered 80% of all over-the-road drivers, and unionized city and road drivers benefited from standards that exceeded the FLSA. The commission considered that adequate protection was provided by complex contractual provisions for daily guarantees, pay for non-driving work, and trip *minima*[67] (see chapter 5).

Unfortunately, the MWSC based its report on pre-deregulation data, between five and 15 years old at the time. The decline in union coverage and the substantial growth of non-union truckload carriers during the late 1970s and following the passage of the MCA of 1980 created an environment in which wage and work rule concessions could thrive.

My research has shown that the industry transformation created a new, low-wage sector in which road drivers for national general freight TL carriers earn 58% of the average mileage wage rate of drivers at national LTL carriers. In fact, after adjusting for the absence of pay for most non-driving labor time and for the absence of overtime pay for work beyond 40 hours, it appears over-the-road truckload drivers' mean earnings average quite a bit less, maybe as low as $7 per hour.[68] Furthermore, while the MWSC report specifically notes drivers usually received pay for their non-driving labor because of collective bargaining contracts, TL and non-union carriers now are significantly less likely to pay drivers for their non-driving labor time.[69]

In my 1991 survey of 225 Class I general freight motor carriers, I found that companies were much more likely to pay LTL drivers than TL drivers for all of their labor. By not paying for non-driving labor time, carriers push the risk for inefficient operations down to the drivers. While inefficiencies can be created by the carriers, more likely than not they are the result of a lack of concern on the part of shippers and consignees for the labor time of truck drivers, whose time has no cost to them. To determine the extent of the risk shift, I created a "Risk-Shifting Index," comparing freight drivers across several dimensions. I found that unionized drivers, in both LTL and TL segments of the trucking industry, were significantly more likely to be paid for all of their time. Comparing LTL with TL, I also found the LTL industry itself was more likely to pay drivers for their non-driving labor than was the TL industry (table 3.1).[70]

Finally, this low-wage, non-union competition has forced concessions on many local unions. For example, during the 1980s, Chicago's powerful Teamsters Local 705 agreed to allow carriers covered by the tank drivers' contract to break down the distinction between city and road seniority boards (the collective bargaining contract specified separate bidding for road and city drivers). This meant that once a driver had worked 40 hours locally at a straight-time hourly rate, the company could force him onto the road for the remaining 20 to 30 hours at a straight road rate, which is paid on a mileage or "piecework" rate. A subsequent contract raised city drivers' overtime standards from eight hours per day to 45 hours per week, exacerbating the situation. Again, the 45-hour workweek at straight time would be illegal in almost any other industry.

Such conditions exist outside the tank drivers' contract as well. In many cities, non-union competition has forced even union drivers to accept compensation based on a percentage of freight revenue, rather than on miles or hours. For example, intermodal (both piggyback and container) drivers frequently earn a percentage of the revenue paid by the freight. Since the rate does not increase along with a driver's weekly hours, all driver compensation is on a straight piecework basis. In addition, if the rate falls, the driver's wage falls as well. Drivers absorb all delay time at rail and container terminals, and percentage rates reduce shipper incentives to improve timeliness and productivity. Also, most piggyback or drayage carriers are local carriers, so they do not file daily driver logs, making enforcement extremely difficult. In practice, drivers may work an unlimited number of hours each week.

Table 3.1 1991 Risk-Shifting Index, by Industry Segmentation and Unionization Patterns

Type of Carrier	Risk-Shift Index	Type of Carrier	Risk-Shift Index	t-Statistic	Significance
National	2.333	Regional	1.653	3.144	***
LTL	1.387	TL	2.475	7.701	***
Union	1.324	Non-union	2.400	7.661	***
Union/LTL	1.127	Non-union/LTL	2.100	4.840	***
Union/TL	2.154	Non-union/TL	2.630	1.750	*
Union/LTL	1.127	Union/TL	2.154	3.990	***
Union/LTL/regional	1.135	Non-union/LTL/regional	2.053	4.458	***
Union/TL/regional	2.000	Non-union/TL/regional	2.688	2.140	*

Source: Belzer survey data 1991. First published in Michael H. Belzer, "Collective Bargaining after Deregulation: Do the Teamsters Still Count?" *Industrial and Labor Relations Review* 48 (1995): 648. Reprinted with permission.

*Statistically significant at the .10 level (two-tailed tests).
***Statistically significant at the .01 level (two-tailed tests).
Risk-shift index measures the extent to which drivers absorb non-driving labor time. Table compares risk-shift indexes for each segment of the general freight trucking industry.
Definitions derived from 1991 industry survey: National carriers operate within all sections of the country; regional carriers operate within one or more regions.
Index Coding: 1 = drivers earn wages for all non-driving labor time; 2 = drivers earn wages for some non-driving labor time; 3 = drivers earn no wages for non-driving labor time

Thus, with the expansion of the truckload sector and the resulting significant de-unionization of the industry, many drivers earn very low wages, some falling below the federal minimum, especially when one accounts for unpaid waiting, loading, and unloading time and labor.[71] But changes wrought by deregulation have gone even further. They have transformed the entire trucking industry, from the firm down to the lowest employee. That transformation is the subject of the next two chapters.

4 An Industry Transformed

The new regulatory regime—designed to subject the trucking industry to market forces—has changed the economic environment for the industry and its workers. Before 1977 the trucking industry was a utility, regulated and tied to the public trust. Regulatory restructuring forced carriers to repackage themselves as niche producers, focusing their energies on definable markets and customer needs. Compelled by the market to redesign business strategies forged over decades, successful carriers that could find markets which fit their expertise and capital structures succeeded. Those that could not went out of business.

Today, employees work longer hours for smaller paychecks. Research shows that drivers exceed hours of service limits regularly, pushing to deliver loads on time to satisfy ever more demanding customers. We also know that real wages have declined by nearly one-third, and by more than one-half in the most competitive sectors. Economic deregulation also accelerated the de-unionization of the trucking industry, contributing to the decline in wages and conditions. As the Teamsters Union represents fewer workers and workplaces and bargains within an extremely lean environment, industrial relations within trucking have become wracked by crisis and conflict.

Collective bargaining within the general freight sector of the trucking industry has become more decentralized since economic deregulation. Bargaining between the Teamsters and general freight motor carriers had been centralized under the National Master Freight Agreement (NMFA) beginning in 1965, bringing about remarkably uniform wage levels and working conditions across industry sectors and regions. With the decentralization of bargaining, the coverage of the NMFA has declined by two-thirds, and the variation of wages and conditions has increased.

But it is not only the relations between employer and employee that have shifted. The business of trucking itself—operations, markets, productivity—has been transformed by intense competition. Profits are harder to come by, and the trucking industry has suffered successive waves of accelerating bankruptcy following both economic and legislative shocks.

What caused such a profound transformation of this industry?

Trucking Operations and Market Structure

The first part of that answer relates to shipment size, which exerts an important influence on the general freight industry. Before deregulation, many full-service general freight carriers hauled a mix of truckload and less-than-truckload freight, balancing between the two types to keep trucks fully loaded on all movements. Take Yellow Freight, for example: before deregulation, the company carried mostly truckload freight on eastward movements, with more less-than-truckload freight going west.[1] Anticipating deregulation, Yellow began to shed once-profitable truckload freight and re-balance its freight network with LTL freight in all movements. Like other successful LTL carriers, Yellow was poised to take advantage of deregulation by a combination of proactive strategic repositioning and the competitive advantage already inherent in its relatively dense route structure.

Deregulation has reshaped the competitive environment. Today carriers that were previously restricted to the commodities, service areas, and routes for which they held certificates are permitted to compete in any market and price according to what the market will bear. Indeed, competitive pressure quickly stripped many carriers of their stable freight bases and required them to find new customers overnight. While regulators were the motor carriers' "customers" before 1980, carriers were forced to recognize very quickly that their real customers were those who would buy the services, and they would buy only the services they preferred at a price that they demanded. Indeed, in the deep economic recession of the early 1980s, and with the tremendous overcapacity created by the immediate deregulatory shakeout, the market for trucking services belonged to the buyers.

Soon after the regulatory structure changed, carriers specializing in TL shipments proliferated. Deep price cuts for these shipments became the norm. Why did these carriers gain such a competitive advantage? The answer can be found in the structure of the general freight industry.

Companies specializing in LTL freight employ a sophisticated network of pickup and delivery (P & D) trucks that "peddle freight" on a local basis. Dispatched from a terminal with a load of small shipments, these trucks deliver and pick up freight throughout the day, returning at the close of business with a load of small shipments destined for locations throughout the carrier's network and beyond. Dockworkers unload these peddle trailers and distribute the freight to linehaul trailers heading to other terminals for subsequent delivery by peddle drivers in other cities.

Many of the large LTL carriers also have "break bulk" terminals located strategically throughout their systems, designed to aggregate freight from end-of-line terminals throughout their region and accept and re-ship freight from other regions. For these carriers, the originating city terminal may ship freight destined for widespread locations to a break bulk. Freight on one trailer may be destined for several cities in a distant region. Once this freight arrives at the break bulk, dockworkers unload the trailer and combine the freight with that from other city terminals. Linehaul drivers then take the freight to its destination—which in some cases is another city terminal, where dockworkers unload the trailer and distribute the freight among several city peddle routes. The pickup and delivery process then begins again.

Once carriers grow large enough to develop super-dense pickup and delivery volume, they may be able to do away with some of the break bulk hubs and deliver more freight directly. The first carrier to restructure operations this way was Consolidated Freightways, a national LTL carrier. In September 1995 the company announced a restructuring of its operations to provide for more direct delivery between major cities. The restructuring, which reverted to the use of sleeper-teams, was intended to provide shorter cycle times for customers—causing significant dislocations, including lost jobs for some drivers and dockworkers, and harder work and arguably a reduced quality of life for the drivers who remain. Yellow Freight System and Roadway Express followed with similar strategic changes, and these carriers have reduced dramatically the number of terminals in their systems. Broadly speaking, all carriers have had to reevaluate their old systems based on a large number of local and intermediate terminals and have optimized operations to deliver freight directly as much as possible, reducing the number of intermediate handlings.

The elaborate system of terminals maintained by LTL carriers, akin to multiple hubs and spokes with many layers of centralization, is unnecessary for truckload freight. The shipper typically loads TL freight at its dock, and the trucker delivers it directly to one or more consignees. There are many variations: for instance, there may be consolidation points from which a TL trucker picks up freight for delivery to another consolidation point across the country. But the basic process is the same. The infrastructure requirements differ fundamentally: TL carriers need not invest in the terminals and break bulks required to handle LTL freight.

To understand the significance of deregulation, however, recall that successful carriers originally built the industry around balanced freight movements. In a broad sense, carriers typically hauled raw materials from west to east and finished goods from east to west. The trucks were loaded all the time, but some of the shipments were LTL and some were TL. In practice, the modal motor carrier earned about 40% of its revenue from TL freight and about 60% from LTL freight. Terminals had to exist at both ends, however, because the carrier had to be ready, willing, and able to handle whatever volume of freight for which it had authority that shippers might tender. The terminal structure had to serve the network at either end. The industrial relations practices and work rules that developed reflected the mixed nature of the industrial process, as well as the job control unionism prevalent within the U.S. industrial relations system.[2] City drivers picked up and delivered both LTL and TL shipments out of city terminals, while linehaul drivers performed intercity transport.

Deregulation also abruptly discarded what were once rigid entry and service requirements. Under the regulated regime carriers had been responsible for hauling the commodities for which they had authority, in whatever volume, and had to be prepared to do so. After deregulation, carriers could pick and choose, discriminating in favor of strategically advantageous freight in advantageous markets. Since others could enter their markets, they had to actively enter the markets of others to protect themselves.

What had been efficient under the original regulatory structure suddenly became inefficient. Once the rules allowed carriers to discriminate in favor of large shippers, carriers needed to provide discounts to them, reflecting the large shippers' impact on the carriers' freight flow. Rate bureaus, which had set the rates and the basis for revenue- and liability-sharing between carriers, suddenly became irrelevant, as rates became only a starting point for actual price negotiations. A price war followed, as carriers cut rates to retain the business, cutting their operating margins and forcing them to demand wage cuts and other givebacks from their employees. The overcapacity in the industry, resulting from large-scale bankruptcies, further intensified the price war, which became a two decade-long battle for survival.

Recall that common carriers under the regulated regime hauled both LTL and TL freight. After deregulation, the business strategy of mixed freight became useless, as rate decontrol meant that TL carriers could cream the TL freight from the common carrier's business base, wiping out the economies gained by mixed freight business. As a result, carriers' carefully cultivated business bases, built over decades, abruptly vanished. The business strategies of the carriers now had to reflect the distinctly different capital requirements of LTL and TL operations, or they quickly went bankrupt.

This regulatory change caused an instant transformation of the industry. The general freight industry further fragmented into national, regional, and local markets, as well as into particular commodity markets. Large carriers, especially ones with a wide geographic scope, had to restructure swiftly as either LTL or TL carriers. Interlining—the sharing of freight and revenue between carriers that use each other's route structures to complete a shipment—became difficult in the unregulated environment. National network carriers no longer needed to share freight revenue with other carriers to complete a transcontinental shipment.[3]

Economic deregulation discouraged interlining by virtually eliminating the institutional framework for shared revenue and liability. With the rate bureaus radically weakened, carriers structured agreements to share revenue and liability either on a contract-by-contract basis or by creating ongoing partnerships. Both of these private contracting frameworks impose high transaction costs[4] and risks and can run afoul of antitrust legislation. Operational economics created by interlining have recently caused many LTL carriers to revert back to the earlier practice of interlining, though often by use of agents that act as pickup or delivery subcontractors.

These changes caused carriers without a national infrastructure to lose their interregional and national shipper clientele. The small special commodities section of the industry suddenly became part of the new TL core segment. New TL general freight carriers, now carrying both common (filed rate) and contract freight, quickly emerged without a developed pickup and delivery framework, using their low infrastructure base, low non-union wages, and correspondingly low rates to take a large share of the original carriers' traditional freight base.

To some extent, pre-existing carriers were at a disadvantage because their experienced, unionized workforce could not accept reductions in wages and conditions forced by the influx of pure TL carriers. Further, the Employee Retirement Income Security Act (ERISA) limited employers' freedom to exit defined benefit pension plans, discouraging firms from exiting the industry (and the plan) other than by liquidation. Potential buy-outs were discouraged because buyers would have to assume a carrier's pension liability, further reducing a carrier's market value. While existing carriers, whose employees generally participated in multi-employer defined benefit plans, had significant withdrawal liability, new entering carriers had no pension liability, as they had no existing pension plans. New entering carriers generally developed neither defined benefit nor defined contribution plans, putting their entire wage bill into the drivers' pockets immediately, but compromising future generations of retirees and creating a ticking time-bomb for society.

Strategically, existing carriers also were at a disadvantage simply because operating rights, an asset required under the regulated environment (and which were expensive to acquire), became nearly worthless. Carriers had to write off as losses a large part of their value that was embedded in these operating rights, accumulated over decades, and for which they paid real money (and which had real value) during the regulatory era.[5] Even worse, for many carriers, their existing terminal structure also became an overhead for which markets offered no compensation. Terminal facilities rapidly became financial liabilities.

Very large carriers already specializing in LTL freight had an advantage. A few carriers had become national or nearly national in scope by making aggressive acquisitions before deregulation. These carriers could pick up a large volume of small shipments and deliver them throughout the country. Some larger carriers were able to convert quickly to regional carriers, offering similar, but expedited, service on a regional basis. The carriers that failed had been perfectly adapted to the pre-1980 system but could not react quickly enough to the new rules, or lacked the management expertise or financial reserves to stave off destruction. They became dinosaurs overnight. Others continued to struggle, offering a mix of LTL and TL service on a regional or local basis.

Interstate deregulation fundamentally restructured the general freight industry, segmenting it into TL and LTL niches. After Congress mandated intrastate deregulation, intrastate and local carriers fell prey to the same forces that had early affected their interstate counterparts, and another round of restructuring and consolidation forced those carriers to specialize as well. Most carriers now haul either all LTL freight or all TL freight.[6]

Market Concentration

The segmentation of the trucking industry into truckload and less-than-truckload sectors was but a part of this radical transformation.

The general freight industry also fractured into national, regional, and local markets, as well as particular commodity markets. This led to significant concentration—a paradoxical limitation on the very competition deregulation was supposed to allow.

It takes some finesse to uncover the real severity of this concentration. Conventional market share estimates understate the concentration of competition because deregulation transformed the general freight industry into so many niches, each of which must be examined individually. It is far more complex than simply comparing the market of an LTL specialist such as Yellow Freight System with that of a TL specialist such as J. B. Hunt. Because their business is in different sectors, there is little direct competition between the two companies.

The differences can be shown quite easily, however, and these two carriers provide apt illustrations. In 1992 Yellow Freight's average shipment weighed 1,153 pounds (89.1% of all shipments were LTL) while J. B. Hunt's average shipment weighed 25,993 pounds (100% of all shipments were TL).[7] Yellow Freight's business requires a complex operation of hub-and-spoke routes between city terminals and regional docks throughout the country, while Hunt's drivers pick up from shippers and deliver directly to consignees. They do not compete with each other.

Just how much concentration has there been? Following deregulation, the number of ICC-certificated carriers tripled, from 16,606 in 1977 to 47,890 in 1991.[8] This would suggest diminishing industry concentration, but concentration must be measured in terms of real markets. Because most of the new entrants are quite small, the number of Class I and II carriers has declined.[9] Meanwhile, the share of the market held by the four largest firms nearly doubled in the first decade of deregulation, as shown in table 4.1.

Within market segments, the picture is even more complex. Table 4.2 shows that LTL carrier concentration has increased dramatically. At the same time, TL concentration, as measured by the market shares of the top four or eight firms, has declined. It helps to be big, however, as the largest TL carriers continue to grow in size and sophistication. Moreover, shippers have become more concerned about reliability of service and recently have acted to reduce their list of carriers to those

Table 4.1 Class I General Freight Industry Market Share

Intercity Motor Carriers	1977	1982	1987	1990
Three Largest Carriers (Total)	12.6%	15.0%	20.0%	17.3%
Roadway Express	4.9%	5.6%	6.5%	5.4%
Consolidated Freightways	4.0%	5.0%	6.4%	5.7%
Yellow Freight System	3.7%	4.4%	7.1%	6.2%
United Parcel Service	15.1%	23.7%	33.0%	31.9%
Four-Firm Concentration Ratio	27.7%	38.7%	53.0%	49.2%
Herfindahl-Hirschman Index	231.6	471.3	823.3	1,147.50
Total Number of Carriers	396	291	266	501

Source: American Trucking Associations, 1978, 1983, 1988, 1991.

Note: The ATA redefined these carriers in 1990, causing the jump in the number of carriers used for analysis in 1990. The ICC classified 191 carriers as Class I general freight carriers in 1990 (see Michael H. Belzer, *Paying the Toll* (Washington, D.C.: Economic Policy Institute, 1994, note 43, page 73).
Class I general freight is the largest category of ICC-regulated carriers hauling other-than-specialized freight (approximately half of all revenue earned by all ICC-regulated motor carriers).
The Herfindahl-Hirschman Index, an accepted measure of market concentration, is the sum of the squared market shares of all firms in the market (Shepherd 1979: 188–90; ICC 1992: 26–34; Paul O. Roberts, "Comments on 'The U.S. Motor Carrier Industry Long after Deregulation,'" Proceedings of the Transportation Research Forum 21–23 Oct. 1992).

they know to be most efficient and dependable (the current "core carrier" practice of shippers), further tightening the market.[10]

The LTL industry does have significant competition at the margins. Fully unionized United Parcel Service, with its volume services, provides an arguably competitive alternative to conventional LTL trucking for shipments that can be broken into packages weighing less than 150 pounds each. Although perhaps two-thirds of unionized UPS employees are part-time workers who load, unload, and

Table 4.2 Concentration in Main General Freight
Market Segments, Excluding UPS

Segment	Share of Revenues Held by		
	Top 4	Top 8	Top 20
LTL			
1977	18.3	26.4	40.6
1987	36.9	48.9	66.6
% change	102.4	85.1	64.3
TL			
1977	14.4	21.6	32.8
1987	10.9	19.1	36.5
% change	−23.9	−11.8	11.1

Source: Thomas M. Corsi and Joseph R. Stowers, "Effects of a Deregulated Environment on Motor Carriers," *Transportation Journal*, 1991, table 2.

sort packages and who earn significantly lower wages than do full-time drivers, many of them still earn respectable wages and benefits. The 1997 contract also established a category of full-time drivers primarily delivering next-day-air packages, earning around $15 per hour (this contract provision has not been implemented as of summer 1999).

Other package delivery carriers, like Airborne Express, subcontract a large volume of their delivery work (in Airborne's case, 60%) to low-wage, non-union carriers paying less than half the wages and none of the benefits paid to Airborne employees.[11] With Airborne able to award contracts to the lowest bidder, they arguably control the level of driver compensation paid by their subcontractors.

For large LTL shipments, freight consolidators and logistics providers use small, frequently non-union, local carriers to pick up freight and deliver it to local or regional terminals. They then consolidate these shipments into a single truckload shipment and arrange for inter-city transportation with a TL carrier. While these freight brokers' operations may be less efficient than those of large LTL carriers, the very low compensation paid by the carriers they use may make them price competitive.

In a new development, some third-party logistics providers have arranged for sequential pickup of freight destined for a particular region or consignee. In this case, the logistics organizer uses information regarding a manufacturer's or distributor's ordering needs to organize freight pickup from the manufacturer's or distributor's suppliers to create a sequential pickup operation. The logistics provider orders the carrier to dispatch a truck on a "milk run" to pick up multiple shipments, each constituting a partial load, and deliver the resultant complete load to the consignee. This same strategy can also be used on the other end of the production system, as a logistics provider might organize the distribution of finished products, using a sequential delivery, or "milk run," system. While these sequential pickup and delivery systems can be used only when the manufacturer or distributor is quite large and when the shipment size is relatively large, the growing presence of such large firms in the economy makes this efficient strategy more effective.

The growth of alternative distribution strategies paradoxically pushes carriers in other segments into narrower service niches. A closer look, analyzing concentration by market, reveals only six transcontinental LTL carriers.[12] This gave that market in 1990 a *very* high Herfindahl-Hirschman Index (HHI) of 2,359—with 80% of the business concentrated within four firms. (The Herfindahl-Hirschman Index, calculated as the sum of the squared market shares of every firm in a market, is a widely accepted method used by economists to measure industrial market concentration as it properly weights the market impact of both large and small firms.)

Even though the industry is more concentrated, competition remains very high because customers are cost driven and competitors can engage in "destructive" competitive practices. That is, any single shipment may rate a high price from one carrier because it comes from that carrier's core territory (its "head haul" lane in which it must charge enough to make a profit) while it rates a low price from another carrier because it comes from an area with high empty capacity (its "back haul" lane in which it hopes to cover variable costs only). The carrier making the back haul sets the rate, in this case, and nobody makes a profit. In other words, variant capacity utilization may systematically justify very different rates, and since at equilibrium every carrier is hauling freight at the lowest possible price, profits remain chronically low. Controlling for information asymmetry, each customer will purchase its preferred bundle of lowest rate and highest service, keeping competition intense.

Regional LTL carriers replicate—and even surpass—this level of market concentration. Identifying all LTL carriers operating in the Southwest, transportation analyst Paul Roberts computed an HHI of 3,059 in 1990, with a four-firm concentration ratio of 100%.[13] With the mandate of intrastate trucking deregulation, and the resultant shakeout of intrastate and small regional carriers, we can expect this phenomenon to become more widespread.

The issue of concentration is so important in part because it confounds the expectations of the pro-deregulation economists, who blithely assumed the entire trucking industry would end up the way the TL sector has developed thus far—that is, with less concentration and intense competition (although it is worth noting that TL appears to be concentrating more and more). They based that expectation on a rather simple view of the trucking firm as little more than a truck and a driver, with no capacity for scale economies, rather than as a complex network of operations in which economies of density might matter.

Even within this highly concentrated LTL sector, though, competition remains evident. Networks of regional LTL carriers—such as USF, the Con-Ways, and others—have thrived in the regional markets while developing the means to transfer freight among sister regional carriers, creating the potential for new interregional or even *de facto* national LTL carriers. With most of the growth in the transportation business at the regional level, however, we can expect any such national effort to be tentative at best. The Viking Freight System debacle during the mid- to late 1990s, in which Caliber tried to unify the former Roadway Regional Carriers into a single firm under the "Viking" name, pushing its successful regional carrier to become national, caused enormous losses and the eventual sale of Caliber to FedEx.

Analytical imprecision prevents us from knowing whether carriers in highly concentrated markets earn monopoly rents. But it is instructive that UPS—the dominant participant in the package delivery market—regularly earns more than $1 billion net profit annually. While most other LTL and package carriers have not been quite so successful, particularly at the national level, they have experienced proportionately even greater success at the regional level. In the regional market, where overnight premium service has become the norm, the most successful carriers earn between 10 and 20 cents for every dollar of revenue and have shared that success with their employees.

Economies of Scale and Scope

What caused all of this concentration? It could be that economies of scale—positive returns to increasing capital investment—give highly capitalized carriers a natural advantage over smaller carriers. Research, however, has shown repeatedly that true economies of scale are slim or non-existent in trucking. Nevertheless, big carriers with many pickup and delivery opportunities (that is, a dense network of customers or potential customers) clearly can keep their trucks loaded more of the time, giving them higher load factors and greater marginal returns on each new shipment. High load factors are critical to making money both for the company and for the driver, whose income derives from the company's success in keeping trucks loaded, so economic advantage appears to favor firms with large, dense networks.

There is broad disagreement among industry analysts over whether concentration comes from economies of scale or scope, or from some other causal factors. George Wilson and others who advocated restructuring rate and entry believed regulation conferred an unfair advantage on large firms.[14] Deregulation advocates like Richard Spady and Ann Friedlaender expected the industry to become characterized by small, competitive firms.[15] John Snow, writing for the American Enterprise Institute, thought these small, competitive firms would exhibit no economies of scale.[16] However, the data clearly show a significant increase in LTL concentration following economic deregulation.

Some analysts—Theodore Keeler and Robert Kling among them—see the post-deregulation development of significant economies of scale and scope.[17] Thomas Corsi and Joseph Stowers continue to claim "there is no evidence of scale economies in any of the industry segments."[18] But in a 1993 review, Corsi noted that more recent research indicates size, combined with particular management strategies, does make a difference.[19] While his study shows medium-size firms perform competitively with large firms, particularly combined with a market differentiation strategy,[20] the connection between size and performance remains important.

The issue of size is important both for LTL and TL carriers. While most of the attention has focused on LTL carriers, and their market aggregating tendencies, we should also look at advantages that large TL carriers have over small ones. These economies demonstrate why successful carriers like Schneider get more freight and are able to deliver it at a lower price. Schneider enjoys such huge economies related to size that it can afford to hire its own engineers to design trucks that can be built to Schneider specifications. Schneider can afford advanced technology and makes technological innovation a source of strategic advantage, and the company was the first in the trucking industry to install a satellite system.

These economies do not diminish the contribution made by Schneider's innovativeness. Schneider is a large carrier in part from aggressive and intelligent investment and strategy. Once established, Schneider's size and scope of operations have given it a further advantage over smaller carriers. Size does matter, however, and the unregulated market puts smaller firms at a disadvantage.

Paul Roberts argues that economies of scale exist in both LTL and TL carriers. The hub-and-spoke-system, into which trucking and other transportation modes have organized, helps carriers build the kind of market density needed to compete efficiently. For LTL carriers, hub-and-spoke systems can generate the kind of traffic flow that keeps trucks full, increases load factors, and may allow them to grow to a level where they can support direct shipments between two points, bypassing the hub altogether.

Traffic density allows TL carriers to achieve greater economies by minimizing empty miles. While truckload carriers do not build hub-and-spoke structures in the strict sense (they have no terminals through which to move their freight), they do offer lower rates to move freight into a region where they have a surplus of outbound freight, making that region a kind of hub around which they build loads. These dense regions allow larger truckload carriers to have more equipment available in that area to take advantage of business opportunities. The more trucks it can position in a revenue-producing region, the closer each truck is to the motor carrier's customers. Since one major goal of any carrier is to reduce empty miles, the shorter deadhead mileage gives larger carriers a considerable advantage.[21]

The dispute actually revolves around the terms analysts use. For economists, economies of scale exist when a production process favors large-scale capitalization. We find economies of scale in steel and auto plants and in the generation of electric power. Where economies of scale exist, production is spread over a fixed capital stock and the greater the capitalization, the lower the unit cost of production. Trucking apparently demonstrates little or no such economies, since even large trucking companies have a relatively low level of capitalization. At the same time, the fact that we observe apparent size advantages suggests that we may be looking in the wrong place for the explanation.

Mark Keaton provides strong empirical evidence that network scope—economies of density or scope—provides modest but persistent economic advantages, explaining the growth of both large and small carrier networks.[22] While economies of scale may be small or even nonexistent, economies of density have a significant effect on the carrier's ability to generate and maintain a sufficient supply of freight to keep its trucks loaded and productive. That is, a motor carrier (or any other transportation carrier, for that matter) derives great economic advantage not by volume alone but by the strategic location of that volume of pickup and delivery. Economies of density allow a carrier to build its business region by region, taking care not to spread itself too thin. As long as it has a sufficient business level in any area, it can profitably maintain its advantage over newcomers and sustain its business economically.

The U.S. Postal Service and United Parcel Service, both able to concentrate service within dense networks, derive enormous economies of scope within these networks. Making deliveries and pickups within a dense door-to-door network takes maximum advantage of labor and capital resources and allows these carriers to waste no time or resources. While both cover thinly distributed regions as well as dense ones, the economies of density gained in dense regions allow them to cover their costs in the thin ones and provide overall efficient and inexpensive service.

In short, although regulatory barriers have disappeared, operational economies of some kind may have created new and perhaps more resistant barriers in particular sectors of the industry.

Employment and Labor Productivity

The transformation of the trucking industry also can be seen in employment and labor productivity figures. Data collected by the Bureau

of Labor Statistics (BLS) show that job growth in the trucking industry has been increasing steadily at an average annual rate of 2.63% since
1947.[23] This increase reflects the continued shift of freight from railroads to trucking over the period, as well as the general increase in
production and consumption of goods. Short-term employment declines, while significant, have been limited to the period of the oil crisis of 1973 and the first years of interstate and intrastate economic
deregulation. Since these initial changes in regulation and recovery
from the recessionary shocks of the early 1980s, though, employment
has increased even more. From 1964 through 1980 employment of
drivers and dockworkers ("production workers") increased 2.1% annually, while employment increased at a 3.7% annual rate since economic deregulation (see figure 4.1).

In addition, structural changes in processes of production and
distribution have elevated the importance of trucking in the supply
chain. Lean inventory management, total quality management, and
lean production all depend on just-in-time delivery, whether defined
as day-definite time windows or by-the-minute scheduling for live
unloading. With regulations changing over the past two decades, allowing for longer, wider, heavier trucks, along with extended use of
double and triple trailers, the expansion of the industry has meant
an ever-increasing demand for drivers.

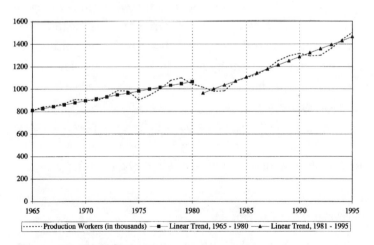

Figure 4.1: Production Workers, SIC 421

Productivity data are less certain. Bureau of Labor Statistics data suggest that labor productivity increased by 169% between 1954 and 1989. This increasing labor productivity has obvious roots. Since the development of the Interstate Highway System, beginning in the late 1950s, both cars and trucks have been able to take advantage of a comprehensive system of limited-access, high-speed highways. With limited access, trucks could avoid the constant gearing up and down required by repeated stops and starts, allowing for considerably greater average speeds. They also could avoid the risks inherent in side and cross traffic, increasing safety. Extensive and sophisticated grading and routing also smoothed out steep up and down grades, allowing trucks to maintain their speed more easily. Perhaps most critical, the scope of the project, extending from congested urban areas to rugged rural terrain, opened up wide areas of the country previously inaccessible by truck. The development and legalization of larger truck and trailer combinations, pulled by ever more powerful diesel engines, took advantage of the Interstate Highway System to produce dramatic productivity gains. The week-long trip from Chicago to New York, common in the 1930s, was replaced by a trip taking no more than 24 hours, including a mandated rest break. During this period, output per employee among Class I and II common and contract carriers increased steadily at an average of 3% per year.[24]

After economic deregulation, the annual rate of labor productivity appeared to increase at a rate nearly 50% higher than before deregulation—apparently caused by the transformation of the industry since the shakeout of the early 1980s, discussed elsewhere. Critical elements of this productivity increase, if it occurred, would include the effects of a dramatic winnowing of less efficient firms and firms without clear blanket coverage or niche identification; the segmentation of the industry into specialized firms; and the legalization of larger and heavier trucks. For these reasons, it appears that deregulation might have resulted in significant annual labor productivity improvement.

However, these labor productivity measurements are flawed and unreliable, so government data do not provide the information we need to evaluate regulatory reform. First, while the BLS measures labor productivity in most industries as both output per employee and output per employee-hour, it reports trucking labor productivity only as output per employee. This creates an analytical problem because most truck drivers do not keep track of unpaid work time. Since the development of exclusively TL carriers after regulatory change corresponds also with the de-unionization of much of the trucking industry, and since the available evidence suggests that TL drivers and carriers systematically underreport their hours of work, competition probably caused more drivers to log more work time as "off duty" in order to make up for lost wages. Clearly, research shows that TL drivers, especially non-union TL drivers, tend to perform a significantly greater amount of unpaid work.[25] Many have also argued that, as ICC/BLS data suggest, the average driver now drives farther and works longer hours than before deregulation.

Government officials readily concede that with the proliferation of small carriers it has become very hard to police the industry and easier for drivers to exceed maximum work hours restrictions. Indeed, the UMTIP driver survey, conducted in 1997, indicates that the median over-the-road driver works 62 hours per week, two hours more than the legal limit. The median union driver works 60 hours, and the median non-union driver works 65. Averages are even higher, reflecting the fact that 10% of all drivers report working more than 95 hours during the last week, with the average driver working 65.7 hours and the average non-union driver working 70 hours, 10 hours more than the legal limit.[26] We have no similar study documenting hours worked before deregulation, but it is a safe bet to assume that competitive pressures increased after economic regulations were eliminated, creating an environment that pushes drivers harder than ever. In fact, a review of ICC data showed that the average road driver's mileage increased from 94,832 to 105,148 between 1977 and 1987—an increase of 11% just among Class I General Freight carriers. At the 90th percentile, driver mileage increased from 115,425 to 135,062, a 17% increase.[27] If employee hours actually increased for the same output, and if the proportion of unreported non-driving time also increased, then productivity declined. One cannot determine actual labor productivity from the BLS data.

Second, output per employee, as published before February 1989, shows post-deregulation labor productivity declining, while revised data published in February 1989 show a 48 to 57% increase over the same period. Figure 4.2 shows decreasing productivity reported in 1988 and increasing productivity reported in 1993. Using the revised data, the BLS most recently reported in 1993 that general freight output was down more than 9% and employment was down 42% from its 1977 peak.[28]

In essence, the high labor productivity is the result of lower reported employment in the revised data. This conflicts dramatically with the BLS employment data for Standard Industrial Code (SIC) 421 (Trucking and Courier Service, except Air) (figure 4.2), which draw from a different and more reliable source. The problem of conflicting data further highlights important underlying problems with data collection and reporting and with data interpretation that insufficiently accounts for structural changes within the industry—and thus fails to provide an accurate picture from the government of deregulation's consequences. It is an important point to make, because the proponents of deregulation stake much of their support on these claims of greater productivity.

Data for the Employment, Hours, and Earnings series derive from the Current Employment Statistics program, known commonly as

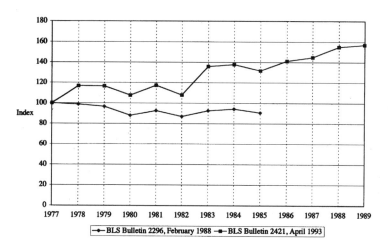

Figure 4.2: Trucking Industry Productivity

the establishment survey. Data for the Labor Productivity series derive from ICC Motor Carrier Annual Report data. The quality of these data has declined significantly since regulatory restructuring in 1980.

The declining data quality stems from several sources. First, the survival rate of Class I and Class II motor carriers has been about 50% over this period, so significant proportion of carriers disappeared. New carriers also have failed to report as required, either because they preferred to remain unknown or because they failed to understand reporting requirements. Some carriers tactfully reported late enough to be excluded from that year's database. Reported data often are inaccurate and incomplete (intentionally or not), reducing the comprehensiveness of the data series. Structurally, the ICC dropped its uniform accounting requirements and dramatically reduced the amount of data required, while raising reporting thresholds to further exclude many important carriers. Finally, since responsibility for collecting and managing these data has transferred to the Bureau of Transportation Statistics in the Department of Transportation, and since the collection of these data is itself a controversial matter, many carriers have applied for and received exemption from reporting, so that the data set now is neither a population nor a representative data sample. In this condition, it is not useful to anyone except the reporting carriers' competitors.

Besides carriers who were supposed to have reported but did not, the number of carriers required to report declined.[29] In addition, the ICC did not require strict compliance with reporting rules, particularly with respect to individual and consolidated carriers. For example, the regional subsidiaries of Consolidated Freightways (except for Con-Way Eastern, the former Penn Yan Express) originally did not report as separate or consolidated carriers, even though they did business as separate carriers, probably reducing the accuracy of parent company reports as well as reducing the overall quality of the data series. Their reporting is uneven, in that Con-Way Transportation Services reported as a single entity for many years, and Con-Way Western reported as a single entity for selected years. After these subsidiaries were spun off from Consolidated Freightways, the Con-Ways still did not report separately, and the commingled data may give a false impression for one regional carrier or another. That said, since the spin-off, Con-Way has declared itself a national carrier with three divisions, and it may make more sense to report as a single carrier than as a set of consolidated carriers (though to my knowledge they have not reported as consolidated carriers either). Despite the good intentions of the American Trucking Associations (ATA), which cleans, error-checks, and distributes the data, problems with the underlying data sources have reduced severely the quality of the data.

These flaws have led to alarmingly biased labor productivity information. Before regulatory restructuring, the population of carriers was relatively consistent and reliable. The BLS carefully collected ton-mile data within general freight, specialized freight, and household goods carrier groups, then weighted the data before aggregating them into a single output index. This procedure distinguished labor productivity characteristics in general freight from those in specialized freight (heavy haulers of truckload shipments), and vice versa.[30] Since the characteristics of the freight hauled have powerful effects on the measure of ton-miles per employee, very fine classification distinctions can have profound effects on productivity results. Each truckload employee can haul much more freight than can a LTL employee, because average shipments are more than 20 times larger and are subject to much less time-consuming physical handling.

Common and contract carriers also tend to differ structurally, as shippers negotiate contracts for larger shipments or groups of shipments. Contract carriers haul freight by the shipment in truckload lots, while common carriers haul freight on a regularly scheduled basis often operating well below physical capacity in order to maintain service commitments. Contract and common carriers therefore require separate analysis. Accordingly, the BLS reported information for two groups: Class I and II intercity common and contract carriers (virtually the entire population of interstate for-hire carriers with more than $1 million in revenue) and Class I and II intercity common carriers of general freight.[31] With both sets of data, analysts could examine productivity changes in trucking and hold constant the type of freight handled, allowing valid comparisons.

After regulatory restructuring, freight characteristics changed dramatically from year to year. Many general freight carriers operated more like specialized carriers, yet they retained their original classification. Common and contract freight became commingled, making it difficult to distinguish underlying differences and hold these differences constant while comparing yearly changes. When the general freight population's underlying characteristics changed, the data gathering did not keep up, so we really do not know what effect economic deregulation has had on labor productivity.

The number of Class I general freight carriers, as defined and reported by the ICC, declined since deregulation, from a high of 354 in 1977 to a low of 191 in 1990.[32] While the ICC listed about 16,000 carriers with operating authority in 1977 and 48,000 by the end of 1991, almost all of them were Class III (less than $1 million in revenue, which is about 10 trucks).

This decline is only partly attributable to a shrinking number of carriers; some of it reflects the ICC's indifferent attitude toward data collection. Although the ICC reported only 191 Class I common carriers of general freight in *Transport Statistics in the United States*, the ATA classified 495 carriers as Class I general freight carriers on their 1990 data tapes.[33] While I agree with the current and former ATA officials who told me that the ATA was justified in reclassifying carriers, this reclassification caused the general freight population to exhibit more TL characteristics than it did previously. The lack of comparability from year to year hampers accurate policy analysis.

Lack of confidence in this measure led the BLS Office of Productivity and Technology to stop issuing new estimates after 1989, declaring that they "have actually lost coverage in [their] labor productivity program for the transportation sector due to the data problems" with trucking and bus carrier industries.[34]

The flawed measures of productivity make some of the pro-deregulation arguments difficult to support. Proponents of deregulation find they cannot demonstrate conclusively that the trucking industry has seen measurable productivity increases. One analyst, Robert V. Delaney of Cass Information Systems, who has been touting his figures for many years purporting to show dramatically decreasing logistics costs since deregulation, suddenly discovered that all of his analysis showing decreasing logistics costs were inaccurate because he did not account for the carrying cost of capital. When accounting for interest, logistics cost remained flat throughout the 1990s at 10.6% of the Gross Domestic Product, further throwing cold water on the magical savings due to deregulation.[35] The problem, endemic to service industries, is that it is very difficult to measure output and output quality, and quality can be produced at widely varying levels.[36]

Several analysts, notably Ann Friedlaender, Richard Spady, and Judy Wang Chiang, have argued that the regulatory framework established by the MCA of 1935 created an economic environment that did not use industry technology maximally. Specifically, they claimed deregulation would increase productivity by increasing average load.[37] But what really happened? Did productivity increase after regulatory restructuring? Did average loads increase?

The conclusion you draw depends on whose statistics you believe. Thomas Corsi and Joseph Stowers claim equipment productivity has improved since deregulation. Annual miles per truck and average haul (ton-miles per ton) have increased in both TL and LTL markets, and average load (ton-miles per mile) has increased in TL general freight. However, without an increase in average load, the increase in annual mileage per truck and average haul in LTL may actually indicate diminished efficiency. In addition, increased size and weight limits, rather than economic deregulation, may have caused increases in average load in TL. Corsi and Stowers plausibly suggest economic deregulation caused the increase in average haul because it cut the use of interlining, though my recent case study research on the LTL industry suggests a resurgence. They argue the segmentation of the general freight industry may have led to more efficient use of LTL networks, because LTL carriers no longer use their resources on simpler TL freight movements.[38]

In contrast, some analysts have argued that productivity—defined as the average load per dispatch—actually has dropped since 1980. Nicholas Glaskowsky argues that these lower average loads mean higher cost of transportation per unit of goods shipped. Since intermediate goods may be shipped several times between the raw material and finished stage of production, the distribution process may add significant new production costs, reducing the competitiveness of U.S. manufactured goods in the global market.[39] While this increased cost may reflect manufacturers' preferences for "Just-in-Time" (JIT) inventory control, such an assumption is purely conjectural. It might just as well reflect a hidden increasing cost driven by the carriers' competition for freight.

While service competition could give each firm an advantage, it can also lead to lower labor and equipment productivity. For example, more frequent and guaranteed on-time delivery may lead to lower load factors, as carriers dispatch lightly loaded equipment carrying freight to satisfy inflated service promises.[40] If load factors are down, it would cause a decline in productivity, measured as ton-miles per employee (as the BLS productivity data show before the 1988 edition).

Bankruptcies and Profits

The transformation of the trucking industry also can be seen in how firms have fared, not only in terms of profitability but in terms of their very survival. There have been big winners *and* big losers.

No one can dispute that deregulation caused a monumental increase in bankruptcies of both small and large firms. The only disagreement is over what led to the bankruptcies, their effect, their appropriateness, and their potential avoidability. While the number of small Class III carriers increased greatly after 1977, the number of reporting Class I and Class II carriers declined.[41]

Class I and II carriers experienced a phenomenal bankruptcy rate. Annual failures among intercity carriers increased 1,280% between 1978 and 1985.[42] Before the MCA of 1980, total failures of ICC-regulated carriers averaged between 200 and 250 per year. After regulatory restructuring, trucking failures boomed, reaching an annual peak of 2,297 in 1991.[43] The failure rate rose every year between 1977 and 1986, irrespective of the nation's business cycle.[44] Since then, failures appear to have become quite cyclical, increasing drastically during the 1990–1992 recession.

According to the Teamsters, 140 Class I and Class II ICC-regulated general freight carriers—all covered by the 1980 National Master Freight Agreement—went out of business between the passage of deregulation legislation and 1993 most of them early in the process. These carriers employed 175,022 workers and earned $8.2 billion in annual operating revenue in 1979 (or more than $20 billion in 1995 dollars). It is difficult to equate historical data with current data, but in 1979 these carriers accounted for 48% of the total employment and operating revenues of the entire regulated Class I and II general freight market. If we add two large non-Teamster general freight bankruptcies—Brown Transport (including Thurston Motor Lines) and Bowman Transportation—these figures rise to more than 187,300 employees and $8.5 billion. One could add many more non-union carriers to the list.[45]

What about profits? First, trucking companies normally have low profit margins. Motor carriers have very high variable costs compared to fixed costs, and they convert a very small proportion of their operating revenue to return on investment. Consequently, even a short-run operating loss can overwhelm assets, quickly causing bankruptcy. In his classic work on transportation economics, the late Philip Locklin argued that for any carrier "the margin of revenues over expenses required to pay a normal rate of return on capital invested [is] so small that a slight miscalculation of probable revenues or expenses could leave the carrier with revenues insufficient to pay operating expenses."[46] Since very small perturbations in operating ratios—the ratio of total carrier operating expenses divided by total carrier operating revenue—can have disastrous consequences for operators, the ICC used operating ratio rather than return on investment as a regulatory standard.[47]

These operating ratios have fluctuated widely since deregulation. The ICC expected an operating ratio of 93% would provide a healthy margin of gross profit with which carriers could afford to maintain their current level of investment. But as can be seen in figure 4.3, which shows average operating ratios for all Class I general freight carriers since deregulation, the linear trend is flat at 95.7% over the entire post–

World War II period—not the 93% ICC standard. In fact, over the past 45 years, the industry has never reached the 93% target for all Class I and II carriers, and operating ratios have worsened steadily since 1970 (see figure 4.3).

Nicholas Glaskowsky presents evidence that the average trucker's profit margin is about half that of the average manufacturer's margin.[48] Figure 4.4 shows that average net profit margins, like operating ratios, have fluctuated widely, but the long-term post-deregulation linear trend for Class I general freight carriers is flat at approximately 4.25 cents per dollar of revenue.

Return on equity (ROE) does not appear to have increased, but the data tell a mixed story.[49] For all ICC regulated carriers, ROE fell sharply during the first five years of deregulation, which surprises nobody given the collapse in carrier equity and the dramatic rise in bankruptcy during this period. Remember that deregulation forced carriers to write off the value of operating authority they previously bought under the old regime, and many carriers invested in a significant amount of new authority before deregulation so that they would be in a good position the moment the new regime took effect. Return on equity was flat over the longer 10-year span, though for all carriers it improved enough in the early 1990s to show a 20% increase over the first 15 years of deregulation (figure 4.5).[50] For Class I general freight carriers, the

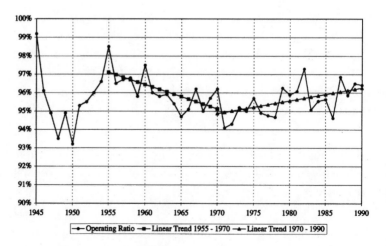

Figure 4.3: Operating Ratio 1945–1990

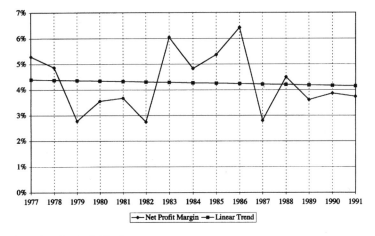

Figure 4.4: Net Profit Margin

hardest hit by deregulation since they included most common carriers, the entire period shows a general decline of 18.7% (figure 4.6). After intrastate deregulation in 1995, however, ROE for all carriers again fell as intrastate carriers experienced a new wave of competition. In fact, average return on equity among these Class I general freight motor carriers has declined 22% since the change of the regulatory framework. This aggregate decline helps explain the steady and alarming increase in bankruptcies already noted. As the aging of carrier equipment suggests,[51] it appears that many trucking firms have be-

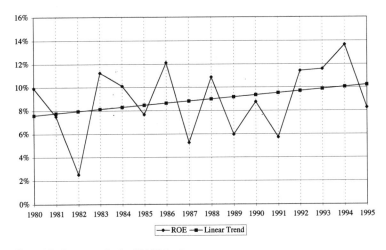

Figure 4.5: Return on Equity, All ICC Carriers

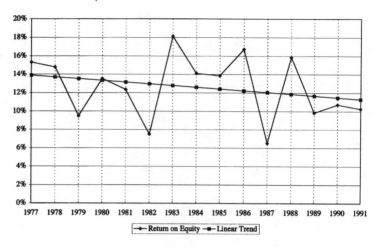

Figure 4.6: Return on Equity, Class I General Freight Carriers

come unwilling or unable to make the kind of investment that can sustain profitability in the long run.

The stock market reflects this increased risk. Since the mid-1970s motor carrier stocks have declined compared to the Dow Jones Composite and Standard and Poor's 500 indices. A 1993 analysis by the brokerage firm Donaldson, Lufkin & Jenrette rated most stocks of large LTL carriers "neutral" or "unattractive."[52] An analysis by Alex. Brown & Sons echoes this assessment.[53] Declining returns within an entire industry signal a public policy problem. Only during the most recent period of expansion, in 1996 and 1997, have LTL carriers' stock prices begun to rise, but they remain sluggish in comparison to other industries similarly invested in information technology.

Some transportation economists argue that the competitive market will drive every transportation producer to offer a large proportion of service at prices that may cover average variable cost but not average total cost. This is a special problem in the trucking industry.[54] If a declining base of motor carriers' revenue-producing business pays fully allocated costs, they may earn insufficient revenue to maintain a healthy return on equity, and the businesses may eventually fail. In fact, ROE has declined because income from continuing operations after taxes has declined in real dollars since regulatory reform. Chronic bouts of low rates, excess capacity, and poor returns have plagued motor carriers.[55]

These characteristics—along with market concentration, declining productivity, bankruptcies, and squeezed profits—are but part of the story. Just as the business of trucking has been transformed, so have industrial relations within the industry. What has the decline in unionization, wrought by deregulation, meant for workers in the industry?

5 Collective Bargaining Still Makes a Difference

Trucking was once among the most heavily unionized industries in the United States. At the beginning of the 1970s, the Labor Department claimed local and intercity trucking was 80 to 100% organized, and scholars considered general freight to be "very close to 100 percent" unionized in local and long-haul freight.[1]

Unionization began to decline during the 1970s, as private carriers, owner operators, and special commodity carriers grew. Between 1967 and 1977 the Teamsters' share of freight dropped by 20 to 25%.[2] Since a high of 1,975,000 in 1974, (not all of which was trucking), Teamster membership levels have declined by 27% overall (see figure 5.1). The sharpest decline was from 1980 through 1984, during the severe shakeout following economic deregulation.[3] Although membership has remained relatively stable since the late 1980s, it has not rebounded significantly. Intensive efforts during the administration of Teamsters president Ron Carey increased organizing activity and at least stemmed the slide, but time will tell whether this intensive organizing will lead to enough growth to begin to increase union density in the trucking industry as a whole.

Union Density: The Root of Bargaining Power

The Current Population Survey shows broadly declining union influence in the trucking industry. Union representation has dropped by more than 50% overall in the last two decades.[4] In the core general freight sector of the industry, however, collective bargaining remains important. The Teamsters represented approximately 48% of all Class I general freight drivers in 1991. With the growth of UPS, recognized

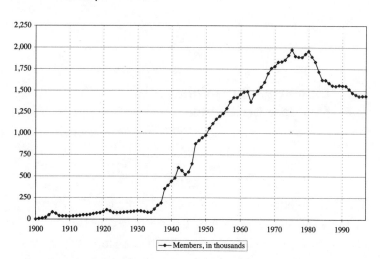

Figure 5.1: Teamsters Union Membership, United States and Canada

by the ICC (and now by the Department of Transportation) as an LTL general freight carrier, and with the growth of the large national LTL carriers, unions represented approximately 65% of all truck drivers in the industry as of 1995 (table 5.1).[5]

Most unionized drivers are represented by the Teamsters.[6] New TL carriers that entered the market after regulatory restructuring, however, almost entirely employ non-union drivers. The union also lost nearly all of its coverage and bargaining power at most previously unionized TL carriers. Schneider, which was heavily unionized until late in the 1970s, is a good example. Schneider began by bargaining a special contract in 1976 that provided for pay based on a percent of revenue and ended up by replacing almost all union drivers with non-union drivers. At other companies, such as Coles Express in Maine, drivers went on strike, permanent replacement workers were brought in, and the union was decertified. Coles limped along for many years as a regional truckload carrier and eventually was bought by Roadway as part of its regional carrier group—which eventually was spun off as part of Caliber. When Caliber decided to make Viking a national carrier, it absorbed Coles and others into its own operation and Coles ceased to exist. Unfortunately for Caliber and Viking, this strategy failed dismally, and in 1997 Viking withdrew to its West Coast base

Table 5.1 Union Density

Year	Hirsch A (%)	Hirsch A N	Hirsch B (%)	Hirsch B N	Belzer A (%)	Belzer A N	Belzer B (%)	Belzer B N
1973–1978	60	1,533						
1977					85	380	88	382
1978								
1979	57	175						
1980	56	94						
1981	61	84						
1982					80	278	86	280
1983	50	127	43	1,034				
1984	30	79	38	1,158				
1985	29	111	34	1,154				
1986			32	1,093				
1987			28	1,136	73	256	85	256
1988			30	1,161				
1989			27	1,166				
1990			24	1,264	48	189	65	190

Source: Data from Hirsch, "Trucking Deregulation and Labor Earnings," *Journal of Labor Economics*, 1993: 284; American Trucking Associations 1977, 1982, 1987, 1990; Belzer 1991 survey.

Table from Michael H. Belzer, "Collective Bargaining after Deregulation: Do the Teamsters Still Count?" *Industrial and Labor Relations Review* 48 (1995): 646. Reprinted by permission.In both measures, union density is the proportion of drivers who are union members.

Hirsch A uses only May public use CPS samples; *N* = number of drivers sampled in the for-hire sector.
Hirsch B uses all 12 monthly CPS samples for each year; *N* is the same as Hirsch A.
Belzer A excludes United Parcel Service; N is the number of carriers analyzed.
Belzer B includes United Parcel Service; N is the number of carriers analyzed.
Analysts of the LTL market historically have excluded UPS, but arguably changing markets makes inclusion necessary. Both figures cited here allow alternative interpretations.

and shed all other operations, completing the Coles saga. Caliber, having lost millions of dollars in this gambit, sold out to Federal Express in 1998 and ceased to exist as well.

Contrast this with the core LTL segment that grew out of the common carriers that dominated general freight before deregulation. As of 1991 the Teamsters still represented employees working for almost 70% of all Class I LTL general commodity carriers, compared with employees in only 24% of all Class I TL general commodity carriers (this does not mean they represent all employees at these firms, but represented at least some of them). My 1991 survey of Class I general freight carriers showed that, although only 36% of all carriers were completely unionized, 49% had enough union representation to make the union a credible threat to organize and hence cause the union threat-effect to produce higher wages for employees. Mileage pay rates, which were indistinguishable between general freight carriers with 100% unionization and carriers with even a trace of membership, were dramatically lower at carriers with no union representation at all. This suggests the union continues to constitute a serious threat to which even most non-union carriers pay attention.

My unionization data, based on a survey of carriers appearing in the Motor Carrier Annual Report (produced for decades by the ICC), suggest a modest decline in union density within the largest intercity general freight motor carriers. The employment gain at large union-ized LTL carriers (and especially at UPS) offsets many of the employment losses of unionized drivers caused by extensive bankruptcies.[7] In segments of the trucking industry other than general freight, union representation varies. Drivers who work for a few specialized commodity carriers, for example, have union representation, but the Teamsters represent nearly all drivers working for carriers that deliver new automobiles. Drivers who work for some private carriers, such as those in the retail food industry, also retain a high degree of unionization.

Overall, Teamster membership today remains large compared with that of other unions in the United States.[8] The Teamsters Union represents trucking employees in many occupations and trucking industry sectors, as well as hundreds of thousands of employees in other industries. In 1996 the Teamsters had 1.44 million members, including approximately 400,000 truck drivers—little more than one-quarter of whom worked under the National Master Freight Agreement.[9]

Decline of the National Master Freight Agreement

The story of the National Master Freight Agreement (NMFA) is linked closely to this declining membership. The number of Teamsters employed by companies directly covered by the NMFA has dropped by approximately 75% since deregulation, although a large but indeterminate number of Teamsters work under contracts patterned after the NMFA. The problem actually involves a broad decentralization of industrial relations, common across many industries.[10]

Before deregulation, most general freight common carriers belonged to carrier associations that bargained centrally. The diversity of needs among these different carriers—common and contract carriers; long-, medium-, and short-haul carriers; and large, medium, and small carriers—was tremendous, and such associations were not without internal discord. The post-1980 regulatory regime sharpened the conflict, exacerbating the differences among firms of different sizes operating in different markets. This forced a change in the bargaining structure.

In fairness, regulatory restructuring was not the only source of tension. The same underlying diversity of needs—even before 1977—put a strain on unity within Trucking Employers Incorporated (TEI), an employers' association that represented between 800 and 1,000 carriers in the mid-1970s. At its peak, the NMFA negotiated by this federation directly covered between 300,000 and 500,000 workers, and many non-TEI carriers either followed the TEI pattern or actually signed the Master Freight contract.[11]

Trouble within TEI began with the 1970 contract when the new wage structure in Master Freight, resulting from a major strike in Chicago led by city drivers' Local 705, made local pickup and delivery operations relatively more expensive than linehaul operations, tilting the cost structure significantly to the detriment of local carriers and others with extensive local operations. While large general freight common carriers devoted only 25 to 35% of their effort to local pickup and delivery, 65 to 75% of the costs borne by small pre-deregulation carriers went into local pickup and delivery operations, putting small carriers at a serious cost disadvantage.[12] The gap between union and non-union, short- and medium-haul carriers also grew wider, giving non-union carriers some advantage as well.

This internal tension caused TEI to break apart in September 1977. When carriers formed Trucking Management, Incorporated (TMI), in April 1978, the breach was healed—at least temporarily. But the new association retained essentially the same representational structure as its predecessor,[13] as well as the diverse constituency and needs that had plagued TEI. In short, TMI was born with the same inherent internal tensions, and stability depended on a firm relationship with a strong union with strong bargaining power.

By 1979 the National Master Freight Agreement was under pressure from several directions. As employers saw it, administrative deregulation and the stagflation crisis of the 1970s really put the squeeze on specialized, truckload, and local and regional carriers. From the employees' perspective, high inflation caused the value of wage packages to deteriorate and heightened the uncertainty these workers felt as consumers. Deteriorating real wages created political pressures within the union and put the heat on bargainers, who needed to respond to charges from militants within the Teamsters that the leadership of the union was corrupt and negotiating inadequate contracts from a position of weakness.

Viewed in historical perspective, the wage bargain set by the 1979 NMFA was not extreme. It did not drive wages up unusually high, especially considering the level of inflation at the time. But such moderation was not enough to save many of the smaller carriers facing the rigors of both deregulation and recession, and membership in TMI began to erode. The vacuum deregulation created within the industry was one from which few carriers could escape.

The new TMI that negotiated the 1979 contract represented only about 400 carriers. Centralized bargaining continued to erode during the height of the post-deregulation and recession shakeout, and by the 1982 negotiations TMI represented only 284 carriers.[14] Between 1980 and 1982 scores of carriers came to the Teamsters at both the national and local levels and asked for contract re-openers and roll-backs. One popular ploy was the Employee Stock Ownership Plan, or ESOP, which became a convenient method of disguising contractual givebacks.[15] Other negotiations confronted the issues more directly, as carriers demanded dramatic concessions that made wages and conditions of these union drivers much more similar to those in the non-union sector. During these years more than one carrier adopted a forcing strategy and used the resulting strikes to decertify the Teamsters.

By the time Master Freight negotiations came around again in 1985, TMI represented fewer than 40 carriers employing about 110,000 working Teamsters. Consolidation in the LTL segment of the general freight industry had been so extensive, though, that both TMI and the union claimed this represented the same proportion of the industry's employees as before deregulation.[16]

These negotiations involved two other employers' associations as well: Motor Carriers Labor Advisory Council (MCLAC) and Regional Carriers Incorporated (RCI), both of which represented small and medium-size carriers in the Midwest. The bargaining with TMI set the pattern, however. Ultimately, the situation forced MCLAC, representing 115 carriers employing between 40,000 and 50,000 employees of smaller cartage carriers,[17] to accept the TMI agreement, while RCI, representing only 20,000 employees, did not sign, leaving its members to negotiate independent settlements.[18] The contract covered between 150,000 and 160,000 employees, although the union estimated that between 40,000 and 50,000 of these employees were on indefinite layoff.[19] Because the contract terms and grievance panel representation incorporated in TMI-negotiated contracts still benefited large carriers over small ones, even more small carriers defected from the pattern.

By 1988 bargaining representation became even more decentralized. TMI retained its representation of the largest carriers, while MCLAC represented 50 smaller cartage carriers and RCI only 18. Published reports again claimed the NMFA included about 180,000 workers,[20] although the number was probably closer to the roughly 150,000 covered in 1985, again with thousands on long-term layoff.

By 1991 TMI had dwindled to 24 carriers, although the association probably still represented nearly as many workers as in previous years[21]—supporting the view that consolidation in LTL had continued to concentrate both freight and employees in the largest carriers. Master Freight bargaining in 1994 represented 120,000 employees directly and 30,000 employees indirectly under related contracts, as well as an indeterminate number of additional employees whose contracts follow the NMFA pattern.[22]

The 1994 Master Freight strike, the longest in U.S. history, profoundly changed the relationship between the Teamsters and the companies whose workers they represented. Negotiations had begun unusually slowly, as internal political conflict had made the Teamsters rather uncertain about their demands and particularly uncertain about how to negotiate such a large and complex contract. Without the usual personal relationships between bargainers and beset with continuous internal political challenges, bargaining came down to the wire in March without the foundation for an agreement.

Management, for its part, knew exactly what it wanted and was prepared to confront the union directly on these issues. In particular, TMI wanted to be able to hire part-time workers for cyclical dock operations (similar to the relationships permitted under the UPS contract and to those favored by some non-union carriers); to limit dockworkers to 40 hours per week; to increase the amount of long-haul freight they could put on rail cars; and to replace the traditional "open-ended" grievance machinery with one ending with arbitration.[23] After a 24-day strike, Teamsters went back to work having defeated the attempt to establish a part-time workforce but accepting very modest wage increases (less than 2% per year); the end of the open-ended grievance system; an extension of carriers' right to rail freight (up to 28%); a rule allowing carriers to send dockworkers home after reaching 40 hours; and other setbacks. The Teamsters Union also was millions of dollars poorer, as strike benefits brought it to the brink of insolvency.

Both sides took heavy blows during this strike. One motor carrier folded and others suffered long-lasting damage to their business bases and reputations as a result. At the 1994 National Trucking Industrial Relations Association meeting, Roadway president and CEO Michael Wickham announced a new era of constructive engagement with the Teamsters.[24] During the following three years Roadway made a notable effort to work with the Teamsters, talking with them regularly about industry issues. They also broke new ground, developing jointly with the Teamsters programs to distribute Roadway stock to union-represented employees (as bonuses for performance and as a stock-purchase opportunity) and a 401(k) program for hourly employees to save additional funds for retirement. These efforts by Roadway, along with efforts by other carriers, will bear fruit in subsequent negotiations.

In October 1997 TMI changed again in response to shifting industry priorities. The "Big Four" LTL carriers—Roadway, Consolidated Freightways, Yellow, and ABF—along with a few regional carriers formed Motor Freight Carriers Association (MFCA) to deal with broad economic and political issues affecting the LTL trucking industry, including bargaining. Carriers in the LTL industry increasingly have felt that the American Trucking Associations no longer represented their interests sufficiently, as the ATA seemed to turn its focus toward TL carriers; some LTL carriers, who were long-time members, even stopped paying dues. Trucking Management Incorporated remained intact but became a subsidiary of the MFCA. Management asked to begin negotiations early in order to head off business threats from non-union carriers.

As negotiations began, non-union LTL carriers began to approach the union carriers' customers and encouraged them to switch their business in advance of any possible strike, indicating they would not take shippers' business if tendered only during a strike. This competitive threat (viewed as raiding by unionized LTL carriers) put early pressure on both the carriers and the Teamsters to settle as soon as possible.

In the 1998 collective bargaining round, the Big Four carriers took the bargaining lead, and regional carriers such as A-P-A Transport, New Penn, and US Freightways stepped aside, agreeing explicitly or implicitly to follow the pattern set by the negotiations between the Teamsters and TMI. Discussions began as early as the spring of 1997 on an informal basis under Article 20 of the existing contract, which established a framework within which the parties could discuss broad issues of industry needs outside the direct bargaining relationship. The resulting agreement, reached some six weeks before the expiration of the old contract, produced a five-year NMFA that signaled new stability for collective bargaining in the LTL industry. Perhaps most critically, both UPS and Master Freight contracts do not expire until after the next national election for Teamster officers, scheduled for 2001.

In sum, centralized bargaining declined far more than did Teamster representation. While NMFA negotiations covered perhaps one-sixth as many carriers as before deregulation, by 1985 industry consolidation had increased the size of these firms by so much that only about half as many employees were represented as before 1980. By 1998 the negotiations included only four very large firms, with many others following the pattern in various ways. In addition, the increasingly divergent needs of many carriers in newly defined markets caused many motor carriers to negotiate with the Teamsters individually, rather than using employer associations. While fragmented pattern bargaining allowed these carriers to follow a general industry pattern while tailoring their contracts to their increasingly diverse market needs, the resultant labor market competition, based on diverse wages and work rules, has limited the union's ability to set the tone in the industry. Unable to keep wages out of competition, the Teamsters have begun to chase the tail of the labor market, "selling labor" for an ever-decreasing market price. Even though the Teamsters can no longer dictate contract conditions, the union makes a significant difference within each market, giving unionized members a decided advantage over their non-union brethren. The union premium remains more than 25%, a differential that has to make a difference in an era of scarcity.

Where, then, does unionization remain strong? Just as breaking down the industry by market segment shows the changing levels of concentration, bankruptcies, and productivity, this approach provides an even more accurate picture of what has happened with unionization. My survey of Class I general freight carriers[25] shows declining union density within carriers that survived the deregulation shakeout[26] (see table 5.2). This means that in many cases the union represents some but not all of the drivers and other eligible employees within the firm, reducing the union's bargaining power. The University of Michigan's driver survey suggests further that the Teamsters may represent as few as one out of every ten over-the-road drivers, suggesting an impending crisis in bargaining power.

Unionization by Industry Segment

Union density levels vary by specific subsector and market. Union membership levels remain high in some parts of the trucking industry and low in others, so unionization remains a powerful predictor of wages and conditions overall. For example, union density in the new automobile transport industry is nearly 100%. Union density among other specialized carriers, however, is quite low. While unionization

Table 5.2 Declining Union Density within Surviving General Freight Carriers

Percentage of Unionization	1977		1982		1987		1991	
	Count	%	Count	%	Count	%	Count	%
0	96	44.0	102	46.4	108	48.6	112	51.1
0–12.5	5	2.3	8	3.6	8	3.6	9	4.1
12.5–25	3	1.4	1	0.5	4	1.8	5	2.3
25–50	6	2.8	9	4.1	9	4.1	9	4.1
50–75	6	2.8	5	2.3	8	3.6	5	2.3
75–100	102	46.8	95	43.2	85	38.3	79	36.1
N	218	100	220	100	222	100	219	100

Source: Belzer survey data 1991.

Union density defined as proportion of carrier's employees who are union members. Percentage columns may not sum to 100% due to rounding. N varies due to data limitation caused by firm creation and mortality.

is still higher in the general freight sector than it is elsewhere in the private sector, it is much higher in LTL than it is in the TL market. The union has pockets of strength in urban areas as well, giving the Teamsters some bargaining leverage in subsectors of the trucking industry that depend on local delivery networks.

By transforming the trucking industry and creating two distinct general freight market segments, however, economic deregulation changed the labor picture in a fundamental way. Employment conditions split dramatically along the industry's new fault lines, creating very different results for different people. While wages and conditions deteriorated for all workers, they collapsed for non-union truckload workers. Further, deregulation diminished the Teamsters Union's ability to secure the best agreements for its members—and in the process influence wages and working conditions for non-union workers as well. Paradoxically, the unevenness of the unionization pattern has left the union more critical than ever in some segments but unable to constitute a credible threat in others. As the threat of unionization declines, collective bargaining power weakens, making it less likely that the market can regulate the trucking industry to benefit everyone working in it.

The change in industry structure produced by economic deregulation created hundreds of significant new truckload carriers. While unions represented most TL and LTL general freight before deregulation, the industry segmentation into separate TL and LTL industries led to changed union representation patterns, and by 1991 there was a sizable difference in union representation between TL and LTL companies (see table 5.3). Many drivers who were laid off went to work for the new, non-union TL carriers that proliferated, and union coverage overall has declined. As a result, TL carriers no longer feel threatened by unionization, which has led to a pronounced decline in average real wages.

Under certain, albeit rare, circumstances, the union represents only individuals rather than whole groups of individuals and has no bargaining authority at all. In some truckload carriers that once had strong Teamster representation but have driven out most Teamsters, the union cannot bargain for the vestige that remains. The union has minority representation, and thus the carrier is not bound to recognize or bargain with the union under the National Labor Relations Act. In some of these cases the parties have reached an understanding whereby the Teamsters Union will accept health and welfare and/or pension contributions but does not represent workers contractually. These workers have no collective bargaining contract. Such carriers may even pay union drivers according to a different schedule than they use for non-union drivers, although these drivers coexist within the same company. In at least one company, unionized owner operators receive lower pay than do non-union operators, shifting a portion of their wages to the union benefit plans to which they have belonged for many years.

As these data show, unionization initially remained relatively stable within the less-than-truckload segment of the general freight industry, especially among the carriers that gained market share

Table 5.3 Unionization in 1991 of TL and LTL Carriers

Union Status	TL	LTL
Non-union	75 carriers (76%)	36 carriers (31%)
Union	24 carriers (24%)	80 carriers (69%)
Total	99 carriers (100%)	116 carriers (100%)

Source: Belzer survey data 1991.

   Union carriers have some union representation, but not necessarily a majority or a contract.

over the last 20 years. Recently, however, and especially since the 1995 elimination of intrastate economic regulation, a number of non-union regional carriers have begun to make inroads in the LTL industry. These carriers include independent interregional and emerging national carriers such as American Freightways (formerly a southern regional carrier known as Arkansas Freightways), Con-Way (formerly a set of three regional subsidiaries of Consolidated Freightways and later spun off as part of a group of carrier and logistics operations), and Old Dominion (formerly a southern regional carrier now emerging as a transcontinental carrier); regionals such as Pitt-Ohio and Ward in the East; subsidiaries of unionized LTL carriers such as WestEx in the West and Saia in the South (Yellow Freight System); and subsidiaries of non-union national carriers such as Viking in the west (originally independent, then a regional subsidiary of Roadway and later of its spin-off, Caliber, which itself was swallowed by Federal Express); and Overnite (a national subsidiary of Union Pacific Railroad operating as an interregional carrier). The recent growth of many of these carriers has reduced union density in LTL considerably.

Some union carriers have opened up new non-union terminals, further reducing the level of union representation within the firm without disturbing representation patterns at old terminals. Unlike the Railway Labor Act, which requires company-wide bargaining, the National Labor Relations Act allows collective bargaining at individual worksites. This means that a unionized carrier can legally open up a new non-union terminal, as long as it does not violate a contract, or as long as the union allows it, or if the company has the leverage to do so. In some situations, the company's bargaining power is such that it can open a new non-union terminal without worrying about the union, defying it to attempt to extend bargaining rights to the new terminal or organize new employees at that terminal. Until 1992 this strategy worked quite well as the decentralized Teamsters, beset with regional rivalries, were unable or unwilling to challenge such carriers. This company strategy contributed to the de-unionization that developed after deregulation under the old Teamster leadership.

Why Is Unionization Important?

The presence or absence of the union has a big effect on the quality of jobs in trucking. The issue of good versus bad jobs has implications not only for the workers and carriers, but for society as well. It raises several questions for public policy that need to be addressed. What is an acceptable effective minimum wage within the U.S. economic system, and should it cover all industries? How far below the poverty line should this minimum wage be? Is it meaningful to speak of an unsafe or unhealthy number of hours to work in a day or in a week? Should work hours be limited for health reasons, or even for quality of life reasons? Even more basically, is it acceptable in a democracy for a majority of workers in any industry or occupation to spend more than 65 hours per week on the job, especially a job that takes them away from home for days or weeks? Such workers have little time for family or religious life, or for education, and uninformed, alienated citizens create social externalities we can only dimly imagine. Broad concerns such as these were addressed long ago in American public policy, when workers toiled in sweatshops, making subsistence wages. We abolished the sweating system decades ago and created the 40-hour workweek to encourage employers to create more jobs that balance labor and leisure. Are we turning back the clock?

Now, with economic deregulation and deinstitutionalization of the labor market, these questions have become important again. Absent institutional and economic regulation of trucking, perhaps only unionization or expanded minimum wage and maximum hours limits can provide the protections for workers Americans have long believed appropriate.

Employers use all sorts of strategies to avoid unionization. Truckers will tell you that it is common in the industry for some TL carriers to hire employees from paper domiciles in widespread locations, defying the union to find them. In cases like this, the carrier (or driver leasing firm) hires its employees out of an arbitrary location, such as a motel, and may not even establish an office in the region. Often, a phone is all that is needed. My own survey in 1991 revealed that at least one carrier employs a labor leasing firm whose purpose is dispersion and obfuscation to ensure the drivers do not organize.

Labor leasing also offers one potent way for carriers to evade the legal responsibility to recognize a union. If a trucking company employs no drivers itself, but rather has a contract with a labor leasing agency that employs the drivers, the carrier can simply cancel the contract if the workers unionize. That is a very effective union avoidance strategy.[27] As long as the leasing firm maintains a minimum legal distance from the motor carrier, the carrier need never concern itself with unionization. If the employees vote to unionize, the carrier severs its business relationship with the leasing firm and contracts with another leasing firm with new drivers.

Trucking companies often pursue a third avenue. Many hire owner operators to haul their freight. Courts have ruled that these drivers, who own their own tractors (or lease them from a firm often owned or controlled by the carrier), legally are independent contractors. Independent contractors, technically defined as independent businesspeople by U.S. law, cannot unionize. Research shows that these workers, on average, earn less than do other non-union truck drivers after costs of operation are deducted from their gross income.[28]

What the Union Means for Wages

As we explore the effects of unionization, it is important to note that many analysts claimed pre-1980 trucking industry regulation created rents—that is, unearned premia resulting from market control—for unionized workers[29] and thus artificially enhanced the Teamsters' bargaining power. Some suggest that labor captured between 66 and 75% of these rents in the form of inflated wages.[30]

What actually happened is more complicated. Real wages have declined steadily since the late 1970s among workers in many goods-producing industries, as well as in trucking. Earnings data from the Bureau of Labor Statistics Establishment Survey show that non-supervisory employee average annual earnings in the trucking industry declined by 29.5% percent between 1977 and 1996. In 1997 dollars the average trucking industry production employee (including truck drivers, dockworkers, and other non-supervisory employees) earned $224 less per week and $11,702 less for all of 1996 than he did in 1977. This compares with an average real earnings decline of $2,541, or 8.2%, for other manufacturing and service production workers, who lost ground as well. In other words, at a time when production workers in general were feeling a real pinch, trucking production employees were feeling a pinch more than three-and-a-half times as bad in percentage terms. As figure 5.2 shows, perhaps the most telling change is the convergence of trucking earnings and earnings in general manufacturing. Recall that data collected by the University of Michigan truck driver survey, corroborated by data collected for the Current Population Survey, suggest truck drivers work very long hours to reach this earnings level; the driver survey suggests that the average road driver works nearly 3,500 hours annually, with perhaps five days of vacation and a couple of holidays.

Between 1978 and 1997 the wealth loss for truckers was $173,556 in 1997 dollars, compared with a wealth loss of $45,376 for the average production worker over the same period (table 5.4). To the extent that truck drivers sweat their labor by working longer hours and driving more miles, they may have reduced the financial loss, but a loss this great within normal work hours constitutes a significant redistribution of wealth.

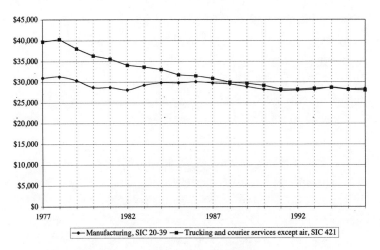

Figure 5.2: Average Annual Earnings of Production Workers

Table 5.4 Annual Earnings Change from Start of Deregulation

Year	Trucking and Courier Services Except Air SIC 421 ($)	Manufacturing SIC 20-39 ($)
1978	—	—
1979	(2,251)	(949)
1980	(3,935)	(2,621)
1981	(4,685)	(2,640)
1982	(6,196)	(3,225)
1983	(6,623)	(2,075)
1984	(7,209)	(1,474)
1985	(8,531)	(1,528)
1986	(8,804)	(1,263)
1987	(9,427)	(1,550)
1988	(10,313)	(1,814)
1989	(10,578)	(2,430)
1990	(11,117)	(3,084)
1991	(12,037)	(3,390)
1992	(12,044)	(3,294)
1993	(11,793)	(3,125)
1994	(11,610)	(2,620)
1995	(12,096)	(3,003)
1996	(12,276)	(2,903)
1997	(12,034)	(2,389)
Cumulative Change in Wealth	(173,556)	(45,376)

Source: U.S. Department of Labor, Bureau of Labor Statistics, *Employment, Hours, and Earnings,* 1991 and Bureau of Labor Statistics Web Site.

Wage trends over the past three decades show that real wages have fallen to their value in the early 1960s. A comparison between wages in trucking and those in other industries confirms the trend (see figure 5.3). In 1958 wages in trucking were comparable to those in manufacturing. Trucking wages rose during the late 1950s and early 1960s, owing in part to the successful development of centralized bargaining, culminating in the 1964 National Master Freight Agreement. By the mid-1960s truckers' wages had become comparable with auto and steel workers' wages and remained so until 1970.[31]

After 1970 real wages increased sharply, though temporarily, in response to both the uncertainty produced by high inflation and the absence of the moderating influence of Jimmy Hoffa, then in prison and out of the bargaining picture. In the political power struggle that followed, many union leaders sought to establish themselves as Hoffa's legitimate successors. Teamster leaders in Chicago, led by Local 705 Secretary-Treasurer Louis Peick, were independent of NMFA bargaining control and were particularly rebellious. They broke from the NMFA

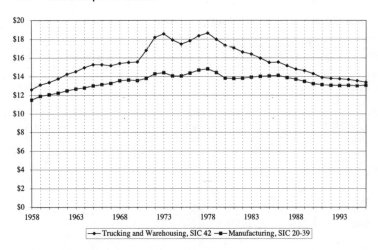

Figure 5.3: Hourly Wages of Production Workers

pattern of a $1.10 per hour raise (over three years) negotiated by General President Frank Fitzsimmons and struck for 13 weeks, winning a wage increase of $1.65 per hour over three years.

The wage increase was important for two reasons. The raise won by Chicago Teamsters embarrassed Fitzsimmons and forced him to go back to TEI and negotiate a further increase, raising Master Freight wages by $1.85, shifting real wages up by 20%. Political conflict within the union therefore caused a kind of competition that gave Teamsters high wage increases by historical standards. Second, the raise disproportionately benefited city drivers, the primary constituents of the Chicago locals, changing the entire structure of compensation in unionized trucking. With greater relative wage increases for city rather than road drivers, carriers with a larger fraction of city work were put at a disadvantage. It encouraged many carriers to think about alternatives to unionized operations and exacerbated the tensions within TEI, almost certainly contributing to its fracture a few years hence.

Under Hoffa, such a distortion would have been unlikely. He always cast a wary eye on the market and avoided pushing trucking wages too far in any segment. The market distortion that fell out of the political conflict not only raised trucking employees' wages to an all-time high, but also destabilized the balance between road and local wages. In hindsight, this destabilization—which brought business and consumer interests together against labor—probably sowed the seeds of support for deregulation to a significant degree.

The Teamsters' pattern was not substantially different, however, from that in other basic industries, as labor and other unrest swept the nation in the late 1960s and early 1970s and upset the post–World War II balance. Rank-and-file groups arose all over the country, most notably in auto, steel, and other manufacturing sectors. In the Teamsters, dissident groups like TURF and PROD developed, leading ultimately to a mature rank-and-file organization—Teamsters for a Democratic Union—that eventually gained a significant degree of power within the union.

Wildcat strikes (illegal and unauthorized strikes by unionized employees during the term of a collective bargaining contract) broke out in many industries during this period, but none were more disruptive than the wildcats and other strikes that occurred in the late 1960s among unhappy truckers hauling steel.[32] These steelhaul wildcats erupted into shooting wars on the nation's highways, particularly in the Midwest in the manufacturing heartland between Chicago and Pittsburgh. In fact, it was weary and, some say, trigger-happy National Guardsmen just returning from a steelhaul wildcat strike who fired on students at Kent State University in Ohio on May 4, 1970, killing four people.

Even the traditionally conservative construction unions saw unrest during this period. Strong union bargaining power combined with a tight labor market and the loss of some young construction workers to Vietnam—and even to college, where these young workers could escape the draft—created unrest in construction as well as low labor productivity. Wages went up to extraordinary levels, bringing calls for the expansion of non-union construction labor from the Business Roundtable, an organization of large business buyers of construction services.

As figure 5.3 showed, these factors—strong bargaining power, low unemployment, high inflation, and rank-and-file militancy—fueled the upward tendency of wages of all production workers during this period. But after peaking at $18.64 per hour (in 1997 dollars), trucking and warehouse workers' wages began the drop from which they have yet to recover. As of 1996, they stand at an average of $13.39 per hour, a 29% decline from the 1978 peak. Again, truckers and warehouse workers were not the only losers but perhaps suffered more than most others: manufacturing production workers' wages dropped 12% over the same period. Construction workers' wages fell the farthest, however, both in nominal and percentage terms, dropping 32% (more than $4.50 per hour) between 1974 and 1995, and now also hover around 1960 levels.

That drop may in part mirror a transfer of wealth from the trucking industry to shippers. A 1990 study of surface freight deregulation by the Brookings Institution claimed that shippers' welfare resulting from motor carrier deregulation averaged $4.78 billion per year in 1977 dollars ($11.48 billion annually in 1997 dollars). Approximately 17% of that gain came from improvements in service time and 83% from rate reductions.[33] While part of the rate reduction comes from more efficient operations, the foregoing wage analysis suggests most of the decrease probably came from workers. Assuming this figure is correct and that the average savings is constant over the past two decades, it suggests that this transfer of wealth was 79% of the savings. The total shift over the 20-year period between 1978 and 1997 transferred a whopping $229.6 billion from truckers to shippers (in 1997 dollars), with $190.6 billion coming from rate reductions and only $39 billion coming from service improvements.[34] In other words, while the service improvements made by competitive markets were an important and visible positive effect of deregulation, most of the savings came from lower real rates charged by the industry for the work performed by its employees. In fact, when we multiply the average annual earnings loss for trucking employees by the number of employees and sum across all years, we find that industry employees (both supervisory and non-supervisory) lost more than $250 billion over the period, about 10% more than the total welfare transfer. The rest probably was caused by the same macroeconomic forces and labor law deregulation that caused the income declines experienced by blue-collar workers in general over the same period; the income of the average blue-collar worker declined 20% as much as did the income of the average trucking employee.

As post-deregulation wages declined, they began to differentiate along several dimensions, breaking the wage solidarity pattern developed from the 1950s through the 1970s. I found wide variation among driver wages in my 1991 survey of current general freight wages.[35] Driver wage variation followed the segmentation of the industry, and certain companies now compete based on low wages paid to employees—a big change from the past, when they could compete only on the basis of efficiency, frequency of service, transit times, reliability, and the low incidence of damaged freight.

How wide are the variations? The mean mileage rate in 1991 for the 132 general freight carriers that pay drivers by the mile was 29.5¢ per mile. This rate, which includes all types of Class I general freight carriers operating within the 48 contiguous states, varied from a minimum of 18¢ to a maximum of 42¢. There were two peaks at approximately 34¢ and 40¢, with another cluster near the lower end. Most of the carriers paying at either of the two higher peaks are both unionized and LTL. The lower of these two market wages (34¢ and 40¢) seems to correspond to regional markets, especially including the few remaining unionized TL or mixed freight carriers, but this characterization is by no means universal. Most of the carriers in the bottom distribution, on the other hand, are both non-union and TL.

The survey showed dramatic contrasts in wages by unionization and industry segment (see table 5.5). While non-union drivers average 24.3¢ per mile, Teamster drivers average 35¢.[36] Industry segment, however, provides a similarly graphic spread. The mean TL wage was 23.8¢, but the mean LTL wage was 33.5¢.

Among LTL carriers, the mean union wage is 35.8¢ while the mean non-union wage is 26.8¢, only 74.9% as much. Non-union TL drivers earn only 80% of the average TL union rate. Overall, the average non-union wage is 70% of the average union rate. Even within market segments, the union premium remains between 20 and 25%.

An important confounding influence is the geographic scope of the carrier, with those hauling freight over longer distances paying much more in the LTL segment than in the TL segment. The average national carrier paid 25.1¢ per mile, while the average regional carrier paid 31¢ and the average local carrier paid 36.2¢. However, the distance effect

Table 5.5 Average General Freight Mileage Rates by Industry Segment and Unionization (cents per mile)

Industry Segment	Pay Rate	Industry Segment	Pay Rate	t-Statistic	Significance
Union	34.7	Non-union	24.3	12.947	.01
LTL	33.5	TL	23.8	10.960	.01
National	25.1	Regional	31.0	−4.478	.01
Union/LTL	35.8	Non-union/LTL	26.8	7.520	.01
Union/LTL	35.8	Union/TL	28.4	2.763	.05
Union/TL	28.4	Non-union/TL	23.1	2.008	.10[.01][a]
Non-union/LTL	26.8	Union/TL	28.4	−0.571	
Non-union/LTL	26.8	Non-union/TL	23.1	3.147	.01
Union/National	34.7	Non-union/National	23.1	3.353	.05
Union/National	34.7	Union/Regional	34.7	0.001	
Union/Regional	34.7	Non-union/Regional	25.0	10.764	.01
Non-union/national	23.1	Non-union/Regional	25.0	−2.033	.05
LTL/National	38.9	TL/National	22.6	12.105	.01
LTL/National	38.9	LTL/Regional	33.1	4.147	.01
LTL/Regional	33.1	TL/Regional	25.1	6.693	.01
TL/National	22.6	TL/Regional	25.1	−2.272	.05

Source: Michael H. Belzer, "Collective Bargaining after Deregulation: Do the Teamsters Still Count?" *Industrial and Labor Relations Review* 48 (1995): 650. Reprinted by permission.

Significance based on critical values of t in two-tailed tests.
Union defined as more than 12.5% representational density.
[a] There are only 8 union TL carriers and 7 degrees of freedom. ANOVA on union/TL compares TL with and without union: F-ratio = 13.363 (p=.0006).

for truckload is exactly the opposite of that for less-than-truckload. National LTL carriers paid 38.9¢ per mile, while national TL carriers paid only 22.6¢. Regional LTL carriers paid less than their national counterparts, while regional TL carriers paid more. Ironically, while the highest-paid LTL drivers work for national carriers, the lowest-paid drivers in the general freight industry work for national TL carriers. As of 1991, long-haul truckload drivers earned only 58.1% as much per mile as did long-haul LTL drivers, and the latter get home much more often and have more regular schedules.[37]

The 1997 University of Michigan truck driver survey confirmed that the patterns found in 1991 generally still apply. Non-union drivers reported driving 115,000 miles per year at the median, while union employees drove only 100,000 miles, a 15% difference. For the added work, the median non-union driver earned $35,000 last year compared to the median earnings of $44,000 for the union driver. The earnings difference has two component sources, the mileage rate and payment for non-driving labor. While the median non-union driver earned 28¢

per mile, the median union driver earned 37¢, a full 33% more. Again supporting my 1991 survey, non-union drivers are about half as likely to be paid for non-driving labor as are union drivers, depending on the activity, and at a much lower rate. Since this non-driving labor constitutes 27% of the average driver's workday, the difference in outcomes can be substantial.

Returning to data derived from the ICC, we can see an empirical basis for the claim that union drivers earn a significant premium over their non-union counterparts, and the premium has increased since economic deregulation. Figure 5.4 shows the extent to which the gap between union drivers and nonunion drivers grew over the first decade of deregulation, from 1977 to 1987. By 1987 union employees were earning 10% more than the average earnings in the industry. Nonunion employees, on the other hand, were earning more than 15% less than the mean. By this measure the gap between union and nonunion drivers, even a decade ago, was more than 25%. But lest union drivers grow complacent, figure 5.5 demonstrates union drivers' decline over the same period. Union drivers' annual earnings declined by nearly 20% in the first decade of deregulation while nonunion drivers' earnings declined 28.5%. In other words, in the simplistic logic of some analysts, including the Teamster leadership at the time, union drivers merely needed to reduce their wage demands or cut their wages

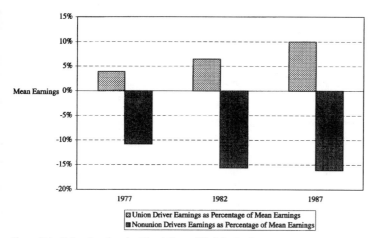

Figure 5.4: Union Premium for Class I General Freight Carriers

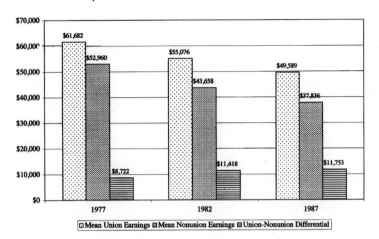

Figure 5.5: Average Annual Earnings, Class I General Freight Carriers

to keep their jobs and remain wage competitive with their nonunion counterparts. We see now that nonunion driver earnings dropped farther, both in dollars and in percentage terms, than did those of union drivers. Nobody wins in the race to the bottom.

This differential especially applies to benefits. While we do not know from the driver survey how much firms contribute to benefits, we do know whether drivers receive them. Union employees are about 3.5 times more likely to qualify for a conventional pension and more than twice as likely to have an Individual Retirement Account. While we cannot easily compare the quality of health benefits, a company is twice as likely to pay for all benefits costs of union drivers than of nonunion drivers.[38]

A central tenet of the pro-deregulationists was the claim that economies of scale in the trucking industry do not exist: there are no advantages to carrier size. Economies of scale, scope, and density have been discussed elsewhere in this book, and evidence of their effects appears when we examine wages also. Looking at unionization and pay scales, it turns out larger carriers pay significantly higher wages than do smaller firms (controlling for other effects). This suggests that industry consolidation has been beneficial for those who work for larger firms. While this effect seems modestly significant for all employees, accounting for perhaps 10% of all attributable variation, it appears most dramatic on mileage driver wages. Using my own data on mileage driver rates, market share accounts for nearly half as much of the accountable wage differences as does Teamsters Union representation, a fivefold increase in explanatory power. In short, big firms pay more than small firms, suggesting a new source of rent shared by drivers and firms and arguably encouraged by market forces.[39]

The University of Michigan driver survey showed that truckload drivers clearly earn less annually, confirming the pay rate analysis in table 5.5. Again, the effect is most pronounced among road drivers, as TL road drivers earn lower wages than their LTL counterparts who perform similar work. This disparity is made worse by the fact that TL drivers' jobs are probably more difficult: they frequently load and unload their trucks without pay, wait for loads and repairs without pay, and drive highly irregular routes over longer distances. Much of this work is uncompensated, and so annual earnings are correspondingly lower (and artificially boosted by illegally long work hours).

It should be noted as well that all employees of trucking firms based in the southern United States earn significantly lower annual salaries than the national average, controlling for other factors, returning to the pattern of regional inequity that existed before the Master Freight Agreement. Although the road drivers' disadvantage is greater than that experienced by other carrier employees, it is notable that all employees of carriers with southern operations experience lower salary levels.[40]

Comparing unionization within the most narrowly defined segments suggests a significant union premium remains in general freight. To determine the size of the premium, however, one must control for other likely factors that reflect the other dimensions I have presented. Clearly market segment is important (in this case, LTL and TL), reflecting the pricing driven by the competition for customers and the cost of delivering the service. Further, carriers earning greater profits should be able to pay higher wages, sharing some of those profits with employees. We also should expect carriers with a greater market share to pay higher wages, as their relative market power would insulate them somewhat from price competition. I use average haul (ton-miles per ton) as a proxy for regional versus local operations, expecting that controlling for other factors regional carriers would pay greater wages than national carriers, suggesting a greater ability for unions to bargain for locally-based firms and a greater need on the part of localized firms to respond to labor markets.[41] The longer the average haul, the greater the expected driver earnings, controlling for other factors.

If we disentangle the union and segment effects suggested in table 5.5, we find that unionization is an overwhelmingly positive predictor of wage levels and a negative predictor of risk-shifting, as shown in table 3.1. Union members likely earn more, and earn wages for all of their work, while non-union drivers earn less and earn no pay for much of their non-driving labor time. Truckload drivers likewise earn less per mile and give away time.[42]

Profits, market share, and intercity operations also lead to higher pay levels. Truck drivers working for large, profitable, intercity carriers make significantly more money than those working for small, unprofitable, primarily local or regional firms. However, these factors do not appear to be associated with risk-shifting. We find compensation regimes that shift risk from firms to drivers primarily in non-union carriers.[43]

There are two explanations for this strong association between unionization and better wages and working conditions. First, the Teamsters Union retains considerable bargaining leverage within the general freight industry, as table 5.1 suggests. While the labor market arguably includes drivers whose experience lies outside general freight, employers in the union LTL sector I surveyed in 1991 indicated they primarily hire drivers laid off from other LTL carriers that have downsized or closed. The 1993 contract between United Parcel Service and the Teamsters, which provided sizable increases in wages (to $19.95 per hour in 1997 for full-time employees) and improvements in conditions, suggests that even the most powerful carrier in the industry has little choice but to respect the Teamsters' ability to disrupt production. The Teamsters graphically demonstrated this power to disrupt operations in their three-week strike of UPS in 1997. Faced with an unsatisfactory final offer that they believed concessionary, the Teamsters struck UPS nationally and won a dramatic victory for full-time jobs and higher pay, particularly for low-paid, part-time workers. Moreover, while the Teamsters' 24-day strike over the Master Freight Agreement in April 1994 cost the union and its members mightily, employers also paid a high price, as freight volume declined 23% that month and did not regain profitability for more than two years.[44] When it came time to negotiate a new Master Freight contract in 1998, TMI carriers pushed hard to settle early and without another strike, which they did.

The second explanation is that the union indicator variable may be in part a proxy for other unmeasured characteristics. Barry Hirsch uses Census Department Current Population Survey (CPS) data in his effort to measure the union premium, controlling for years of schooling and potential experience, race, marital status, veteran status, and region. He finds these factors explain very little of the union premium.[45] He does find that those who entered the period as nonunion drivers and later became union members earned more in their first period of the CPS survey in the industry than did the drivers who never joined the union. In other words, some union drivers presented unmeasured characteristics that caused them to earn a higher wage even before they joined the union. This suggests union carriers hire drivers superior to those hired by non-union carriers, a result predictable by efficiency wage theory. In other words, although union carriers paid substantially more wages and dramatically higher fringes, they hire from the front of the labor market queue. That is, they can and do hire the best available drivers, leaving much less qualified drivers to the non-union truckload sector.

But just what kind of power does the union still wield?

Union Bargaining Power

Barry Hirsch maintains that ICC regulation allowed the Teamsters to have greater bargaining power than they would have in a "more competitive" unregulated environment.[46] Some analysts go even further to declare that wage declines after deregulation prove that the union enjoyed substantial unearned market power in the regulated regime and that wages now seek their appropriate market level. Assuming high wages could only result from these unearned "rents," asserts Michael

Pustay, the reduced wages prove the Teamsters Union lost "much of its bargaining leverage" (its ability to capture the rent) as a result of regulatory restructuring.[47]

While collective bargaining has become more difficult since regulatory restructuring, for workers it has become more important. To what extent, then, has the union really lost bargaining power since deregulation? To find the answer, we need to disentangle market and unionization effects from each other.

The results (detailed in the Appendix) demonstrate that it is an oversimplification to assert that the Teamsters Union has lost "much of its bargaining leverage," as claimed by Pustay and others. Rather, it appears that the Teamsters Union used its leverage mainly to minimize the fall of real wages for its members, even as real wages fell dramatically among non-union workers elsewhere in the industry. The Teamsters Union has retained considerable bargaining clout for its own members within general freight, contrary to what most observers predicted. They figured deregulation would broadly weaken the bargaining power of the Teamsters.

Since the beginning of administrative deregulation in 1977, the union has had a strong and systematic positive effect on wage outcomes in general freight, and the strength of the effect has grown steadily over the years. Controlling for industry niche, scope, market share, net profit margin, urbanization, and region, the Teamsters Union has the largest effect on annual salaries and wages, raising earnings of union workers relative to those of non-union workers, as unions do elsewhere in private industry.[48] The Teamster wage effect was significant in all years, and increased dramatically between 1977 and 1990.[49]

Among Class I general freight carriers, the influence of the Teamsters on wages of unionized workers has increased significantly, slowing the decline of its members' real wages. On the other hand, its ability to draw non-union wages up has declined, reflecting employers' diminishing fear of successful Teamster organizing drives. For LTL drivers, this does not mean that union drivers' wages are up, but rather that union drivers' wages have declined while non-union drivers' wages have declined as well. Strong bargaining power within markets, however, along with the decline of this unionization threat, has caused an increasing union/non-union wage gap (controlling for various firm effects), fueling the race to the bottom for a large number of trucking employees.

The overall earnings gap between employees of general freight union and non-union firms increased 34.7% between 1977 and 1987, the first ten years of intense competition (see figure 5.4).[50] However, just as a rising tide lifts all boats, a falling tide beaches all boats. While there is an increasing gap between union and non-union employees, the differential is based on declining earnings for all employees.

Even economists who claim consumers have benefited from deregulation admit that it has been at the expense of the trucking industry and its employees. "The LTL sector of the trucking industry has lost $5.3 billion in profits annually from deregulation . . . [benefiting] the American economy, while redistributing wealth from labor and one segment of the motor carrier industry, the LTL carriers, to consumers and to railroads."[51] How bad has the earnings decline been? Mean earnings in general freight declined 24% between 1977 and 1990. Union employees fared better, as their earnings dropped by only 19.6%. Non-union employees did much worse: their earnings dropped by 28.6% (from a lower base) over the same decade.[52] Consequently, the union premium climbed from 14.1% in 1977 to 24.3% in 1990. As of 1997 the overall gap between wages paid at union carriers compared with their non-union counterparts averaged one-third.

These data show that the Teamsters did a reasonably good job protecting the wages and working conditions of their members under very adverse circumstances. However, the data show a dramatic deterioration of wages among the increasing number of employees of non-union carriers. As the proportion of unionized carriers declines, non-union wages may continue to decline, dragging unionized wages with them. The increasing union premium is small consolation, however, for union drivers who see their earnings fall.

The wage and earnings effects of deregulation can be summed up in a few words: the market on its own has been unable to "regulate" a reasonable minimum wage. Deregulation and deinstitutionalization have torn the industry apart. The surviving carriers have been the winners, and the losers have no voice.

Meanwhile, the workers have lost much of their claim to middle-class status. It is true that membership in the Teamsters Union provides truck drivers with their best earnings opportunities. While the industry segment matters—drivers do best in LTL, especially with the national LTL carriers—union members do better than non-union drivers across all sectors. While all truck drivers, including unionized drivers, have lost ground since economic deregulation, union members have lost the least and non-union drivers have lost the most. As a result, a significant union premium exists in all segments—with implications for the entire industry.

On the whole, however, much of the trucking industry has sagged to the bottom of the industrial pay scale.

6 Labor Market Failure and the Role of Institutions

Until the late 1970s trucking was an occupation with above-average wages and reasonable working conditions, lucrative enough to produce a stable and relatively skilled workforce. But the labor market institutions that once sufficed to ensure some measure of equity and efficiency have proved inadequate. While the steady erosion of Teamsters' real wages presents a problem for policymakers who want to retain a broad middle class, the concomitant and more severe decline in non-union wages has created a problem for the industry as well.

What produced this reversal in a mere 15 years? Could the wage profile of all industries in the United States come to look like trucking? What would it take?

As we have seen, industrial relations patterns have changed to fit a shifting industry structure. Wage scales narrowed during the period within which earlier Teamster leaders built and consolidated centralized bargaining.[1] As the Teamsters Union consolidated its power, James Hoffa and his allies kept wages down in some regions, while bringing them up in others, and as a result established a national scale for truck driver wages. Though not uniform, wages fluctuated within a narrow range in general freight and among other Teamster truck drivers following the freight pattern, generally taking wages out of competition. Since 1980, however, driver wages have stratified to follow a segmented industry organization, as I have shown in chapter 5.

Meanwhile, new risks have developed for drivers.

Competition Puts Compensation at Risk

The current broad trend in human resource management is to put more of each worker's wages "at risk." The theory suggests that the

more employees' earnings depend on personal or company performance, the greater productivity we can expect from them. With company and employee interests aligned, the organization will pursue
common goals more smoothly.

While most non-supervisory workers outside of trucking are paid
on an hourly basis, pay structures in trucking vary widely. From the
driver's point of view, payment by the hour is the surest way to ensure
a direct link between the number of hours worked and total compensation. Decades ago, however, the Teamsters agreed to mileage as the
basis of pay for over-the-road truck drivers. This kept driver and company incentives in line with each other in an unmonitored environment, benefiting drivers as well. They agreed to mileage pay along with
full hourly pay for non-driving labor time, however, which has always
constituted a significant component of total time on the job. In the
general freight industry, mostly consisting of the common carrier sector before economic deregulation, union contracts ensured that carriers paid drivers for all time spent in service to the employer, whether
driving, working on the dock, or performing other tasks. In this case,
the shipper's and consignee's incentives were in line with those of the
carrier and the driver: minimize on-duty, non-driving time and maximize the number of hours spent driving.

While compensation schemes tied to production, such as mileage-
based pay, have a long tradition in trucking, schemes that limit pay
to revenue-producing activity have proliferated over the last two decades. If carriers cannot charge their customers for waiting time because the market has competed this charge away, for example, they
have become increasingly reluctant to pay drivers for that time. Carriers even are loathe to charge shippers and consignees for unreasonable detention time, called "demurrage," that results from excessive
loading or unloading time, customarily beyond two hours. For many
of these drivers, therefore, pay has become contingent on mileage only,
forcing drivers to give away many hours each week while waiting for
freight, waiting for a trip assignment, or loading and unloading. These
changes in the drivers' wage structure also follow the lines of market
specialization, making non-payment of labor time consistent in some
sectors. If the driver absorbs labor time in this fashion, he has absorbed

the risk for operational delays and the vagaries of the market. This risk shifting has become one of the more serious problems endemic to the truckload sector of the modern competitive trucking industry.

When pay systems limit compensation to revenue-producing activity, they shift the risk for mechanical or system breakdown to the employee. If a similar pay structure was in place in a factory, this kind of risk-shifting might allow an employer to stop paying workers when an assembly line shuts down due to a temporary shortage of components or a mechanical breakdown on the line. In this way, the company would shift the risk of system failure to the employee. In trucking, if a driver waits "off the clock" for a shipment to be ready, for a truck to be repaired, or while somebody loads or unloads his truck, both carriers and their customers have shifted the risk of production delays to the employee. Since this kind of risk shifting generally is not permitted elsewhere in the economy, trucking becomes the exception that proves the necessity of the rule. Given different expectations across various sectors of the labor market, it should be no surprise that there is a labor shortage in the trucking industry segments most vulnerable to this abuse.

How Risk-Shifting Works

The most common compensation regime is mileage pay. Under this system, the driver earns a mileage rate for driving labor, and he may or may not earn an hourly rate for other duties.[2] Carriers pay for driving labor according to distance traveled, and the driver almost always assumes responsibility for traffic and weather delays.

Most unionized carriers pay by the hour or by the mile, and pay all drivers the same (see table 6.1). These carriers also usually pay drivers an hourly rate for time spent performing non-driving labor or waiting for loads and other non-driving responsibilities. They pay for non-driving time because of the collective bargaining power of organized drivers, compared to the individual bargaining power of non-union truck drivers. Some carriers pay all drivers at one rate, and others pay varying rates for different operations, seniority, experience, commodities, location, and other factors.[3]

Table 6.1 Contingency Table Showing Basis of Driver Pay in 1991

	Hourly	(%)	Mileage	(%)	Percentage of Revenue	(%)	Total
Non-union Carriers	0	(0.0)	29	(25.4)	16	(14.0)	45
Expected Values	2.8	(2.4)	33.9	(29.8)	8.3	(7.3)	45
Union Carriers	7	(6.1)	57	(50.0)	5	(4.4)	69
Expected Values	4.2	(3.7)	52.1	(45.7)	12.7	(11.2)	69
Total Carriers	7.0	(6.1)	86.0	(75.4)	21.0	(18.4)	114

Source: Belzer survey data 1991. First published in Michael H. Belzer, "Collective Bargaining after Deregulation: Do the Teamsters Still Count?" *Industrial and Labor Relations Review* 48 (1995): 647. Reprinted by permission.

Chi Square = 17.61 with 2 degrees of freedom
$p=0.0002$

Non-driving labor time has long been a major issue between trucking companies and their drivers. Intercity carriers use three basic schemes to pay for non-driving labor time, which includes inspecting equipment, loading and unloading, waiting for equipment, waiting to load or unload, waiting for repairs, road closure due to disaster or severe weather, and excessive layovers.[4] Except for time spent actually loading and unloading, carriers call non-driving labor "non-productive time" (NPT) because it does not produce revenue. Carriers that pay for loading and unloading or for NPT put a lot of energy into reducing their exposure through more efficient operations. Obviously, carriers that do not pay for NPT have less incentive to increase efficiency. The customers of those carriers, shippers and consignees, also have no incentive to improve operational efficiency when it comes to shipping and receiving, as they no longer pay for delay time.

The most comprehensive method of payment for non-driving time is to pay drivers for all time spent in service to the employer. Companies that strictly follow this model generally do so because of a collective bargaining contract that requires the carrier to pay for all non-driving time on an hourly basis. Many truckload and other non-union carriers pay drivers a flat rate by the stop, or for mandated pickup or delivery. This method is less comprehensive, but it compensates drivers somewhat for their labor time while keeping the driver's incentives in line with the carrier's production needs. Frequently companies pay drivers only for intermediate stops required in addition to the origin and destination; drivers must donate some or all of their time for the original pickup and final delivery. Carriers sometimes pay the driver by the hundredweight to load or unload the freight by hand. Again, time spent inspecting equipment and waiting for equipment or loads, maintenance or repairs, layovers, and road closure due to severe weather is the responsibility of the driver. These carriers only have an indirect incentive to reduce NPT, as it ties up the equipment but entails no labor cost.

Many companies simply choose not to pay their drivers directly for any non-driving labor. The carrier that uses a mileage scale might treat all loading and unloading, along with other delay time, as incidental labor. If the carrier pays by percentage, the freight rate includes loading and unloading. Tariffs charged by carriers (freight rates quoted by contract or formerly filed with the ICC) often include loading and unloading grace periods for which the shipper does not pay separately. Once again, drivers absorb any delays.

Some drivers are paid according to the percentage system—that is, they earn a percentage of the rate the carrier charges the shipper to deliver the freight. In this scheme, drivers assume the risk of weather, traffic, loading and unloading delays, breakdowns, and waits between jobs (which usually happen away from home) and may perform loading and unloading duties or pay someone else to do them either with a carrier allowance or out of their own pockets. Most important, drivers paid a percentage of the revenue also assume a market risk, since their pay depends on the freight rate the motor carrier can secure. Low-rated goods, such as fresh food, require a great deal of driver care and labor, including responsibility for the refrigeration unit and timely delivery, yet frequently pay drivers less than other freight.

Most non-union carriers pay by the mile but a significant number pay percentage. Few union carriers pay percentage rates because this scheme long has been considered manipulable, and union contracts usually specify miles and hours.

While unionized carriers usually pay their employees a standard negotiated rate, non-union carriers can pay a myriad number of rates depending on experience, seniority with the firm, region of hire, and on-time and other performance factors. Only 22% of carriers paying variable rates are unionized, compared to 61% of carriers paying a uniform rate, and the union has no impact on wages among carriers that do not pay a uniform rate, suggesting low bargaining power. The product market apparently drives the rates of carriers that pay variable rates to drivers.[5]

I created a risk-shifting index to measure the extent to which carriers assign this operational risk to their drivers. A carrier that pays all labor time gets a value of 1. These carriers pay for driving, loading and unloading, waiting for freight, breakdowns, and excessive layover time. If the carrier pays by the stop, the value is 2. In this intermediate case, carriers do not pay hourly for loading and unloading but rather a flat rate. They also do not pay for delays waiting for freight and for breakdowns or extended layovers and other irregular activities. Carriers that pay no compensation other than mileage or percentage—that is, pay only by the mile, not by labor time—get a 3. Carriers with a higher index number make compensation more contingent on the production of revenue, shifting the burden of risk to the employee (see chapter 3, table 3.1 for descriptive statistics and the Appendix for statistical analysis).

This analysis also shows the influence of the union on non-driving labor pay. The broad patterns are similar to those for mileage wage scales, though they are not quite as pronounced.[6]

- National carriers appear to be more likely than regional carriers to shift risk to employees, suggesting that local labor market pressures may exert a countervailing influence. Local or regional drivers are more closely tied to local labor markets influenced by fair wage laws that require employers to pay employees for all labor time.
- LTL and union carriers are more likely to pay for all labor time, absorbing the risk of inefficient operations. This may be the heritage of the pre-deregulation era, but it also reflects the bargaining preferences of the union and its members, who value their non-driving labor time.
- The gap between union and non-union in the less-than-truckload segment is large and significant, while the same gap in truckload

is much smaller. The truckload product market seems to force contingent wages on all competitors.
- Collective bargaining does not counteract entirely the effect of market segmentation: unionized truckload carriers shift more risk than do unionized less-than-truckload carriers.

One of the reasons the carriers can get away with shifting of the risk has to do with the rules governing the trucking labor market. It is a different story than that of other industries.

Institutions at Work: Minimum Wage and Maximum Hours Rules

Most of us take for granted the Fair Labor Standards Act (FLSA) of 1938, which established minimum wages and maximum working hours for American workers. While the Act originally covered only one-fourth of all private-sector workers, Congress has amended the FLSA several times. Minimum wage standards now apply to 92% of all non-supervisory employees. But employees of interstate trucking companies, from the outset, have been excluded from the maximum hour standards, as specified in Section 13(b)(1) of the Act. That means that, although these employees cannot legally be expected to work for less than minimum wage, they do not qualify for overtime pay at time-and-one-half after 40 hours in a single week. Since their pay structure may be contingent on many factors, including miles and revenues, it may be very difficult to determine for each individual whether he or she is even earning minimum wage.

In 1977 a Minimum Wage Study Commission (MWSC) was created to evaluate potential amendments to the Fair Labor Standards Act. Congress funded the Commission for three years, charging them with evaluating whether regulations such as those in the FLSA of 1938 harm or benefit workers.[7] Finding that 80% of trucking employees were Teamsters—and finding that the presence of the union had a strong effect in establishing the very guidelines it was charged with examining—the MWSC elected to omit trucking from its reform recommendations.

The Commission's report, submitted to Congress in May 1981, stated:

Most employees in the transportation sector are represented by labor organizations and over 90 percent of the approximately 2.2 million transportation workers
with exempt status from FLSA overtime pay provisions are employed in the interstate transport of passengers or goods by rail, truck, air, or water. The four major
interstate transportation sectors (rail, truck, air, and water) have a long history of
determining wages, hours, and working conditions through formal labor/manage-
ment collective bargaining procedures.[8]

The MWSC also found that while 90% of mechanics and loaders
worked under collective bargaining contracts providing for time-and-
one-half after 40 hours, all of them not earning overtime premia were
in the non-union sector.[9] The explosive growth in this non-union sector since deregulation had led to a large increase in unpaid time.[10]
Perhaps most telling, pressure from the non-union sector has led the
union sector to weaken standards for unionized employees as well,
breaking down the reliance on the 40-hour week even in Chicago, long
a bastion of Teamster power.[11]

According to the MWSC, Section 16(b)(1) of the Fair Labor Standards Act exempts trucking because the Department of Transportation (DOT) has the authority to limit hours. This power to regulate
hours-of-service, even though never exercised for anyone but drivers
and helpers, has provided the rationale to continue the exemption. In
addition, the DOT views the regulation of hours of service entirely as
a safety issue, not as a labor market issue, so pay rates are immaterial
to the DOT as long as carriers maintain safe operations.

The FLSA exemption, however, extends to all employees, including loaders and mechanics as well as to white-collar support staff,
because the Secretary of Transportation's unexercised power to regulate blocks the Department of Labor from acting. While arguably there
is a substantive difference between the Labor Department's interest
in regulating the labor market and the DOT's interest in safety, substantial unionization in trucking appeared to provide satisfactory private regulation.

The problem arose because the MWSC based its recommendation
on old data. Economic deregulation began administratively in 1977
and became law in 1980, just before the Commission issued its report.
The massive industry restructuring after 1980, bankrupting hundreds

of common carriers and creating a new and turbulent truckload general freight sector, reduced unionization dramatically[12] and thus erased much of this private regulation. The market also became super-competitive, putting extreme pressure on driver hours and wages, the only variable cost over which carriers retain direct control.

All of this has caused the conditions in the trucking labor market to deteriorate. Today, trucking employers find it very difficult to hire the same quality of employee they once could. Carriers are forced to go way down the queue to hire "quality" drivers. Just how far? An uneven decline in wages in a highly competitive industry with limited Fair Labor Standards Act regulation probably has stimulated wages to drop consistently—perhaps as low as the minimum wage, if one accounts for the number of hours the typical trucker works. This translates into wages that may be below the effective reservation wage of the skilled employees one would think the industry desires and that certainly lie below the poverty level.[13]

How do I come up with the near-minimum wage calculation? I developed it by first using firm-level data self-reported by motor carriers annually to the Interstate Commerce Commission in their Form M report.[14] In 1993 the average truckload (predominantly non-union) employee earned $29,831 in 1997 dollars. That amounts to $8.16 per hour at straight-time rates, assuming a 70-hour work-week, as determined by the UMTIP driver survey, and a 52.25-week year (3,657.5 hours worked annually, including five vacation days).[15] If the FLSA overtime-pay provision applied to interstate drivers, which would cause them to be paid time-and-one-half after 40 hours per week or 4,446.25 hours per year, the average interstate truck driver would have earned only $6.72 per hour in 1993 (again, in 1997 wages for purposes of comparison). For drivers working more hours for the same earnings, the average FLSA-based hourly wage goes down since each hour after 40 is at a straight time, rather than at an overtime rate.[16] The 1993 minimum wage, in 1997 dollars, was $4.73, according to calculations provided by the Economic Policy Institute, which suggests these drivers earned just 42% more than the minimum wage. With these low wages, accompanied by the high cost of living out of a truck and eating at truck stop restaurants for days or weeks at a time, it is a safe bet that most industrial workers would choose more lucrative occupations given the opportunity, exacerbating the labor market crisis (the driver shortage) in trucking.

In table 6.2, I present several hypothetical scenarios to estimate hourly wage rates, using 1990 data from Form M, submitted to the ICC by Class I and Class II motor carriers, as reported on tapes provided by the American Trucking Associations. While the average road driver earned $40,746, the average LTL general freight road driver (primarily union, at least at that time) earned $55,232 and the average TL road driver (primarily non-union) earned $30,293 (all in 1997 dollars). Again, the annual earnings figures understate estimates of hourly wages because of the FLSA exemption compounded by the long hours drivers work. The University of Michigan driver survey suggests the average union driver (predominantly LTL) works 60.7 hours per week and is paid for all of his labor. Assuming a 60-hour week, the average union driver earns about $17.62 per hour at a straight time rate (remember, they do not earn overtime pay in interstate trucking unless provided by contract) or $15.10 adjusted for overtime pay (time-and-one-half after 40 hours).

Truckload drivers' hourly pay was a very different matter. The driver survey suggests the average non-union driver (predominantly TL) works 70 hours per week, 10 hours more than the DOT limit. Some of this is unpaid on-duty time they do not log, and some may be in trips they do not log in their regular logbook (these drivers tell us they sometimes use multiple logbooks to account for all of their time). Assuming 70 hours of work, in 1990 the average straight time hourly rate comes to $8.28 (in 1997 dollars). Again, comparing these drivers' wages with workers in the non-trucking labor market (where they earn time-and-one-half for overtime), the hourly wage works out to $6.82. Thus, the FLSA exemption may cause the TL carriers to push wages so low that they find themselves competing with non-trucking employers who pay little more than the minimum wage. Given that they are asking these low-wage truck drivers to work long hours, stay away from home for several weeks at a time, sleep in the truck, and buy all of their meals on the road, the churning of this labor market is no surprise. Their reservation wage may approximate the minimum wage, and it should not surprise anyone that these workers are indifferent about their jobs and careers.

We also think that these workers today drive more miles than their predecessors. Between 1977 and 1992 the median per-driver mileage for reporting Class I and Class II general freight carriers increased nearly 29%, from 78,899 to 101,538 miles per year.[17] Calculated on a conservative overall average of 40 miles per hour overall, this represents an increase from 1,972.5 to 2,538.5 hours per year of driving alone. The driver survey both corroborates these calculations and suggests a further increase, as the average driver in 1996 drove 109,965 miles, with union drivers logging 103,016 and non-union drivers putting in 111,726 miles (2,575.4 and 2,793.2 hours of driving, respectively).

The large national LTL carriers' road drivers operate approximately this many miles, and they perform very little non-driving labor. Drivers who work for truckload firms, many of whom haul irregular loads and frequently load and unload, probably work many more non-driving hours than do the LTL drivers, further extending their work hours. We have known for some time that 75% of all interstate drivers regularly violate hours-of-service rules, suggesting most drivers work more than 60 hours per week at least some of the time.[18] In fact, the best data available indicate that the average driver worked 65.7 hours, with the average union driver working 60.7 and the average non-union driver working 70.0 hours.[19]

These rough wage calculations, originally based on data self-reported by the carriers, now have been tested with direct survey data. The University of Michigan driver survey shows that the median road driver puts in 62 hours per week, so let us look at this driver. The median union driver works 60 hours per week while the median non-union driver works 65 hours per week. Compare 65 hours per week in an FLSA-covered industry (in which a worker would earn 77.5 hours of pay for 65 hours of work) to 65 hours of work in trucking, not covered by the maximum hours provision of FLSA. Our driver would earn at most 65 hours of pay, though our research suggests he would more likely work 65 hours and earn only 48.75 hours of pay, since he would be giving away 25% of his time. This median driver earns $35,000 per year, or $670 per week, which is $10.31 per hour for 65 hours (alter-

Table 6.2 1990 Average Annual Earnings of Class I General Freight Drivers, Converted to Hourly Wage Estimates in Current Dollars: Alternative Scenarios with and without Section 13(b)(1) Exemption

Average Road Driver $33,352
TL Road Drivers[a] $24,796

Hours per Week	Hours per Straight-time Year	Annual Overtime Work Hours	FLSA Overtime Paid Hours	Annual Work Hours	FLSA Annual Paid Hours	Straight-time Hourly Rate ($)	FLSA Hourly Rate Adjusted for Overtime ($)
60	2090	1045.0	1567.50	3135.5	3657.50	7.91	6.78
70	2090	1567.5	2351.25	3657.5	4441.25	6.78	5.58
80	2090	2090.0	3135.00	4180.0	5225.00	5.93	4.75
90	2090	2612.5	3918.75	4702.5	6008.75	5.27	4.13
LTL Road driver[b] $45,209							
50	2090	522.5	783.75	2612.5	2873.75	17.30	15.73
60	2090	1045.0	1567.50	3135.5	3657.50	14.42	12.36

Average Local driver $31,653

TL Local driver[c] $23,590

60	2090	1045	1567.5	3135	3657.5	7.52	6.45
70	2090	1567.5	2351.25	3657.5	4441.25	6.45	5.31
80	2090	2090	3135	4180	5225	5.64	4.51
90	2090	2612.5	3918.75	4702.5	6008.75	5.02	3.93

LTL Local driver[d] $32,069

50	2090	522.5	783.75	2612.5	2873.75	12.28	11.16
60	2090	1045	1567.5	3135	3657.5	10.23	8.77

Source: Interstate Commerce Commission Form M data (motor carriers), as reported on tapes provided by the American Trucking Associations. Limited to carriers reporting separate TL and LTL revenue, and reporting driver wages paid and hours worked. The University of Michigan Trucking Industry Program Driver Survey replicates results shown in this table, using data collected directly from truck drivers. Previously published in Michael H. Belzer, "Labor Law Reform: Some Lessons from the Trucking Industry," *The 47th Annual Meeting of the Industrial Relations Research Association,* 1995. Reprinted by permission.

[a]N = 83 carriers.
[b]N = 85 carriers.
[c]N = 33 carriers.
[d]N = 116 carriers.

natively calculated at $13.74 per hour on 48.75 hours of paid work; the end result is the same). The same driver earning $10.31 per hour for 65 hours but working in an FLSA-covered industry would earn $799 per week, or 19.2% more. Looking at it the other way, our typical non-union over-the-road truck driver apparently earns an effective rate of only $8.65 per hour ($670 divided by 77.5 hours of pay).

Here is another way to illustrate the impact of the FLSA on wages and earnings. The 1997 Current Population Survey of truck drivers shows drivers' wages increasing from a low of $8.18 per hour for those working fewer than 35 hours to a high of $12.88 for those working between 41 and 49 hours, then decreasing again; those working 80 hours or more earn only $7.99 per hour of work. This does not mean that individual drivers' wages follow that pattern, but it does suggest that those who work just a little overtime make the highest rate of pay and those who work the most hours earn the lowest rate of pay and make up for the low rate of pay by working long hours. A driver who works 80 hours per week can expect to earn $640 for that labor at $8 per hour. If the FLSA maximum hours provision applied to this group, this same driver would earn $800 per week, bringing his effective wage up to $10 per hour (a 25% higher rate of pay). Under the current regime the driver has the option of quitting at 60 hours at $480 or continuing to work the extra hours for $640—not much of a choice.[20]

This analysis suggests that not only do wages in an industry with an unregulated labor and product market tend perilously close to mere subsistence, but clearly the rational employee who is worth $10.00 per hour and who can choose between the FLSA-covered job and over-the-road trucking would be irrational to choose trucking, where he would suffer a 20% pay cut. This enormous discrepancy may well account for the labor shortage perceived by the truckload trucking industry.

Unpaid work-time, along with the absence of full coverage by the Fair Labor Standards Act, thus contributes significantly to low effective wages. Non-union TL drivers are significantly less likely to earn wages for all work-time, contributing to low hourly earnings.[21] While little research beyond the driver survey exists on this phenomenon, non-union TL drivers certainly work many unpaid hours per week.[22]

Much, perhaps most, of that time goes unreported and does not show up in anyone's data, since drivers do not log unpaid time.[23]

It would appear, then, that a significant and growing number of truck drivers may be earning little more than the minimum wage. Exacerbating this problem is the fact that these drivers must eat most of their meals in restaurants, making for a very high cost of living on the job. Many, if not most, sleep in their trucks for days and weeks at a time, further suggesting a rather substandard quality of life. Drivers who live in their trucks take up a large share of the parking spaces in private truck stop lots and public rest areas, pushing off this externality on uninvolved parties, including taxpayers. Subtract from those poverty–level earnings the cost of living on the road for an average of three weeks at a time, and truck drivers have very little left to send home to support their families. This hard life buys them little more than the necessities.

Does Trucking Look Like a Labor Market Failure?

These sweatshop conditions raise a problem for employers. The non-union carriers, predominantly in truckload over-the-road operations, are experiencing "the first major, widespread labor shortage since the 1980s," according to Allen Sinai, chief economist for Lehman Brothers.[24] The situation is so severe that TL carriers have asked for the right to hire workers from other countries to drive trucks in the United States.[25] The Truckload Carriers' Conference of the ATA also wants to extend hours of service to a possible 96 hours weekly by allowing drivers to "reset" their weekly hours-of-service clocks, when they reach their legal limit of 70 hours in an eight-day week, by logging off duty for 24 hours, after which they can begin working again. In the current hours-of-service controversy, truckload carriers have continued this line of reasoning while advocating "performance-based" regulation rather than direct prescriptive regulation. Performance-based regulation would take the labor market dimension out of the picture entirely and base allowable hours entirely on safety performance. Anxious about possible hours-of-service changes that might further restrict their options, some LTL carriers also advocate this simple prescription.

Why? The problem may be both the low pay (or no pay) for nondriving work performed and no pay for forced waiting time. In the truck driver labor market an instability may have developed because of the tension between drivers in very different markets. I have shown that a large wage gap has developed among drivers in different sectors and between union and non-union drivers, although their work is substantially the same. The drivers working in the most competitive sector earn little more than the minimum wage. Accounting for overtime, paid and unpaid, wages in TL may be one-half of average manufacturing workers' wages. Elsewhere trucking wages are much higher, as drivers in the unionized LTL sector may earn up to 50% more than the average manufacturing worker. These sectoral gaps could account for the chronic labor shortage the industry has experienced over the past decade, which both truckers and shippers believe has prevented many TL carriers from expanding to serve their customers fully as the industry has expanded.

Liberalization of the hours-of-service rules is opposed by most safety advocates, including the insurance industry. Research shows drivers are very tired now, and extending work hours cannot be expected to make this better. Fatigue research shows negative effects on driver alertness as a result of long hours of driving and extended hours of wakefulness, as well as nighttime driving.[26]

One of the unintended consequences of any liberalization of the hours-of-service rules might be to drive more potential employees away from the industry, and even drive some current drivers out of that labor market. In this case the single-minded focus on the safety aspect of driving hours rules overlooks the social aspects. Not only are drivers earning a rather low wage for this effort level, but they may be getting ground down to such an extent that any increased work hours would push them out of the industry, either voluntarily or involuntarily. If the average worker in the United States works around 40 hours and over-the-road drivers currently average more than 50% more hours than that, then an increase to 96 hours would push them up to 2.4 times as many hours as the average worker; that is 2.4 jobs worked by one person. Regardless of whether this workload is physically possible for a wide range of workers, it may discourage those workers not accustomed to that pace from entering or sticking with the industry once they are trained.

Between low pay, the high cost of living on the road, and the pressure on the family caused by the trucker's irregular lifestyle, it is little wonder the job attracts fewer high-quality employees than it is used to, and puts the least desirable workers behind the wheel. When asked about human resource quality, unionized LTL carriers indicated they had no complaints with their workers, indeed suggesting they were exemplary. Non-union TL carriers, on the other hand, reported great difficulties finding and retaining workers skilled enough to keep their operations fully staffed. Unionized LTL carriers reported a turnover rate averaging only 5%, compared with a reported 52% turnover rate among non-union LTL carriers. The differential between union and non-union carriers extended to the TL side, as union TL carriers experienced a 24% turnover rate while non-union carriers experienced a turnover rate averaging 82%. Non-union carriers reported a turnover increase since deregulation while union carriers generally reported workforce stability.[27] We face a crisis: as the economy expands, the pinch may worsen and freight may not move.[28]

It is a problem created by the intense competition triggered by the policy of economic deregulation. The labor market of the over-the-road truckload driver today approaches the unregulated ideal. With the disappearance of economic regulation in the industry, truckload firms face minimal entry barriers (no institutional barriers, very minimal capital barriers) and no restrictions or guidelines on rates. With the decline of collective bargaining generally (and the virtual disappearance of collective bargaining in the TL sector), there is no collective or institutional pressure to support wage rates. Neither institutional nor legal barriers restrict competition enough to support wages sufficient to attract needed labor. The only reason they stay at their current level and do not drop below our current minimum wage is the competition for labor created by the minimum wage itself, as set by Congress. Further, the virtual disappearance of welfare, and the threat posed to the minimum wage system by the Republican leadership of

Congress during the mid-1990s, means that we need to consider what the labor market would look like if all such institutions were to disappear. Would we return to the sweatshop of the nineteenth century?

Under current circumstances, why should unionized or LTL or special commodity drivers enter the TL general freight market? For that matter, why should even semi-skilled workers from other industries enter the truck driver labor market? Workers from other industries and occupations, not conditioned to accept these low wages and hard conditions, certainly will not remain for long once they figure out what they really earn.

Given the persistence of the current regime, the trucking industry can probably expect this chronic understaffing to last indefinitely. That's why Schneider has hired Irish workers, M.S. Carriers has recruited British drivers with continental experience, and the TL Carriers Council has even asked the Labor Department to declare an emergency so that they can hire Mexican nationals.[29]

Trucking firms are forced to lure drivers from outside the very labor force from which they ought to be able to recruit. If the market were doing its job, this problem would not exist—which brings us back to that question of rents.

All of those lost wages resulting from deregulation: were they rents—again, unearned premia resulting from the Teamsters' monopoly control of the labor market—or compensating differentials? Compensating differentials are premia paid to companies for superior products and to workers for superior qualities, such as higher education, training, experience, or various unmeasured attributes.

If the lost wages were rents, we may be better off without them. If they were compensating differentials, though, declining labor quality behind the wheel may make us worse off—and point to yet another risk.

A 1993 study of trucking wages by Barry Hirsch suggests that "a substantial proportion (half may be a good guesstimate) of the union/non-union differential for truck drivers is a compensating quality premium."[30] My own research shows union wages remain considerably higher than non-union wages, even after two decades of supercompetitive markets, so one suspects much of this aggregate earnings loss (in my judgment, perhaps more than half) represents a decline in the quality of labor, especially in the non-union firms.

This conclusion is corroborated by carrier executives, who maintain that labor quality has declined, particularly in the mostly non-union truckload sector.[31]

In sum, it appears at least some of the higher wages paid to certain trucking employees may not be rents, but rather a premium to attract a higher-quality workforce. Once known as knights of the highway, today's trucker faces the travail of the low road while trying to support his family. Something needs to be done to get the industry back on the high road.

7 What If the Rest of the World Looked Like Trucking?

Has the restructuring of the trucking industry been a success or a failure? The answer depends to some extent on your perspective. Each constituency is a "special interest" when it comes to public policies that regulate motor carriers. The task of public policy is to balance those interests and maximize social welfare.

Much has been made of the fact that trucking, as a transportation industry, is not like other industries. While economies of scope and density appear to be important, traditional economies of scale may be rather small in this industry. The industry effectively is exempt from the Fair Labor Standards Act, which acts as a floor for labor market competition elsewhere in the economy, because the maximum hours provision of the law does not apply to interstate trucking. Significant sectors of the industry, mainly the long-haul truckload sector, currently are out of the reach of labor organizers. Market forces are extremely powerful, and arguably they are strong enough to impede a competitor's ability to earn a normal profit on invested capital. Economic theory tells us that firms should earn normal profits when the market is perfectly competitive and perfectly contestable, but perhaps the trucking industry is mobile enough to constitute an industry on roller skates—where one carrier's revenue haul is another's back haul—preventing firms from earning even normal profits. What if the rest of the world operated like the trucking industry?

This book has shown that economic deregulation of the trucking industry has brought intense competition, low wages, long hours, and a constant struggle to maintain safe operations in a hyper-competitive environment. Neither private nor public safety and health regulations may be able to place effective enough constraints on the trucking industry in the absence of economic regulation to keep competition within socially acceptable bounds. While it has not been proven that the long hours required by the industry are responsible directly for a significant proportion of all truck traffic crashes, the onus remains on the industry to show otherwise, and this is an impossible task. The problem of long hours puts the industry on the defensive, which may not be fair in view of the extreme level of competition society has forced on truckers, but trucks are large and ubiquitous and tend to take the blame politically. If the rest of the American economy, including both manufacturing and service industries, suddenly found itself without the FLSA, and the minimum wage and 40-hour rules disappeared, we likely would see an explosion of low-wage work and a significant expansion of the working poor, pushing a sizeable number of workers to nineteenth-century levels. Arguably the only brake on sub-minimum wage work in trucking is the presence of the FLSA elsewhere in the labor market.

If the minimum wage were cut to $2.00, as suggested by Senator Phil Gramm (R-Tex.), or eliminated altogether, as suggested by Representative Richard Armey (R-Tex.) in January 1995, what would become the floor? We already know that many over-the-road truck drivers earn little more than the minimum wage and make up for it by working extremely long hours. These hours likely impose a direct social cost in the form of health problems and an indirect social cost in the form of family dysfunction and separation. Very few of these low-wage, non-union employees will ever see a pension and or have made enough money to be able to save, so they will rely entirely on Social Security. Who pays the social cost of low retirement savings?

Regardless of whether growing inequality in America is caused by the expansion of skill-biased reward systems (higher returns to college and other education) or by the tournament effect in a mass consumption society (the "winner-take-all" syndrome[1]), a significant majority of Americans could face impoverishment in a truly market-driven regime. The trucking industry has shown us the way after deregulation. Is that the way we want to go?

A World of Winners and Losers

Consumers

Some constituencies have been winners, and sometimes we merely have to switch hats to move from one constituency to another. Consumers are one such constituency. They want to pay low prices for the goods they buy. Because the cost of getting those goods to them is passed on as part of the price of goods, they also want low shipping costs. Regulatory restructuring has been a boon for consumers. Real truck freight rates (per ton-mile) declined 11.4% after little more than a decade of deregulation. As a broad measure of consumer savings due to deregulation, transportation has declined from 7.79% of U.S. gross national product (GNP) in 1980 to 6.29% of GNP in 1992. While the overall producer price index (PPI) increased from 100 to 140 between 1980 and 1992, LTL revenue per ton-mile increased only from $18.00 to $22.40 during the same period (index 100 to 124). Trucking, therefore, became relatively cheaper—and consumers benefited. Insofar as world trade has brought American workers of all kinds into a purely market-regulated world economy, perhaps these low transportation costs made it easier for them to compensate for their own lower wages.

Air freight (including FedEx and UPS) ton-mile revenue actually decreased in nominal terms. The air freight index was 100 in 1980 and 95 in 1992, up against the same PPI. During the same period, the total revenue for small shipments carried by truck (including UPS) increased 136%, reflecting the modal shift from rail and the increase in trade and network manufacturing.[2]

Shippers

Shippers, another constituency, want to reduce their overhead, of which trucking costs are a significant part. For shippers, the competition brought on by economic deregulation has meant lower rates, better service, and increased customer responsiveness. Truckers now tailor services to their customers' needs. Truck drivers, including those represented by the Teamsters, also are very sensitive to customer needs and represent a strong link in the logistics chain.

Motor Carriers

Trucking companies, yet another constituency, want a stable business environment in which they can earn a return on their investments and manage their business with a minimum of interference. Deregulation cleared some of the direct economic interference, but many of the carriers went bankrupt in the process. Broadly speaking, returns continue to be low, and the industry may be weakly capitalized. We also know that many loads sit undelivered and that trucks sit empty because the carriers cannot find the drivers they need at the rate they are able to pay.

Employees

Trucking employees want jobs with decent pay and working conditions, career stability, and job security. We have seen a wide disparity develop in these areas as a result of regulatory restructuring. While Teamster drivers have done better than their non-union counterparts, it is a matter of degree. Real wages among Teamsters have declined for years, averaging perhaps no more than 20% more than they were 20 years ago in nominal dollars and 25% less in real dollars. Real hourly wages among non-Teamsters, now the great majority of all drivers, have fallen through the floor.

The Public

The public wants safe highways and a reliable transportation system. For this largest constituency, deregulation has been fraught with danger. Truckload drivers, under pressure to deliver quickly and at low cost, may push well beyond safety limits to deliver the freight. The low wages in the industry also drove out hundreds of thousands of experienced drivers, who were replaced by workers from much further down the labor market queue.

From the public's perspective, the bottom line is this: the TL industry has had to make do with workers who will put in long hours away from home for low wages—workers who will sweat their own labor—trading long hours for middle-class incomes. This workload comes with a price: there probably are more drivers with fatigue problems than ever before. An influx of drivers with poor driving records has led to intensive drug and alcohol testing and the introduction of the Commercial Drivers License, designed to raise standards for truck drivers and prevent multiple licenses that hide moving violations, accidents, and DWI convictions. Drug use is down due to stringent, intrusive, and expensive social regulation by the Department of Transportation. Periodic exposés of trucking and truck drivers focus the public's attention on "dangerous trucks" or "behemoths of the road," doing nothing for trucking's image and nothing to correct problems either. No wonder public concern has been on the rise.

The Trucking Industry Marketplace

These interests contend with an industry transformed by regulatory change. Deregulation paradoxically led to both greater concentration and greater competition in some markets. While less-than-truckload market concentration far outstrips that in truckload, there are some indications that TL carriers are catching up—meaning the industry may become more concentrated, possibly taking us in a direction even further from deregulation's competitive intent.

The bankruptcy rate remains high in trucking. As stock values suggest, the trucking industry generally offers a weak return on investment, particularly in LTL. This encourages those who might otherwise supply capital to the industry to invest their money elsewhere.

The Labor Market

Even positive job growth in the industry raises problems. Job growth in trucking has been a bright spot in the U.S. economy since the mid-1980s, but few of these new positions are "good jobs." The pay is low, there are limited effective standards capping hours of work (either for safety reasons or for limiting labor market competition), and minimum wage protections do not work well. These new jobs offer limited benefits, provide poor working conditions, have no union representation, and are insecure. Jobs like these reflect the meager bargaining power of the individual truck driver and the decline of union representation, especially in the TL segment of general freight trucking. While investors have evaluated the opportunity costs and shunned trucking's low returns, drivers whose human capital is best invested in trucking have been stuck with the tab.

This combination of poor compensation, hard work, long hours, and the prospect of being away from home for days or weeks at a time provides little incentive for workers seeking good career opportunities. The driver shortage reported by TL carriers attests to the unattractiveness of these jobs[3] and to the imbalance of supply and demand at today's low wages. Even management has suffered in trucking companies, as all wages (except those of company officers) have remained depressed.

If markets work, then market forces ought to raise wages and eliminate the driver shortage. Remarkably, though, some motor carriers have been forced to go well beyond the U.S. trucking labor market to find workers—an attempt to circumvent the very laws of supply and demand that are supposed to rule the market. To the extent that the Immigration and Naturalization Service allows the hiring of British, Irish, or Mexican drivers, as some carriers have sought, the government prevents the domestic market from correcting the problem through higher wages and better working conditions.

While we must allow market forces to work, market forces may become dysfunctional when left completely unregulated. In a properly functioning but regulated market, the labor shortage problem caused by the unattractiveness of low-wage jobs could be corrected through collective bargaining. Collective bargaining balances the scales of power so that individuals can bargain collectively with a "collective" employer, the corporation, and when collective bargaining works it allows private market processes to function as effective social regulation. For truck drivers, the most potent force for accomplishing this is the Teamsters Union. Workers earn more money and enjoy better working conditions when the union is present, as my analysis shows.[4] Few other effective institutional brakes on work intensification exist in the trucking industry and they generally involve imposition of "one size fits all" regulation.

Labor Market Institutions

The protections most workers take for granted—such as time-and-one-half for overtime and the health and safety protections of the Occupational Safety and Health Act (OSHA)—do not extend to truck drivers as employees of motor carriers engaged in interstate commerce. The Minimum Wage Study Commission concluded in 1981 that full FLSA protection was unnecessary because union protections made it redundant (see discussion in chapter 6). As we have seen, however, regulatory reform has de-unionized significant sectors of the trucking industry, leaving employees no protection at all.

Not only do most truckload drivers earn low mileage wages, most get no pay for much of their loading, unloading, waiting, breakdown, and other non-driving time. The University of Michigan driver survey shows that only 46% of non-union drivers are paid for loading and unloading (30% are paid for waiting while being unloaded), and a meager 23% are paid to drop and hook loaded trailers. Since 27% of drivers' time is spent doing tasks other than driving, and since less than half of that time appears to be paid, drivers' total hourly rate of pay necessarily is quite low. Many drivers, dependent on load revenue for their pay, put in very long hours for alarmingly low wages.[5]

A 1992 study conducted by the Insurance Institute for Highway Safety found that nearly three-quarters of all road drivers admitted violating DOT hours-of-service regulations, and two-thirds admitted doing so regularly.[6] The University of Michigan driver survey supports this finding: nearly 56% of drivers say they have worked more hours than they logged in the past 30 days, with 54% indicating they drove more than 10 hours without the legally required eight-hour break at least once in the last month, and more than 10% drove more than 10 hours per day at least five days per week. As the driver survey shows, the average driver worked 65.7 hours and the median driver worked 62 hours. With 60 hours being the maximum weekly hours of service allowed by federal regulations, the average driver is working more than the legal limit. Worst of all, one-third of all drivers admitted to having dozed or fallen asleep at the wheel at least once during the past 30 days, and such self-reported data likely is an underestimate. Truck drivers working in unregulated intrastate commerce, out of reach of the DOT, may have no standards at all.

Policy Options

There are several steps that we, as a nation, can take to correct the situation in which truck drivers and the trucking industry find themselves. These suggestions are not a call for re-regulation of the trucking industry nor a call to implement any specific changes, but a recognition that the trucking industry may be like the dying canary in a mine: it lets us know the hazards we face if we do not change our method of operation.

This therefore is a call to level the playing field. Everyone needs to work under the same rules, and comparability of these rules across the blue-collar labor market can ensure that the trucking industry will be able to attract the labor it needs.

Option 1: Extend the Fair Labor Standards Act to Cover Truckers

We could extend the protection of the Fair Labor Standards Act to employees of trucking firms engaged in interstate commerce. The FLSA applies to most of the U.S. labor market, so coverage would put the market for truck drivers on the same footing. For the labor market to stay in balance, arguably truck drivers and other employees of trucking companies need to earn wages comparable to those earned elsewhere. The high industry turnover and chronic labor shortage suggest that wages are not high enough to attract quality workers. The trucking industry is not covered by the 40-hour workweek, so extension of the FLSA to trucking would mean that carriers would have to pay drivers time-and-one-half for all work over 40 hours, creating a disincentive to work drivers excessively while creating more jobs.

An overtime premium also would create disincentives for employers thinking about making employees work every hour permitted by law—or human endurance. We have restricted the safety focus to the single issue of "fatigue," as if drivers were automatons that needed an electroshock to keep functioning. If the 65-hour week were not standard (and the 80-hour week common), trucking might attract workers with reasonable expectations.

Carriers also could pay employees for all work time, including loading, unloading, waiting for loads, and breakdowns. Manufacturing workers cannot be docked if their assembly line goes down or for selective portions of their work, and the same rules could apply to drivers. Disparate rules create an unstable relationship between the labor market for truck drivers and the rest of the labor market for suitable workers, putting trucking companies at a disadvantage. Truck drivers do not hold salaried positions; they are not "exempt" employees. Why should the public expect truck drivers to give away their time?

The sweatshop environment is exacerbated by some specific pay regimes peculiar to trucking. While "contingent pay" is a growing phenomenon in the U.S. industrial relations system, payment by percentage of revenue is a particularly extreme form of contingency. Drivers paid by "percentage" find their earnings dependent on the market for trucking service and may earn extraordinarily low wages as a result. Percentage pay could be eliminated for all but bona fide subcontractors, because it allows carriers to violate the minimum wage provisions of the FLSA and would defeat the purpose of reform.

Drivers who do not get paid for non-driving time have an incentive to falsify their log books and work more hours than is legal or safe. Although they may be loading or unloading, standing on a dock waiting to pick up or deliver a load, repairing their trucks, or waiting for repairs, if drivers do not get paid they have a powerful incentive to log their time as "off duty." Our inability to measure these hours does not mean they do not exist. This unrecorded work time allows drivers to work longer hours than the law allows, probably contributing to unsafe highways and the premature destruction of drivers' health. They sweat their own labor by hiding these work hours. In sum, unlimited competition creates the opportunity for abuses for which the rest of society eventually pays.

There is another reason to impose FLSA rules on the trucking industry—one with wider implications for our economy. Paying drivers below minimum FLSA standards allows carriers to compete strictly on the basis of low employee wages; this sort of competition drives everyone toward the low road. These donations of time by drivers camouflage sloppy operations management, and competition of this sort discourages carriers from investing in efficiency and productivity enhancements. It also discourages shippers and consignees from improving the efficiency of their practices, encouraging a waste of capital and human resources.

Admittedly, record-keeping in this industry is difficult, and we must devise new means to keep track of hours of work. Enforcement of minimum standards of pay and maximum standards of work will require a creative effort. Truck drivers typically do not punch a clock, and they often are away from home for weeks. The Department of Transportation would be spending our tax dollars wisely to develop an efficient and enforceable system.

Option 2: Revise Hours-of-Service Rules

Other corrective steps involve hours-of-service rules. The original purpose of these rules was to put all carriers on the same footing, while making the job less destructive to individual truck drivers. But the rules have gone unchanged for more than half a century. Besides being antiquated, they are inefficient and ineffective.

Three specific policy suggestions emerge from the analysis. First, the hours-of-service rules in trucking ought to prohibit competition among carriers based on overwork of human beings. Trucks have become rolling sweatshops during the 1990s. Overwork—with companies forced to "sweat" labor to compete in the marketplace—supports today's unregulated market.

Second, hours-of-service rules should structure work schedules to maximize driver alertness and support a healthy lifestyle. While research continues to determine the optimum safe limits for driver effort, new rules should emphasize circadian rhythms to make hours of work fit the human body's natural schedule. New hours-of-service rules should also structure work schedules to enhance the long-term health of employees, as irregularity must have a deleterious effect on drivers' long-term health, a negative external cost shifted to other taxpayers.

Work scheduling and limitations must reflect prevailing social standards, as well as known limits to human health and endurance. Studies were conducted during the 1970s to evaluate the effectiveness of current hours-of-service rules and to develop rules that reflected new learning on human health and safety. New research in the 1980s and 1990s has revealed the role of fatigue, or sleep debt, in safety and health problems. The current regulations, which allow companies to dispatch drivers without warning on a completely irregular schedule, are hazardous to commercial and private drivers alike.

Several studies have identified fatigue as a significant contributor to safety problems. The federal Office of Technology Assessment found that excess work, irregular hours, and inadequate sleep clearly cause physical and psychological disorders that jeopardize the health of over-the-road drivers.[7]

One example among many illustrates the problem. In July 1994 a propane gas tank truck driver was killed and 23 people were injured in a fiery explosion on Interstate 287 in White Plains, New York, just north of New York City. Federal investigators later found that the driver had been on duty for more than 35 hours without eight consecutive hours off when he presumably fell asleep at the wheel and hit a bridge and that he had falsified several timesheets. Witnesses saw him drift in and out of his lane prior to the crash. The tank truck company was cited for keeping false daily driver logs, which indicated that truckers were off duty when in fact they were driving. "Investigators from the National Transportation Safety Board concluded that [the driver] probably fell asleep at the wheel," reported the *New York Times*.[8] The company later pleaded guilty to one criminal charge and was fined.[9] The hours of work and the fatigue are perhaps most alarming because the driver was not a longhaul driver but engaged solely in local work.

This tragedy need not have happened. Updated studies likely will support the argument that hours-of-service rules need to be restructured to ensure that they strike the appropriate balance between the industry's productivity needs, workers' health needs, and public safety.[10] We must develop a means of enforcing these rules, since studies like the University of Michigan driver survey suggest that a majority of drivers work more hours than the law allows.

Surely fatigue and stress lead to accidents or to the deteriorated health of drivers. There is plenty of evidence of negative health effects of working swing shifts, and what truckers do may be worse because it is irregular. Other evidence suggests the general importance of circadian rhythms to healthy lifestyles.[11]

Other effects take a toll. For instance, while carriers pay the costs they incur when a driver has a wreck, they are less likely to pay the cost of long-term deteriorating driver health in higher health insurance bills. The worst jobs have the highest turnover, and high turnover transfers the cost of deadly operations to others. Ultimately, society picks up the bill for truck drivers' premature disability and mortality.

Option 3: Strengthen the Industry through Collective Bargaining

One solution would be to put collective bargaining back into the trucking industry equation. Through collective bargaining the need for government intervention—which deregulation sought to limit—might be minimized.

The bedrock of trucking labor market self-regulation—what might be called "private" regulation—lies in the pervasive private-sector collective bargaining relationships that governed the industry for more than half a century. The emergence of the interstate general freight industry mirrored the emergence of the Teamsters Union as a national force. Despite the fact that the Teamsters have retained their significant influence in the traditional crafts (grocery, milk, bread, beer, and some other local product delivery occupations) and in LTL freight, we have seen that they have lost influence in the emergent TL general and specialized freight industries. Indeed, the Teamsters now are losing ground even in the LTL market, as non-union regional and interregional carriers have developed market strength since intrastate deregulation. In short, regulatory restructuring hurt collective bargaining and forced competitive carriers to race to the bottom in pursuit of cheap labor. Unfortunately, the lower wages encouraged by these market forces make it more difficult for the carriers to attract qualified labor, increase training and recruitment costs, and even leave essential services unmet. Ironically, even as the exodus of older drivers leaves a void in the truck driver labor market, many carriers have been forced to cut back on training because their private training investment is squandered when other carriers poach the very drivers they have trained.

The trucking industry is hard to organize. Besides the usual economic, legal, and political pressures that make all union organizing difficult, truck drivers and their employers often are quite mobile. The proliferation of labor leasing and truck leasing operations, as well as the easy market entry by owner operators, makes it even more difficult to conduct organizing campaigns within truckload freight carriers.

Unions will not be able to organize, however, without a level playing field. Drivers will not be able to form unions unless Congress changes three labor law provisions that have resulted from the Taft-Hartley Act and its successors. These changes will give unions the ability to conduct successful campaigns in the trucking industry.

First, unions will not organize successfully unless the strict prohibition of the secondary boycott is lifted, at least for interstate trucking. Without the leverage this boycott provided in the past, it is unlikely that any union would ever have organized the trucking industry. While any new law should discourage top-down organizing—where instead of a rank-and-file election the union leadership appeals directly to the company for recognition—it should permit union members to support their co-workers' efforts to organize and pressure their employers for better wages and working conditions.

Second, collective bargaining reform would require Congress to amend Section 14(b) of the Taft-Hartley Act to allow truck drivers to vote for a union shop in any state.[12] In interstate trucking, employees and operations are spread over a wide geographic area and across state lines. Some carriers intentionally locate within mandatory open-shop states to prevent their drivers from organizing a union, thus distorting economic development and resource allocation. Since interregional and national truckload carriers can locate their operations anywhere without significantly affecting their business, Section 14(b) gives these employers institutional protection that contravenes the very purpose of the National Labor Relations Act.

Third, collective bargaining reform needs to include provisions allowing the parties to bypass the difficult process for voting for union representation as currently recognized by the National Labor Relations Board (NLRB). Since truck drivers—especially in long-distance TL—work all over the country, unions find it exceedingly difficult to organize and certify a bargaining unit by a regular vote. Even when a majority of drivers at a carrier desires union representation, the fact that they cannot easily meet face-to-face—as in a manufacturing plant—frustrates organizing efforts. They cannot even get together for a meeting, let alone an election.

One approach would be to allow truck drivers to select union representation through authorization cards. Cards for the trucking industry should clearly specify that the driver's signature constitutes a vote for representation, and the NLRB could certify a bargaining unit based on authorization cards signed by a 60% supermajority, a tradeoff for allowing the card-check approach.

Making it easier for employees to certify a union would provide an opportunity for collective bargaining to play its role as a private regulatory mechanism, allowing employers and employees to negotiate issues of equity and productivity in this private-sector setting, with minimal government interference. While employment law protects certain individuals' rights, such as the right to equal protection of the laws, it does not substitute for the collective bargaining mechanism as a way to negotiate wages and working conditions. As we have seen, non-union truck drivers—isolated from one another and vulnerable to abuses—have fared particularly poorly in the absence of collective bargaining.

Collective bargaining might benefit the employers as well, although that may seem counterintuitive. As a group, employers stand to gain as the low-wage road closes. Individually, employers can impose lower wages and worse working conditions than is in their collective self-interest. This makes truck driving a relatively undesirable occupation. Unless wages and working conditions improve, the labor shortage will become chronic, and it will take many years to make the industry attractive again even to semi-skilled workers. Indeed, the *Jobs Rated Almanac* ranks truck driving 230th among 250 jobs, considering income, stress, physical demands, growth, job security, and work environment.

Collective bargaining could create gains for society as well. The costs of the social regulation designed to improve motor carrier safety—required because of reduced labor quality caused by poor wages and conditions—may be greater than the costs of the wages and working conditions saved through regulatory reform. Better wages and conditions would attract a higher quality workforce to the trucking industry, ultimately reducing society's regulatory costs. One carrier, J. B. Hunt, found that higher wages reduced turnover, increased safety, and added to their "bottom line."

What Have We Learned?

What have we learned from this analysis? It appears that following the deregulation of the trucking industry that began in 1977, union bargaining power declined in that section of the industry specializing in truckload shipments but held relatively firm for a time in the sector specializing in less-than-truckload shipments. Like other deregulated industries, such as airlines and telecommunications, union strengths and weaknesses follow market dynamics within the industries' new segments.

The union's failure (or inability) to organize any new, exclusively TL carriers since economic deregulation has made "union scale" for truckload freight movements uncompetitive. It is unlikely that any union productivity effect, if it exists, could outweigh the large difference in wages. The relative low value of TL freight encouraged carriers to establish low-wage special commodity divisions to haul TL freight, or caused them to reconstitute themselves as low-wage (union or non-union) TL carriers. Truckload carriers that remain unionized pay significantly higher wages than their non-union counterparts.

For companies that specialize in less-than-truckload freight, the union has retained considerable bargaining power. The relatively high union density within the LTL sector of general freight allows the Teamsters to continue to try to take wages out of competition. These higher wages also allow carriers to maintain the skilled and reliable workforce needed to provide the level of service demanded by their customers. The firms' commitment to the relationship remains high: LTL firms do not usually risk confrontation to reduce unit labor costs.

The Teamsters' influence in LTL may be waning, however. The surging growth of non-union regional and interregional carriers suggests the balance of power may be tipping in favor of non-union firms. While the decline of union influence may be welcomed by some, we need to be concerned that this declining influence is not accompanied by a new round of wage and benefit reductions. My research suggests that collective bargaining is the strongest predictor of wage and earning levels, including a union premium that ranges between 20 and 30%.[13]

There is evidence that union influence still exists within the truckload segment, although less than before economic deregulation. Whether due to custom, drivers' unwillingness to accept lower wages, the effect of the unionization threat, or actual bargaining power, union wages and conditions in TL remain somewhat better than non-union wages and conditions, controlling for other factors. Although TL drivers will not do as well as their LTL counterparts, research shows they are better off with a union.

The evidence confirms that most motor carriers and their employees have been big losers as a result of economic deregulation. Average wages for all truck drivers dropped 30% between 1978 and 1995. For non-union TL drivers, the decline is closer to 50%. Less-than-truckload driver wages have declined less severely, although the evidence suggests that they have become significantly weaker in regional markets than in national markets.

Truckload drivers earn very low wages compared either to LTL drivers' wages or general manufacturing wages. We have seen that in 1997 the average non-union driver earned $35,551, while the average LTL driver earned $43,165.[14] Assuming the average TL road driver works 70 hours per week, as indicated by the University of Michigan driver survey, he works 3,539.5 hours per year, assuming 10 days of vacation and holidays,[15] earning $10.04 per hour worked. If the Fair Labor Standards Act covered intercity truck drivers so they earned time-and-one-half for overtime, we would calculate this as an $8.24 average hourly wage.[16] Contrast this to BLS data showing that the average durable goods manufacturing production worker earned more than $13.60 per hour, and it becomes obvious that truck drivers are working more for substantially less. Perhaps most important for motor carriers themselves, they are competing for labor with manufacturing industries effectively paying about 70% more per hour for labor, making it quite difficult to attract qualified workers.

Taking different approaches to the analysis produces similar results. According to ATA data (derived from ICC data originally), the average general freight road driver working for a carrier earning 75% of its revenue from intercity freight logged 109,322 miles in 1990. The same data set shows that the average non-union long-distance driver made $29,993 (in 1997 dollars) for 3,539.5 hours of labor (using the driver survey to estimate hours), and spent much of his personal time on the road. Again, assuming time-and-one-half for overtime—the standard for employees outside interstate trucking—we arrive at $7.08 per hour in 1997 dollars, compared with $13.60 per hour for manufacturing production workers. It seems that no matter how we calculate it, truck drivers are among the worst paid workers in the nation. At best, that is weak compensation for a job that requires mechanical and driving skill, independent judgment, literacy, and the willingness to work around the clock in the most inclement weather—providing an erratic schedule demanding that drivers be away from home for weeks at a time. This compensation is not high enough to attract the kind of employees carriers need for safe and reliable operations.

Finally, we have seen that those who claim that the bargaining power of the Teamsters has collapsed have oversimplified significantly, or at least declared the Teamsters "dead" prematurely. Although little union bargaining power exists in the national general commodity truckload segment of the industry, the Teamsters retain significant bargaining power within LTL markets and in other specific markets, such as package and car haul. The gap between Teamster power in LTL and TL encourages two worlds to develop, however, one of winners and one of losers. The combination of broadly lower wages and profits supports truckers' contentions that bargaining power has shifted to shippers, who lie outside the trucking industry and outside the collective bargaining relationship, creating negative repercussions for more than just the trucking industry.

If our goal as a nation is to provide our citizens with good jobs— like those in trucking once were—we could make it possible for those citizens to choose union representation. Once chosen, we need to make sure those unions can engage in fair collective bargaining. The value arguably would be shared by employees and employers alike.

As we opt for more market and less institutional regulation in other industries, let us remember how pure economic regulation has affected one industry that we know well. Do we want the rest of the American workforce to look like the one within the competitive trucking industry?

Good jobs would attract high-quality workers. Benefits and protections would reduce the negative consequences of the tough life truckers face on the road. Society would be the ultimate winner.

8 Deregulation as Public Policy

Competition's Winners and Losers

Over the last 25 years, arguments for economic deregulation have dominated the policy debate. While it is true that our nation continues to enact certain types of regulations—primarily social regulations, such as the Americans with Disabilities Act and the Family and Medical Leave Act—the primary goal of legislators in the last two decades has been to increase competition by lifting many of the economic regulations that have long governed U.S. industry. Less and less of an institutional framework exists for markets as markets operate more freely. The general trend has been to eliminate economic regulation and allow markets to allocate resources and prescribe winners and losers.

Increasingly, price mechanisms have come to regulate markets, including those in the core transportation industries of airlines, trucking, and railroads, as well as in telecommunications, banking, and others. Meanwhile, government has sharply curtailed its direction of the economic functions of labor markets. Since the 1970s federal and state policymakers have loosened, repealed, and reinterpreted a wide variety of laws that have traditionally governed employment relations. Laws relating to area or "prevailing" wage standards, minimum wages, working at home, eligibility requirements for unemployment insurance, and disability standards under workers' compensation have all come under attack as part of the move toward unfettered competition. This has been coupled with a growing boldness of employers with respect to labor relations. As James Gross has shown, the original intent of the National Labor Relations Act (Wagner Act)—to balance the scales of power between individuals and corporations—has been blunted by the National Labor-Management Relations Act (Taft-Hartley Act), creating an unresolved contradiction within the nation's labor policy.[1] Labor policy and labor law now are seen as a neutral between contending parties, fundamentally altering the conceptual framework for U.S. labor market institutions. As the government has become less inclined to intervene in labor disputes on behalf of workers, employers have become more free to adopt an aggressive policy resisting organizing and have taken a harder line in collective bargaining.

Meanwhile, there has been a dramatic growth in the number of U.S. workers employed as subcontractors or temporaries. This growing contingent workforce is employed only as needed and generally does not benefit from many of the protections available to regular employees. The subcontracting process exposes an even greater number of workers to the forces of the unconstrained market, as independent contractors enjoy virtually no protections—even compared to members of the weakened unions or compared with non-union workers who at least fall under the protection of employment law. Social regulations that have remained on the books to protect full-time workers are rarely extended to this growing number of nonstandard employees.

The "free trade" movement sought by trade negotiators, embodied by the North American Free Trade Agreement (NAFTA) and the General Agreement on Tariffs and Trades (GATT; now governed by the World Trade Organization), has also enhanced the significance of markets. These agreements, arguably constituting "deregulation" of international trade, have brought the same power of markets to manufacturing that I have described above for other industries.

The bottom line is that workers now compete with one another on the basis of wages and working conditions in ways we have not seen since well before the Great Depression and the growth of unions internationally. To find such a competitive environment in the industrialized western world, we may have to go back as far as the latter half of the nineteenth century, during which time workers fought unsuccessfully for regulations creating the eight- and ten-hour workdays, and for the right of unions to organize. The future promises more of the same: current state and federal legislation heralds a continuing movement toward letting the market regulate the economy with minimal limitations.

The Construction Industry:
Another Deregulated, Decentralized Industry

Deregulation and deinstitutionalization take different forms in construction than in trucking. Deregulation of construction labor markets stemmed from repeal of certain prevailing wage laws, court decisions widening contractors' ability to divert business from their unionized core operations to non-union subsidiaries, and court decisions broadening employers' right to subcontract work.

Construction differs from most industries in that workers are more attached to their occupations—electrician, carpenter, and so on—than to their employer. Much of the industry's employment is project-based. While contractors try to keep their best workers busy, many employers are too small to retain large staffs between projects, so employees must be highly mobile. They also must possess considerable skill and experience, especially since they usually work without direct supervision.

Thus the employment structure poses significant challenges, including the need for access to a steady, skilled labor pool; the need to support training programs; the need to provide industry-wide benefits within a fragmented industry; and a host of other specific issues. Unions have provided a framework that resolves these issues, earning them a central role in the construction employment relationship. Hiring halls, union dispatching, and personal relationships have organized the pool. Apprenticeship programs—jointly established by construction firms and unions, and funded as a part of the overall wage package—have ensured training that all unionized contractors and apprentices pay for, largely eliminating free-rider problems. These programs also have set standards for worker skills, providing necessary certification. Jointly managed insurance programs have made it possible for employees to move between employers while retaining the benefits that have made construction an attractive career.

Prevailing wage laws for public works also act to regulate employment conditions in construction, providing some assurance that these human resource development institutions are not destroyed by competition from foreign labor markets. If contractors employing workers from lower wage parts of the country are free to "raid" work originating in high-wage areas, construction wage standards in high-wage regions will collapse, stripping these regions of the ability to reproduce skilled labor. In the long term the race to the bottom will drive skilled workers out of the industry and may hamper development. To the extent that conservative politicians have successfully repealed or weakened these prevailing wage laws, training, safety, and labor supply have all suffered.[2]

Deregulation in construction has taken two forms. First, a series of decisions by the National Labor Relations Board in the 1970s undermined union organization in the industry by making it easier for contractors to operate without construction unions. One series of decisions, known as the *Kiewit* decisions, weakened limitations on a practice called "double-breasting"—the shifting of work from a company's union subsidiary to its non-union subsidiary. Second, federal and state prevailing wage laws have been weakened or even repealed since the mid-1980s.

What are the consequences of this deregulation of employment relations in construction? One result has been the erosion of the craft unions' role as the central institutions in the industry. This weakening of construction unions has threatened construction's training system. While unionized firms in the industry help fund the apprenticeship programs jointly with contributions from the unions and the apprentices (who contribute by accepting a lower wage during the training period), non-union firms "free ride" by poaching trained union labor. But with the decline in unions comes a decline in the apprenticeship system, which results in a declining supply of trained employees for union and nonunion firms alike.

The deinstitutionalization of employment relations in construction may also be adversely affecting safety and construction quality. After Hurricane Andrew struck South Florida, inspectors found shoddy homes shredded while properly constructed homes remained standing. Deinstitutionalization also may compromise safety standards. One researcher finds that accident rates are lower in states with prevailing wage laws and decline directly with stronger laws.[3] The inspector general of the U.S. Department of Housing and Urban Development found that the use of low-wage/low-skill labor in public housing projects was associated with substandard work and increased maintenance costs—both of which cost taxpayers in the end.[4] Obviously, shoddy construction leads to high maintenance costs and early replacement needs for both public and private sector construction customers.

A final consequence of the deinstitutionalization in the construction industry has been the casualization of employment. Before deinstitutionalization, a construction worker could spend most of his working life in the industry. The emerging structure is radically different. What were once career jobs that supported families have become, thanks to deregulation, jobs attractive only to younger, unmarried workers with limited commitment to the industry. Lower pension investments, also in the non-union sector, shift old age costs back to society, and those who invested in their youth later find themselves supporting those who did not. The construction industry now decries its labor and skills shortage, and the same people who caused the problem raise the loudest voices against the situation they have created.[5] Again, the costs to society are self-evident.

Regulatory trends matter because, as a nation, we always have argued that capitalism was good for employer and employee alike. We always have sought to maximize the economic gain of all participants in markets; that is part of why the United States of America has long enjoyed one of the highest standards of living in the world. But as markets become more dominant and operate with fewer constraints, we are beginning to see that the social consequences of unfettered competition may outweigh the economic gains.

Some may say it is the only way, that if we are to have a market-based economy we have to live with these consequences. But I believe the issue is not whether the economic functions of society should be organized around markets. Rather, the question is how markets are best organized. Should we leave economic processes completely unrestrained, or is the well-being of individuals and society better served if we harness some of the market processes through regulation and institutionalization?

Government's Role

Government, once an interventionist force in the labor market, has pulled back—both de facto and de jure—from enacting laws and administrative rules that govern the employment relationship. The pullback leaves this relationship, which in the United States has always been a private one between employer and employee, with a weaker legal structure than it once had, and within which the private agreement is struck.

This legal framework, however, is a prerequisite to complex market transactions. Imagine if we had to negotiate the rules for complex market transactions for each employment situation. How would you like to sit down with your boss and figure out, for example, what constitutes legal tender for payment of wages? How far do you think you would get negotiating with your employer over every condition under which he can fire you—including if he does not like the color of your skin or that you can bear a child or that you are over the age of 45?

Many of the rules that govern the employment relationship affect both the process and rewards of that relationship. Others affect employment practices, taking certain aspects of the relationship "out of competition" or restoring them to competitive determination.

Workers' compensation legislation is a good example. These rules hold employers financially responsible for injuries on the job and assure employees both compensation and due process where payment was challenged. Workers' compensation also is a trade for the right to sue; while workers' compensation allows you to draw medical and disability benefits if you are injured on the job, it also protects the employer by prohibiting you from suing him. Imagine if this risk had not been "taken out of competition" through the imposition of common requirements. You would be at the mercy of your employer, who would likely want to minimize any costs incurred as the result of a worksite accident, like paying for medical costs or time lost due to a work-related injury.

The examples are myriad. What if employees had to fight over each and every working condition, on a workplace-by-workplace basis? Where the employees have strong individual bargaining power, asbestos exposure might be limited and the provision by the company of special masks to protect from toxic fumes might be won. In another workplace, workers might not be so lucky.

As deregulation changes the landscape, though, these sorts of common requirements often fall by the side of the road. Many of the results are easy enough to see, as long as one keeps in mind that social regulation of labor is meant to ensure socially desirable outcomes that would not be achieved were market processes left to themselves. But today, rules regarding money supply and interest rates, laws governing imports and exports, and other such macroeconomic and competitiveness policies have become the key determinants of conditions in labor markets.

Macroeconomic and competitiveness policies have evolved in ways that increase competition in labor markets—with serious social consequences. Free trade policies, as they have been embraced by the United States, encourage nations to compete against one another without restrictions. These free trade policies may encourage one country to support neo-liberal institutions that encourage workers to compete against one another to provide more labor at a lower price, thus reinforcing a downward cycle of impoverishment of workers without the skills that would give them individual market power. The reduction or elimination of social welfare policies—the safety net—provides an incentive for unemployed or underemployed workers to undercut the wages of the employed, creating and reinforcing a vicious cycle that discourages workers from investing in their human capital. These policies may also encourage individual countries to compete by allowing environmental damage (reduced only by costly intervention that leaves its goods less competitive) and by providing tax breaks for powerful corporations whose investment dollars they court. All of these represent regulatory regimes, though they are regulatory regimes built around the power of the market.

The proponents of complete deregulation argue that government ought to stay out of the economic functions of markets. Their view— bolstered by economic theories of firm and consumer behavior—is that government intervention cannot improve, and is likely to impair, market outcomes. Sure, they will admit, some specific groups might be hurt by deregulation, but society as a whole will surely benefit from the efficiencies that come with letting the market make its own way.

Put bluntly, these proponents have constructed a model of market behavior that does not correspond to the real world. In this model, firms always maximize their profits and consumers (their employees) always select the best bundle of commodities and leisure. Prices are always competitive, reflecting what the market is willing to bear. Competition provides the goods, services, and leisure most valued by society. Taken as a whole, society's fortune is rising.

The argument against government intervention through regulation in this picture-perfect world is that it has no constructive role to play. Regulation only gets in the way of market forces ensuring efficiency, productivity, competitiveness, and all the other good things the proponents argue can only make our lives better. In addition, government intervention too often is a consequence of pressure from special interest groups manipulating public policy to their economic advantage. The unfettered market is fair because we define efficiency as fairness and concern ourselves little with the distributional consequences.

To be fair, I must point out that the efficiency-enhancing dimension of deregulation has many significant positive consequences. Air travel costs, on the one hand, have declined for the median flyer since deregulation, providing consumers with significant incentives for frequent travel; full fare coach rates for non-discretionary business travel, on the other hand, have gone up. Long-distance telecommunications service is better, and costs are lower, than they were before the breakup of AT&T, though local rates are higher. Thanks to lower trade barriers, we can buy clothes and electronics for less, though this leaves fewer jobs for Americans. Real trucking rates have not increased since deregulation; in fact, they have fallen while service has improved.

Nor are the gains of deregulation to be found only in the consumer arena. Several researchers have found that deregulation of trucking led to increased minority employment in for-hire truck driving.[6] Unfortunately, as wages have declined in this industry, many of the jobs finally open to these minority workers turn out to be "bad" jobs, with much worse wages and conditions than characterized them in the past.

Government intervention, though, can actually improve on market outcomes under some circumstances. If the best market outcomes are best for society, then some regulation can be better for society than none at all. For example, where there are externalities, due to the presence of public goods, incomplete information, monopsony or monopoly power, or economies of scale or scope, markets without some regulation may simply fail to achieve the efficient outcomes so desired by the proponents of unfettered competition.[7]

While public debate since the late 1970s has been dominated by arguments for deregulation, I would like to explore a bit more arguments in favor of some regulation.

The Argument in Support of Regulation

The first of these arguments relates to public goods and concerns a problem that is created when we rely on the market and its price system—unfettered—to establish market conditions. Sometimes efficiency is best served by shared investment and cooperation among producers. But if the market is unrestrained, firms may take advantage of the results of such cooperation and "free ride"—that is, take advantage of the benefits without paying for them.

The apprentice training system in construction provides an excellent example. Construction skills training has long been shared between construction employers and employees through the institution of their union. Unionized construction workers forego some of their wages for several years as they invest in their skills (taking little advantage of their role in a joint product), and union contractors contribute to a joint apprenticeship training fund. Contractors also contribute training effort through the on-the-job portion of the apprenticeship program, as well as through the high wages they promise to graduates. With the joint labor-management apprentice training system, contractors will invest in human capital rather than poach from their competitors; the system ensures an adequate labor supply for all. As the nonunion sector grew, however, fueled by the effective deregulation of the labor market, it poached trained labor from the union sector and failed to replenish that labor. Hiring marginal crafts-men in boom years and skilled union tradesmen in recessions, the nonunion contractor's lower price (especially during downturns) ensured more regular work. The current alleged labor shortage in construction is the consequence, as the low wages paid by nonunion contractors have failed to attract new workers or support training.

The problems caused by unregulated markets emerge starkly from an analysis of the British construction industry. Back in the late 1960s widespread "self-employment" was endorsed by both Labour and Conservative governments and became a fixture of the British construction economy. This employment system began to have a deleterious effect on the tax structure by the mid-1970s, as unregulated "lump" labor did not pay its fair share of taxes. The Thatcher government reinforced this system, however, and as a result some 800,000 construction workers now are self-employed sub-contractors, working at construction sites. They still do not pay taxes or payments to the national insurance system, costing the government between 2 and 4 million pounds per year, amounting to a taxpayer subsidy paid to extremely low-wage employers. They likewise have no employment security or unemployment benefits, no health insurance or sick pay, and no pension. Without the right to collective representation, their pay also drops by 40 to 50% between economic peaks and valleys. Not surprisingly, training has ceased and a construction labor crisis has developed, created by deregulatory pro-competitive labor market policies.[8]

Another argument for regulation relates to economies of scope, which exist where the costs of the joint production of a set of commodities is less than the total cost of producing each commodity individually. From a societal perspective, joint production is beneficial because it lowers overall costs. However, economies of scope themselves do not ensure the commercial success of joint production; production of one or several of the joint commodities may be more profitable than joint production of all the commodities. These conditions lead some producers to "cream skim"—that is, produce only the individually profitable commodities. As a result, the cost of producing a full range of goods increases, production becomes less efficient, and some commodities may not be produced at all. This probably is not in society's best interest.

For an example of how this phenomenon affects the labor market, consider a teaching hospital. These facilities produce a complex joint product, comprising conventional hospital services, the development and testing of new health care devices, and training for physicians and other personnel. They may also produce low-cost or free medical services to low-income populations. As deregulation forces competition into the world of the teaching hospital, though, the financial burden of some of this production becomes too much to bear—often resulting in the short-term loss of indigent medical services and, over the longer term, the potential to subvert the nation's system of medical education. This also is not in society's best interests.

Workers who find themselves subject to monopsony labor markets more often than not suffer substandard wages and working conditions. Deregulation encourages the situation; only some form of regulation can prevent it. Such is the well-known problem of the "company town." Solutions, while imperfect, have included prohibition of the use of company scrip for wages, the elimination of the company store (the only place to exchange scrip), and the broad imposition of minimum wages paid in legal tender currency. These prohibitions are regulations designed to limit abuses that grow in the unregulated private market, and arguably they serve a useful social purpose.

There are many other instances of imperfect competition that are not ameliorated by an unfettered, or deregulated, market. Long-term employees may be subject to imperfect competition if there are large costs associated with leaving a job prior to retirement. Pension payments in many retirement plans are based on the employee's last year of work and hence give the employer increasing leverage over employees as they grow older. Similarly, job changers may lose health insurance benefits, shifting the cost to local taxpayers via increased Medicaid cost, or shifting the cost to health providers who had nothing to do with producing charity cases. Many service sector jobs, such as those in the grocery, fast food, or retail industries, do not come with health benefits (let alone pension benefits), forcing those employees to turn to the government as the insurer of last resort. Since "the government" really is the taxpaying public and businesses that pay their own health care costs, the same responsible people pay them again to backstop those industries that do not provide benefits themselves. Such factors decrease the mobility of workers between firms, shift external costs on uninvolved third parties, and provide individual irresponsible employers with public welfare. In game theoretic terms, we reward the cheaters and penalize those who play by the rules. This regime also shifts external costs to uninvolved third parties, undeniably an inefficient outcome.

How much information do we really have in the free market? One strength of competition is that it motivates producers to find ways to lower product costs, which increases efficiency and social well-being. At the same time, though, that incentive may cause firms to lower the quality of a product, or even alter the terms of employment in ways that are not so clear to all the parties involved.

Adverse Consequences of Competition

Left to their own devices, with no regulatory oversight (be it economic or social), firms may find it too attractive to engage in competitive practices that are harmful to society as a whole. Some industries may be too competitive, destructively so, in the sense that their competition actually reduces efficiency and produces terms of employment that hurt society. For example, the textile industry not only stripped New England of jobs as it searched for cheap labor, it used conservative southern institutions and values to prevent the organization of unions in the South, creating impoverishment that northern taxpayers had to pay to ameliorate. While not beyond using police and other state agencies to help drive out organizers and break up union activity, they successfully passed to the public the cost of a low-wage heritage and the cost of occupational diseases such as brown lung. Most dramatically, these low southern wage scales became the root cause of the chronic impoverishment the Kennedy and Johnson Administrations sought to overcome in the War on Poverty during the 1960s, paid for by northern taxpayers left behind by these runaway shops.

In my view, the truckload segment of the trucking industry, which is analyzed extensively in this book, fits many of the characteristics of a destructively competitive industry. Research suggests that long-haul drivers earn a modest annual income despite working more than 60 hours a week. Long hours of driving, combined with many uncompensated hours spent waiting and performing non-driving tasks, have driven compensation down toward—and in some cases below—the legal minimum wage. Owner operators, a large component of the trucking industry, work long hours every week, all the while watching their initial investment in a costly rig disappear. Each of these conditions has negative consequences for society as a whole.

Another adverse consequence of unfettered competition is unemployment, which remains chronically high (though the concept of "high" has been redefined over the past three decades). This flies in the face of the neoclassical model of markets, which assumes that all resources—including labor—will be fully employed, particularly in an expanding economy. According to this theory, full employment assures that resources are allocated efficiently. Holders of resources such as labor are protected, in this model, against the consequences of shifts in economic conditions and policies (such as deregulation) by the rapid reallocation of resources implicit in full employment. Any negative consequences are supposed to be transitional and limited.

It is a wonderful model; if only the world actually worked that way. In the United States, we do not have full employment. Our Federal Reserve Board, in fact, has a deliberate policy of keeping inflation low by maintaining slack labor markets, and they prefer at least a level of unemployment between 5 and 6.5%. What happens under conditions of less than full employment? Increased competition in product and labor markets will depress wages and working conditions for extended periods. Thus policies that increase competition in markets are likely to worsen—perhaps substantially—the conditions of labor in particular markets, as well as limit the improvement of wages, compensation, and working conditions for most employees.

Of course, not all the arguments for unlimited competition are purely economic. A good example is the restriction on child labor. In a completely market-driven scenario, the exploitation of children as workers may lead to high short-term levels of economic efficiency, but it certainly doesn't assure an outcome desirable from society's perspective. Long-term investment in human resources declines as parents compete with one another to put food on the table today. The downward spiral is familiar to all who know something about nineteenth-century social history.

The distributional consequences of markets also can be quite troublesome. Differing rules may affect the distribution of income, working conditions, and what might be called the life chances—the opportunity to live a more pleasant life, to send one's children to good schools, to enjoy adequate health care—of different social groups. What, then, are the distributional consequences of extreme competition brought into play by unrestricted deregulation?

In the United States, we have an historic regime of rules that favors property rights, or "liberty of contract," and formal equality of legal and economic power. The employer makes the rules and the employee either accepts them or seeks a more satisfactory contract with another employer. This is the underlying structure—and the one to which we revert almost in toto as deregulatory policies dominate. Paradoxically, deregulation and freedom of contract reduce employee rights while placing fewer restrictions on employer prerogatives, due to the inherent imbalance of power.

Distribution may be an issue even with the more narrow scope of economic deregulation. There is no assurance that the gains from reduced product prices and improved services will be distributed evenly throughout the population, nor that the portion of the gains employees realize will balance out any loss of wages or employment.

Sweatshops: A Recapitulation

In the first chapter of this book I addressed issues that might arise in the reader's mind regarding the title of the book. Looking back into industrial history I found that sweatshops had three common characteristics on which scholars and social reformers agreed.

1. Low pay
2. Long hours
3. Unsafe and unsanitary conditions

This book has shown that super-competitive markets introduced by deregulation have driven truckers' wages, hours, and working conditions off the high road. I have documented the low wages for which truck drivers work, averaging little more than half that of the average manufacturing worker. I have documented wage differences depending on industry segment and unionization; the union premium increased since deregulation and drivers depend more on unionization for good wages than ever before.

This book has documented the long hours that truck drivers work, averaging more than 60 hours per week. For many of these drivers, much of this work time is unpaid, providing incentives for drivers to increase their overall work load to maintain their earnings.

While I have not dwelt on safety and working conditions, the issue has received a great deal of attention in recent years. Rest areas and truck stops fill to overflowing every night with truckers who live in their trucks, obtaining sanitary facilities where they can find them. Bureau of Labor Statistics data shows that truck drivers lead the nation in the number of occupational illnesses and injuries requiring lost work days, and while other leading occupations have reduced their work-loss illnesses and injuries by 20% from 1992 through 1996, those of truck drivers have increased 5%. While truck crash rates are stable or declining per million miles traveled, the increased reliance on trucks means exposure increases every year along with the incidence of crashes, injuries and fatalities, putting truck safety high on our political agenda.

America's economy has become heavily dependant on trucks. Buyers want their goods immediately if not sooner and often insist that carriers adapt their operations to provide disruptive delivery appointments and just-in-time service. With this intense competition on the basis of service and price, drivers are caught in the squeeze. As a result, for purposes of both individual and collective bargaining, drivers compete for jobs on the basis of low wages, long hours, and difficult working conditions. Drivers and carriers are locked into this race to the bottom that nobody wants to win.

Does this mean trucking company owners and managers exploit their workers to force drivers to produce? The concept of exploitation is a very fuzzy one and it doesn't explain why wages and working conditions should decline relative to others in the economy. Even nineteenth-century sweatshop operators did not make much more than the people who worked for them. The very competition that drives the industry forces the standard of living of everyone working in the industry to suffer together. Recent research which we have conducted at the University of Michigan shows that carrier management works similar hours just to keep up with the daily battle to deliver the goods and stay ahead of the competition. While the fast-pace of innovation in trucking is exciting and the daily battle to deliver the freight is a stimulating challenge, the fact remains that trucking managers work hard just like their drivers, and their earnings have suffered as well. While both employees and employers would like to change this undesirable pattern, the dynamics of the marketplace make such changes difficult and unstable.

Laws have been passed and regulations implemented intended to reduce this competitive menace. Economic regulation, sought by states and implemented by the Federal government in 1935, sought to reduce the level of competition in trucking and create incentives that would lead to safer operations. Regulations added later in the 1930s designed to limit hours of work were effective as long as economic regulation remained in place but apparently have become less effective as competition forces everyone to a higher level of performance.

Three solutions were recommended by nineteenth-century sweatshop opponents: the minimum wage, collective bargaining, and limits on work hours. It may not be coincidental that these three solutions have been suggested in recent years by those who want to limit the sweatshop environment today. Some argue that the only way to improve safety incentives is to extend the Fair Labor Standards Act to trucking, requiring employers to pay for all work performed and pay a premium for overtime, disregarding the impact on employment. Others focus on hours of service reform and ways to limit drivers' hours of work, disregarding the impact on earnings. Some advocate collective bargaining, which provides a privatized wage-and-condition-setting environment more closely tailored to the particular needs of each business.

Wages (rate of pay per hour of work), earnings (amount earned by the week, month, or year), and hours of work clearly are interrelated. We can drive up wages by limiting hours of work and we can drive down hours of work by increasing wages, but people will do what they can to reach their target earnings. This undeniable relationship, or its inverse, is responsible for the squeeze we see today.

Some in the industry have forecast dire consequences if any of these policies is implemented. If we limit hours of work, the freight will not move or the industry will be forced to hire hundreds of thousands of drivers, bringing logistics to a halt. Recent research conducted by the University of Michigan Institute of Labor and Industrial Relations suggests that while more than a hundred thousand additional drivers might be needed, that is in a static world that assumes no other changes. Indeed, if shippers and receivers were given strong incentives not to waste drivers' time—reducing by just 25% the unpaid and wasted hours drivers work every week—we might eliminate the need for additional drivers.

It seems clear that the public will not be satisfied with the status quo. While an individual firm's profits or an individual driver's wages and hours may be a private problem, increased safety consciousness has put these underlying issues in the spotlight. While we can increase enforcement all we like, we will need to address the underlying economic forces if we want to make a change. Unlike the proverbial Dutch boy with his finger in the dike, we cannot expect to hold back the tide of economic competition.

The Road Ahead

The road ahead looks a bit foggy, and danger lurks in the fog. We have accepted the notion that if competition is good, more competition is better, and survival of the fittest is best. This book shows us why this may not be the only choice. Indeed, it shows us some of the potential consequences of total all-out competition.

We have seen wages and working conditions drop significantly in some sectors of the trucking industry, as in other industries. We also have seen how competition separates winners and losers, with the losers outnumbering the winners in the long run. We have seen a real world case of labor market competition without some of the customary restrictions that work elsewhere in the economy. Indeed, we have seen the future of complete "deregulation," and the vision is not entirely positive.

It is important to remember that these same cautions apply to employers in other highly competitive industries. In trucking, as in construction, unfettered competition may yield great service at a great price, but in the long run will the market be able to support the investment in human capital needed to generate the next generation of workers? We have seen a skill crisis in construction that threatens to bring large and complex construction projects to a halt. While truck drivers may be easier to find than skilled tradesmen, we see signs of a labor market crisis in trucking that has limited output and provoked employers to demand the right to work drivers on double shifts as a regular method of operation. Such a situation is unstable, and untenable in the long run.

What if the rest of the labor market looked like trucking? We need to revisit the question of labor market competition and decide whether it leads our nation along the high road of good jobs in value-added production, or along the low road of bad jobs in a devalued economy. The choices we make during the next several years may answer this question for the next generation.

Appendix

The following equations test union effects on earnings and working conditions (the latter proxied by the variable "risk shift" which is discussed herein. In Equation 1, average annual earnings is a function of the sum of economic, industrial organization, and industrial relations effects.

$$\text{average wage} = f(\text{industrial characteristics} + \text{industrial relations} + \text{firm-level economic factors})$$

Algebraically, this model can be represented as

$$(1) \quad w_{ikt} = \alpha_{ik} + \beta_1 S_{ikt} + \beta_2 IR_{ikt} + \beta_3 E_{ikt} + \beta_4 L_{ikt} + \varepsilon_{ikt}$$

where w_{ikt} is the average annual wage w for individual trucking employees i at motor carrier k at time t; S_{ikt} represents firm-specific industrial characteristics S indicating industry segment and regionalism; IR_{kt} represents a firm-specific industrial relations variable indicating unionization; E_{ikt} represents firm-specific economic environmental variables E indicating market share and profitability; β_1, β_2, and β_3 represent parameters of these predictors; and ε_{ikt} is the error term.

First let us look at the effect of region by itself. I do this by regressing each region against wages, excluding all other variables. Wages differ by region generally in the United States, so we should see regional differences. While drivers in some regions earn slightly better wages, clearly the strongest single regional effect is the South, where workers earn markedly lower wages. Alaskan wages are markedly higher, but in the broader regression equations I excluded Alaskan carriers because they employ many fewer drivers yet exert a powerful leverage on the regression equation; they are outliers.

Canadian drivers also earn more, but they are paid in nominally higher terms merely due to the exchange rate. They therefore are anomalies, and I excluded them also from the general wage equation.

T-tests with ratios of 1.96 and above reach the .05 level of significance, meaning that we can be 95% sure that the differences are significant. Many of these regional differences barely reach this level of significance when controlling for none of the other possible influences posited in the models above. This would suggest that regional differ-

Appendix Table 1 Regions as Predictors of Average Earnings

Constant	Coefficient	23243.7
	(standard error)	(695.3)
	t-ratio	33.4
Canada	Coefficient	3941.30
	(standard error)	(1806)
	t-ratio	2.18
Alaska	Coefficient	12853.5
	(standard error)	(3438)
	t-ratio	3.74
Northwest	Coefficient	−2936.83
	(standard error)	(1492)
	t-ratio	−1.97
Southwest	Coefficient	2732.07
	(standard error)	(1432)
	t-ratio	1.91
Rocky Mountain-Texas	Coefficient	−2465.49
	(standard error)	(1201)
	t-ratio	−2.05
Plains	Coefficient	950.421
	(standard error)	(1234)
	t-ratio	0.770
Midwest	Coefficient	2109.94
	(standard error)	970.2
	t-ratio	2.17
New England	Coefficient	−2093.76
	(standard error)	(1704)
	t-ratio	−1.23
Mid-Atlantic	Coefficient	1732.33
	(standard error)	1534
	t-ratio	1.13
South/SE	Coefficient	−4449.58
	(standard error)	987.6
	t-ratio	−4.51
F-ratio		6.65
Adjusted R^2		31.5%
N		126

ences are weakly significant. That is, controlling for no other possible sources of variance, wages in the Northwest and Texas-Rocky Mountain areas tend to be slightly lower than average, while wages in the Southwest and Midwest appear to be slightly higher. Wages in the Southern and Southeastern states, however, are much lower.

Looking at wage equations after deregulation had become fully established, we see that unionization makes a profound difference in wages, disentangling this effect from the others (table 2). The adjusted partial R^2 measures the effect of each variable after the confounding effects of other independent variables has been removed, removing all multicollinearity from the equation. "Truckload," an indicator variable set to a value of "1" if the carrier is in that market, and "average haul" (ton-miles per ton, a measure of the carrier's shipment weight and distance) contribute to the prediction of driver wages but account for none of the wage differences experienced by other employees. Market share also provides a significant predictor of wages, as larger carriers pay all employees more money than do smaller carriers (a well-known firm-size effect), and profitability has a positive effect on non-driver employee wages but not on driver wages. Employees of Southern carriers earn less money, whether they are drivers or not, and all employees of carriers that bargain centrally with the Teamsters (those employed by TMI carriers that bargain the National Master Freight Agreement) earn higher wages, on average.

Table 3 suggests that this effect has increased following deregulation. Early in the period of administrative deregulation we can see that the union's effect was quite modest. This reflects the fact that most carriers were unionized and the wage differences among carriers were modest. After deregulation markets came to govern wage outcomes, and the only way employees could reduce these market effects was to unionize.

I used an analogous equation to determine whether wages or unionization made a difference for profits. While technically not a model for profit analysis—these are industrial relations models—this does provide some evidence of whether higher wages or unionization actually depress profits. In Equation 2, the same model tests the effects of these variables on profits.

Appendix Table 2 1990 Earnings Equation

Variable		1990 Average Compensation, All Employees	1990 Average Mileage Driver Compensation
Carriers		N=97	N=72
Constant		22656.9	46929.6
Teamsters	coefficient	4140.95	6478.54
	(t-ratio)	(4.56)	(4.08)
	adj.partial R²	**32.6%**	**29.3%**
Truckload	coefficient	−657.16	−3518.82
	(t-ratio)	(−0.685)	(−1.87)
	adj.partial R²	**−0.6%**	**3.9%**
Log of Average Haul	coefficient	1054.39	−2654.39
	(t-ratio)	(1.32)	(−1.52)
	adj.partial R²	**0.1%**	**4.1%**
Log of Market Share	coefficient	1872.55	5393.26
	(t-ratio)	(2.36)	(4.09)
	adj.partial R²	**3.0%**	**12.6%**
Net Profit Margin	coefficient	14630.0	−6763.96
	(t-ratio)	(1.81)	(−0.543)
	adj.partial R²	**5.5%**	**−1.1%**
Urban	coefficient	245.67	1088.33
	(t-ratio)	(0.342)	(0.957)
	adj.partial R²	**−0.8%**	**−1.2%**
South/SE	coefficient	−2691.72	-2860.33
	(t-ratio)	(−3.03)	(−1.92)
	adj.partial R²	**8.4%**	**4.1%**
Centralized Bargaining	coefficient	2239.62	2850.66
	(t-ratio)	(2.17)	(1.82)
	adj.partial R²	**3.0%**	**2.9%**
R² adjusted		**55.5%**	**68.0%**

$$(2) \quad \pi_{kt} = \alpha_{ik} + \beta_1 S_{kt} + \beta_2 IR_{kt} + \beta_3 E_{kt} + \beta_4 L_{kt} + \varepsilon_{kt}$$

where p_{kt} is the net profit margin of individual motor carriers k at time t; S_{kt} includes firm-specific industrial strategy variables representing industry segment and average haul; IR_{kt} represents firm-specific industrial relations variables including annual wages, unionization, and bargaining structure; E_{kt} represents firm-specific economic environmental variables including market share and profitability; L_{kt} represents locational variables including urbanism and regionalism; β_1, β_2, β_3, and β_4 represent parameters of these predictors; and ε_{kt} is the error term.

The results are illuminating, even though they are inconclusive. Table 4 shows that unionization and centralized bargaining, individually and together, have a slight downward effect on profits. When testing for the effect of driver wages in the equation the union effect is very

Appendix Table 3 Earnings Equations for 1977, 1972, and 1987 Using Repeated Cross Sections

Variable		1977 Average Compensation, All Employees	1982 Average Compensation, All Employees	1987 Average Compensation, All Employees
Carriers		N=333	N=222	N=198
Constant		32054.6	16400.3	21807.5
Teamsters	coefficient	2119.46	3884.95	3240.27
	(t-ratio)	(4.22)	(6.19)	(5.71)
	adj.partial R²	7.5%	15.9%	14.1%
Truckload	coefficient	−2854.03	−1837.86	−1463.40
	(t-ratio)	(−3.67)	(−2.34)	(−2.20)
	adj.partial R²	4.7%	2.0%	2.0%
Log of	coefficient	−2221.99	192.72	−1106.01
Average Haul	(t-ratio)	(−2.81)	(0.186)	(−1.27)
	adj.partial R²	2.1%	−0.4%	0.3%
Log of Market Share	coefficient	2265.38	425.93	1550.42
	(t-ratio)	(4.11)	(0.666)	(2.89)
	adj.partial R²	2.9%	−0.1%	3.7%
Net Profit	coefficient	−7094.24	8208.69	1754.50
Margin	(t-ratio)	(−1.65)	(2.07)	(0.416)
	adj.partial R²	1.4%	1.6%	−0.4%
Urban	coefficient	478.18	1285.97	258.98
	(t-ratio)	(1.09)	(2.28)	(0.522)
	adj.partial R²	0.1%	1.4%	−0.4%
R² Adjusted		18.3%	23.4%	29.0%

weak and insignificant, though the effect of centralized bargaining is stronger. When looking for the effect of all employee earnings (not just drivers and dock workers but every employee in all occupations) the negative effect is more pronounced. This suggests these variables might be picking up the effect of unmeasured characteristics of union firms rather than the effect of the union itself. Wages themselves have little effect—none using driver wages and some effect using earnings of all employees, again suggesting that unionization may be picking up other spurious unmeasured effects.

The strongest effects on profits come from market share and region (see table 5). Controlling for other factors, the larger the firm the higher the profits, echoing an effect found in the wage equations above. Again, just as wages are lower in Southern and Southeastern firms, so are profits, suggesting small Southern firms are most likely to have the lowest profits.

Finally, I tested for the effects of risk-shifting, a concept introduced in chapter 3 and on which I expanded in chapter 5. Carriers shift the

Appendix Table 4 Definitions of Indicators

Variable Name	Type of Variable	Meaning
Average Wage	Continuous	Average annual salaries and wages of all carrier employees, in 1982 dollars, using GNP deflator
Average Driver Wage	Continuous	Average 1990 mileage driver salaries and wages in 1982 dollars, using GNP deflator
Teamsters	Categorical	Teamsters union present, regardless of density
Centralized Bargaining	Categorical	Carrier a member of TMI, MCLAC, or RCI during the preceding bargaining round
Average Haul	Continuous; logged to base 10	Ton-miles per ton. A ton-mile is the transportation of one ton of freight the distance of one mile. Average haul is expressed in miles. It is a measure of weight and distance.
Market Share	Continuous between 0 and 1; logged base 10	Share of general freight market excluding carriers not in analysis (excludes United Parcel Service)
Net Profit Margin (NPM)	Continuous	Ordinary income (loss) from continuing operations before taxes divided by freight operating revenues
TL	Categorical	Carriers which earn most of their revenue from shipments over 10,000 pounds; defined at 70% of revenue from TL freight in 1977 and 1982, and 95% of revenue from TL freight in 1987 and 1990
ESOP	Categorical	Employee Stock Ownership Plan or profit sharing plan authorized by NMFA
South/SE	Categorical	All or part of carrier operations are in South or Southeast states, excluding national carriers
Urban	Categorical	Carrier home office in city of 100,000 or larger
Operating Ratio	Continuous	Total operating expenses divided by gross operating revenues

risk of operational inefficiency when they pay drivers only for driving time and do not pay them for loading and unloading, as well as other waiting and labor tasks. In Equation 3, the same model tests the extent of risk shifting. I hypothesize that the same factors determining wages will also determine the extent to which carriers shift operational risk to their drivers.

$$(3) \quad R_{ikt} = \alpha_{ik} + \beta_1 IC_{ikt} + \beta_2 IR_{ikt} + \beta_3 E_{ikt} + \varepsilon_{ikt}$$

where the dependent variable is the risk-shift index and the independent variables are as specified above. See chapters 3 and 6 for discussion of risk-shifting.

The number of carriers in this analysis reflects only those carriers in the population which pay by the mile and for which information is

Appendix Table 5 The Effects of Wages and Unionization on Profits, 1990

Variable		1990A Net Profit Margin	1990B Net Profit Margin
Carriers		N = 94	N = 74
Constant		0.129324	0.260493
Teamsters	coefficient	–0.025877	–0.015331
	(t- statistic)	(–2.31)	(–1.17)
	adj.partial R^2	**2.1%**	**–1.1%**
Average Wages, All Employees	coefficient	0.000001	
	(t- statistic)	(1.51)	
	adj.partial R^2	**5.0%**	
Average Mileage Driver Wages	coefficient		0.000000
	(t- statistic)		(0.001)
	adj.partial R^2		0.7%
Truckload	coefficient	0.012634	0.017836
	(t- statistic)	(1.13)	(1.29)
	adj.partial R^2	**0.4%**	**4.2%**
Log of Average Haul	coefficient	–0.006884	–0.027793
	(t- statistic)	(–0.485)	(–1.79)
	adj.partial R^2	**–0.3%**	**2.6%**
Log of Market Share	coefficient	0.036885	0.053225
	(t- statistic)	(4.26)	(5.29)
	adj.partial R^2	**10.6%**	**11.2%**
Urban	coefficient	0.007380	0.016301
	(t- statistic)	(0.893)	(1.80)
	adj.partial R^2	**–0.8%**	**1.6%**
ESOP	coefficient	–0.009989	–0.015623
	(t- statistic)	(–0.831)	(–1.14)
	adj.partial R^2	**–0.8%**	**0.6%**
Centralized	coefficient	–0.023142	–0.022085
Bargaining	(t- statistic)	(–2.01)	(–1.69)
	adj.partial R^2	**1.9%**	**2.9%**
South/SE	coefficient	–0.025383	–0.045334
	(t-statistic)	(–2.49)	(–3.93)
	adj.partial R^2	**5.8%**	**17.8%**
R^2		32.5%	44.2%
R^2(adjusted)		**25.3%**	**36.4%**

available on all variables. Analysis excludes carriers that pay by the hour or by a percentage of the revenue.

For detailed statistical analysis see Belzer, Michael H, "Collective Bargaining in the Trucking Industry: The Effects of Institutional and Economic Restructuring" (Cornell University, 1993); and Belzer, Michael H, "Collective Bargaining after Deregulation: Do the Teamsters Still Count?" *Industrial and Labor Relations Review* 48.4 (1995): 636–55. Sources include Belzer 1991 survey data; ATA Financial and Operating Statistics 1977, 1982, 1987, 1990, and 1991.

Appendix Table 6 Determinants of 1991 General Freight Truck Driver Wages and Risk Shifting Index, Using Ordinary Least Squares Regression

		1: General Freight Truck Driver Wage	2: Risk Shifting Index
Intercept	coefficient	0.214***	2.328***
	(t-statistic)	(16.00)	(10.10)
Union	coefficient	0.089***	−0.655***
	(t-statistic)	(10.1)	(−4.30)
	adj.partial R²	**48.3%**	**13.6%**
Truckload	coefficient	−0.030***	0.403***
	(t-statistic)	(−2.81)	(2.35)
	adj.partial R²	**5.9%**	**3.9%**
Net Profit Margin	coefficient	0.101*	0.444
	(t-statistic)	(1.94)	(0.35)
	adj.partial R²	**2.5%**	**−0.8%**
Market Share	coefficient	0.814***	−5.877
	(t-statistic)	(3.12)	(−1.05)
	adj.partial R²	**7.4%**	**−1.05%**
I-27†	coefficient	0.056***	−0.314
	(t-statistic)	(3.61)	(−1.42)
	adj.partial R²	**9.9%**	**0.9%**
Adjusted R²		69.1%	28.8%
N		110	112

*Statistically significant at the .10 level (two-tailed tests).
**Statistically significant at the .05 level (two-tailed tests).
***Statistically significant at the .01 level (two-tailed tests).

†Carriers that earn at least 75% of revenue from intercity shipments

Risk-shift index measures the extent to which drivers absorb non-driving labor time.

National carriers operate within all sections of the country. Regional carriers operate within one or more regions. Definitions derived from 1991 industry survey.

Index coding: 1 = drivers earn wages for all non-driving labor time; 2 = drivers earn wages for some non-driving labor time; 3 = drivers earn no wages for non-driving labor time.

Bold=adjusted R² for individual partial regression equations. Partial regression coefficients measure the effects of each independent variable on the dependent variable, with the linear effects of all other independent variables removed.

Glossary

back haul   The secondary freight loading from a point near the consignee, a region often outside the trucker's primary customer base, returning to the trucker's home terminal; often low revenue.

casuals   Workers hired on an irregular basis and without a position on a seniority board; they may be hired out of hiring halls.

certificated carrier   A carrier authorized to offer common carrier service to the public on the basis of published tariffs.

Class I   Carriers grossing more than $5 million annually.

Class II   Carriers grossing between $1 million and $5 million annually.

common carrier   A carrier that offers its services to the public according to published rates; discounts now privately negotiated.

contract carrier   A for-hire carrier whose services are available only through a private contract between trucker and shipper.

dockworkers   Persons who work on a loading dock, loading and unloading freight.

economies of scale   Economies that develop when the average cost of producing a good or service declines continuously with an increasing volume of goods produced. Generally, economies of scale correspond directly to the size of the capital investment used in production.

economies of scope   Economies that develop when a firm can produce several joint products more cheaply than a single firm can produce each product. The trucking industry demonstrates an unique application of economies of scope because trucking produces a virtually infinite number of individual services. Each route or lane—indeed each individual shipment—constitutes a separate product produced jointly. Taken together, the firm that can deliver the most such service products efficiently has a terrific market advantage.

exempt carrier   Carriers that were exempt from ICC regulation: haulers of certain commodities, haulers of shipments that are part of continuous airfreight movements, intrastate and local cartage, and private carriers.

externalities   Also known as external effects, external economies and diseconomies, spillovers, and neighborhood effects—involve the interdependencies between the utility and/or the production function of economic activity. For example, if a factory discharges something upstream in a river, it imposes an externality on people fishing downstream.

for-hire carrier   A motor carrier that offers its services to the public.

front haul   The primary freight loading from a trucker's home terminal to the consignee.

general freight   Non-specialized freight that generally requires no special handling or equipment.

hiring hall   An employment mechanism, originally designed by unions to allocate work to members (particularly skilled trades people). Commonly members are sent to jobs on a first-in, first-out basis, depending on particular skills needed by the employer.

imperfect information   When transactors have incomplete knowledge and foresight with regard to present and future prices, and with regard to the location of goods and services.

interline   A single freight movement shared by at least two carriers, neither of which can deliver the freight within its own system.

less-than-truckload (LTL)   A shipment weighing fewer than 10,000 pounds; also, a carrier primarily hauling these small shipments. A full trailer load for an LTL carrier typically consists of 20 or 30 shipments. LTL operations require elaborate terminal, pickup, and delivery operations.

linehaul   An "over-the-road" freight movement; also, drivers who do intercity and interstate work, either from terminal to terminal or shipper to consignee.

local cartage   Trucking operations limited to a single city or metropolitan area.

monopoly power   Power wielded by a producer that is the only, or the dominant, seller of a good or service. Monopolists restrict output and increase price, causing an inefficient allocation of resources.

monopsonist Someone with "monopsony power" is a sole buyer of a good or service; more specifically for our discussion here, workers face a monopsony purchaser of labor power when there is a limited number of potential employers. This is often the case when employees are restricted to a particular market by geography or skills. Employers with monopsony power hire labor at below-market cost because they are market-makers, not market-takers, and they must pay to all individuals any premium wage offered to one individual similarly situated.

operating authority The ICC grants operating authority to for-hire carriers, specifying the commodities to be hauled and services to be offered.

owner operator Persons who own and drive their own trucks, either under their own authority or under contract to a carrier. Some owner operators own more than one truck and employ other drivers.

piggyback An intermodal configuration in which a railroad flatbed carries a complete semi-trailer. In a related usage, the rail car holds a container, a semi-trailer box or tank without wheels, undercarriage, or king pin.

private carrier A company that uses its own trucks to deliver goods it produces or distributes. Deregulation allows private carriers to do limited for-hire hauling.

public goods Commodities or services that, if supplied to one person, are available to others at no extra cost.

secondary boycott A secondary boycott is an action taken by a union, in a primary labor dispute with one employer, to put pressure on another employer to cease doing business with the employer with which the union has a primary dispute. Such actions include strikes of technically uninvolved employers in an effort to achieve this pressure. In trucking, if the union has a dispute with one trucking company it may put up a picket line around that company, or it may place roving pickets around that company's trucks wherever it goes to load or unload. If in the course of placing a roving picket on a truck that is loading at another carrier the picketers ask the other carrier's employees to refuse to work (either to refuse to load that truck or to stop work altogether), they are engaging in a secondary boycott. If the employees of the uninvolved carrier refuse on their own to load the struck carrier's truck, they may be engaging in a primary labor dispute of their own against which the uninvolved carrier may take its own action. If they are union members and have a signed contract with the "uninvolved" employer, for example, and if that contract has a no strike clause, they may be in violation of their own no-strike clause.[1]

special commodities   Specialized freight that requires special handling and special equipment; e.g., bulk solids or liquids, refrigerated commodities, automobiles.

ton-mile   An output measure defined as the transportation of one ton of freight the distance of one mile.

Trotskyist   A revolutionary socialist who believes the working class will be the source of ultimate social change. Trotskyists generally believe that workers' power derives from "bottom-up" organizing based on rank-and-file action. The Minneapolis Teamsters, led by Farrell Dobbs and others, developed effective forms of organization that not only unionized that city but led to the first multistate over-the-road contract and 11-state agreement for the Midwest.

truckload (TL)   A shipment weighing more than 10,000 pounds; also, a carrier primarily hauling these large shipments. A full load for a TL carrier typically consists of between one and four shipments. TL operations do not require terminal infrastructure.

Notes

Chapter 1

1. The definitions and characterizations that follow were drawn from a number of classical sources. See the following texts for more information on sweatshops. Black, Clementina. 1907. *Sweated Industry and the Minimum Wage*. London: Duckworth & Company; Dulles, Foster Rhea. 1949. *Labor in America: A History*. New York: Thomas Y. Crowell; Hobson, John A. 1913. *Problems of Poverty: An Inquiry into the Industrial Condition of the Poor*. London: Methuen & Company; Schmiechen, James A. 1984. *Sweated Industries and Sweated Labor: The London Clothing Trades, 1860–1914*. Urbana: University of Illinois Press. For a succinct definition, see Doherty, Robert E. 1989. *Industrial and Labor Relations Terms: A Glossary*. Ithaca: ILR /Cornell University Press.

2. See Black, page 83.

3. For a description of a driver's life on the road in the nineteenth century, see Gerhold, Dorian. *Road Transport Before the Railways: Russell's London Flying Waggons*. Cambridge: Cambridge University Press, 1993.

4. Cynthia Engel, "Competition Drives the Trucking Industry," *Monthly Labor Review* 121, no. 4 (Apr. 1998): 34. Note that this article references my 1995 *Industrial and Labor Relations Review* article, but the citation omits the author's name.

5. Dale Belman, Kristen A. Monaco, and Taggert J. Brooks, "And Lord, Let It Be Palletized: A Portrait of Truck Drivers' Work and Life" (Ann Arbor: University of Michigan Trucking Industry Program, 1998).

6. See James A. Gross, "The Demise of the National Labor Policy: A Question of Social Justice," *Restoring the Promise of American Labor Law*, ed. Sheldon Friedman, Richard W. Hurd, Rudolph A. Oswald, and Ronald L. Seeber (Ithaca, N.Y.: ILR Press, 1994). See also James A. Gross, *Broken Promise: The Subversion of U.S. Labor Relations Policy, 1947–1994* (Philadelphia: Temple University Press, 1995).

7. In 1997 the LTL sector of the trucking industry finally regained profitability after years of stagnation. This profitability may be due to completion of the market consolidation that began early in the competitive period as well as an effect of consolidation arising from intrastate deregulation. It also may

be due to a persistent and near-record expansion. Time will tell whether this new profitability continues.

8. Jeffrey D. Sachs and Howard J. Shatz, "Trade and Jobs in U.S. Manufacturing," *Brookings Papers on Economic Activity* 1(1994): 1–84.

Chapter 2

1. All figures from *Employment, Hours, and Earnings,* published regularly by the U.S. Department of Labor, Bureau of Labor Statistics. Note that recent revisions of some of these series make historic comparisons impossible, hence the decision to report until 1995 or 1996 only. All dollars deflated using the Jan. 1998 Consumer Price Index for All Urban Wage Earners and Clerical Workers.

2. Robert D. Leiter, *The Teamsters Union: A Study of Its Economic Impact* (New York: Bookman, 1957) 17.

3. Donald Garnel, *The Rise of Teamster Power in the West* (Berkeley: University of California Press, 1972).

4. Leiter, *The Teamsters Union*, 19.

5. "Craft" unionism refers to the organization of workers into unions according to their specific jobs, while "industrial" unionism refers to the organization of workers in all jobs in a given industry. A useful comparison exists today between railroads and auto factories. On the railroads, workers are organized into separate unions such as maintenance-of-way employees, clerks, and engineers. Workers in unionized auto factories, regardless of their specific job, typically are all members of the United Auto Workers.

6. Farrell Dobbs, *Teamster Rebellion* (New York: Monad, 1972).

7. Ralph James and Estelle Dinerstein James, *Hoffa and the Teamsters: A Study of Union Power* (Princeton, N.J.: Van Nostrand, 1965) 89–101.

8. See the classic works by Clark Kerr, "The Balkanization of Labor Markets," *Labor Mobility and Economic Opportunity*, ed. E. Wight Bakke (New York: Technology Press of the Massachusetts Institute of Technology, and John Wiley and Sons, 1954) 92–110; and Clark Kerr and Abraham Siegel, "The Inter-Industry Propensity to Strike," *Industrial Conflict*, ed. Arthur Kornhauser, Robert Dubin, and Arthur M. Ross (New York: McGraw Hill, 1954).

9. The union's structure is based on local unions (generally with a geographic scope) that report to joint councils, conferences (in some cases), and the International, which is the highest body.

10. The NMFA is an agreement covering general commodities carriers represented by the Teamsters Union. It establishes grievance panels at the local, regional, and national levels. Actual wages and many rules are set in regional supplements. While it once covered hundreds of carriers, most have opted out since deregulation. The NMFA is discussed in greater length in chapter 4.

11. See both the classic James and James, *Hoffa and the Teamsters*, and Arthur A. Sloane, *Hoffa*, (Cambridge, Mass.: MIT Press, 1991). Hoffa invited both sets of academics to observe his negotiations and interactions.

12. See Thomas A. Kochan, Harry C. Katz, and Robert B. McKersie, *The Transformation of American Industrial Relations* (New York: Basic Books, 1986) 137–43, for an excellent account of this process at Schneider Transport, which in 1976 was a unionized truckload carrier. Schneider anticipated deregulation and the consequential erosion of business at the relatively high rates that supported their Teamster contract. A series of fostering, forcing, and escape tactics, including direct bargaining with individual workers, eventually weakened the union's bargaining power and forced drivers to accept markedly lower wages. The strategy eventually forced the union out and allowed Schneider to escape its relationship. See Richard E. Walton, Joel E. Cutcher-Gershenfeld, and Robert B. McKersie, *Strateguc Negotiations: A Theory of Change in Labor-Management Relations* (Boston: Harvard Business School Press, 1994) 23–40, for a description of these industrial relations strategies.

13. See Grant M. Davis and Norman A. Weintraub, "Labor-Management Relations: ESOPs in the Trucking Industry," *Profit Sharing and Gainsharing* (1990; Metuchen, N.J.: IMLR Press/Rutgers University; London: Scarecrow Press), 97–108.

14. See Dan La Botz, *Rank-and-File Rebellion* (New York: Verso, 1990), and Herman Benson, "Union Democracy Triumphs over Organized Crime," *Dissent* (1992):138–42.

15. Centralized bargaining and grievance panels make local leaders dependent on regional and national grievance committees. This dependence, combined with the open-ended grievance procedure (no arbitration) and even representation between management and labor, makes it difficult for nonconformists to win grievances for their members.

16. Bureau of National Affairs, *Daily Labor Report* 13 June 1985: A-2.

17. Perhaps TDU's greatest strength lies in the carhaul division. See La Botz, *Rank-and-File Rebellion* 271.

18. See Teamsters for a Democratic Union, *Convoy Dispatch* Oct. 1987 and July 1988; see also the Bureau of National Affair's *Daily Labor Report* 24 Aug. 1987: A-9 and 20 May 1988: A-9.

19. Presser, dying from cancer, took a 120-day leave of absence on 5 May 1988, and Secretary Treasurer Weldon Mathis became acting General President.

20. Bureau of National Affairs, *Daily Labor Report* 31 May 1988: A-11, D-1.

21. Teamsters for a Democratic Union, *Convoy Dispatch* July and Nov./Dec. 1988.

22. La Botz, *Rank-and-File Rebellion* 286–88.

23. See Steven Brill, *The Teamsters* (New York: Simon, 1978).

24. See Michael H. Belzer and Richard W. Hurd, "Government Oversight, Union Democracy, and Labor Racketeering: Lessons from the Teamsters Experience," *Journal of Labor Research* 20, no. 3 (1999): 343–65, for a detailed analysis.

25. See Dale Belman, Kristen A. Monaco, and Taggert J. Brooks, "And Lord, Let It Be Palletized: A Portrait of Truck Drivers' Work and Life" (Ann Arbor: University of Michigan Trucking Industry Program, 1998).

26. Michael D. Reagan, *Regulation: The Politics of Policy* (Boston: Little, 1987).

27. See Lawrence J. Ouellet, *Pedal to the Metal: The Work Lives of Truckers*, (Philadelphia: Temple University Press, 1994), for an excellent description of TL drivers' competitive behaviors.

28. Occasional decertifications occurred in isolated carriers that permanently replaced striking employees.

29. Many of the non-union subsidiaries of some of these and other companies either do not report or report as part of their larger holding companies, while as many as 80% of all carriers refuse to comply with legal reporting requirements. Therefore, these data may overstate unionization levels.

30. Hours and earnings data from the University of Michigan truck driver survey. See Belman, Monaco, and Brooks, "And Lord, Let It Be Palletized."

31. See Michael H. Belzer, "Labor Law Reform: Some Lessons from the Trucking Industry," *The 47th Annual Meeting of the Industrial Relations Research Association* (Washington, D.C.: Industrial Relations Research Association, 1995) 403–13.

Chapter 3

1. See also Edward J. Kane, "Interaction of Financial and Regulatory Innovation," *American Economics Association Papers and Proceedings* 78.2 (1988): 328–34.

2. Michael D. Reagan, *Regulation: The Politics of Policy* (Boston: Little, 1987). See also Dennis Swann, "The Regulatory Scene," *The Age of Regulatory Reform*, ed. Kenneth J. Button and Dennis Swann, (Oxford: Clarendon Press, 1989) 1–23.

3. Robert D. Leiter, *The Teamsters Union: A Study of Its Economic Impact* (New York: Bookman, 1957), 16.

4. Charles A. Taff, *Commercial Motor Transportation* (Centreville, Md.: Cornell Maritime, 1986) 350.

5. *Buck v. Kuykendall*, 267 U.S. 307, 1925. See Paul Stephen Dempsey and William E. Thoms, *Law and Economic Regulation in Transportation* (Westport, Conn.: Quorum, 1986) 17–20. See also Taff, *Commercial Motor Transportation.*

6. William R. Childs, *Trucking and the Public Interest: The Emergence of Federal Regulation 1914–1940* (Knoxville: University of Tennessee Press, 1985) 35–40.

7. Stephen G. Breyer, *Regulation and Its Reform* (Cambridge: Harvard University Press, 1982). See also Martha Derthick and Paul J. Quirk, *The Politics of Deregulation* (Washington, D.C.: Brookings Institution, 1985), and Dorothy Robyn, *Braking the Special Interests* (Chicago: University of Chicago Press, 1987).

8. For Derthick and Quirk, the contest is between "procompetitive" and "anticompetitive" forces (*The Politics of Deregulation*, 11). Their analysis rests primarily on the capture theory, and the players are either pro-reform or anti-reform. In the capture theory of regulation, developed by economist George Stigler, the regulated industry can benefit from its regulation by "capturing" the pertinent regulatory agency. The "capturing" can occur in several ways. The regulatory agency may be forced to rely on the industry for technical knowledge. Appointees to regulatory commissions may come from the industry itself. The industry may hold out the promise of future employment to regulators. It may be through lobbying and political influence. Often, the agency's simple need for recognition and cooperation from the regulated industry can result in capture. This is a charge levied frequently against regulators such as the Federal Aviation Administration.

9. Ann F. Friedlaender, *The Dilemma of Freight Transport Regulation* (Washington, D.C.: Brookings Institution, 1969) 153, 155–59, 165–68.

10. See Alfred E. Kahn, *The Economics of Regulation*, 2nd ed. (Cambridge: MIT Press, 1988), vol. 2, 14–28. Indeed, Kahn argues that "in the airlines and trucking competition has exerted powerful downward pressure on egregiously inflated wages—painful for the workers affected but healthy for the economy at large."

11. John W. Snow and Stephen Sobotka, "Certificate Values," *Regulation of Entry and Pricing in Truck Transportation*, ed. Paul W. MacAvoy and John W. Snow (Washington, D.C.: American Enterprise Institute for Public Policy Research, 1977) 153.

12. Michael W. Pustay, "Deregulation and the U.S. Trucking Industry," *The Age of Regulatory Reform*, ed. Kenneth J. Button and Dennis Swann (Oxford: Clarendon Press, 1989) 244–46.

13. See Thomas Gale Moore, "The Beneficiaries of Trucking Regulation," *Journal of Law and Economics* 21.2 (1978): 327–43; Nancy L. Rose, "The Incidence of Regulatory Rents in the Motor Carrier Industry," *Rand Journal of Economics* 16.3 (1985): 299–318; Barry T. Hirsch, "Trucking Regulation, Unionization and Labor Earnings: 1973–85," *Journal of Human Resources* 23.3 (1988): 96–319; and Hirsch, "Trucking Deregulation and Labor Earnings: Is the Union Premium a Compensating Differential?" *Journal of Labor Economics* 11.2 (1993): 279–301. Nancy Rose claims unionized employees captured between two-thirds and three-quarters of regulatory rents. See her "Labor Rent Sharing and Regulation: Evidence from the Trucking Industry," *Journal of Political Economy* 95.6, (1987): 1175.

14. For a cogent classic view, see Harry C. Simons, *Economic Policy for a Free Society* (Chicago: University of Chicago Press, 1948).

15. James P. Rakowski, "Marketing Economies and the Results of Trucking Deregulation in the Less-Than-Truckload Sector," *Transportation Journal* 28 (1988): 11–22. See also Nicholas A. Glaskowsky, *Effects of Deregulation on Motor Carriers*, 2nd ed. (Westport, Conn.: Eno Foundation, 1990), and Tom

Furlong, "Gasoline Tankers Seen as 'Rolling Bombs' of the Road," *Los Angeles Times* 21 Sept. 1992: A1.

16. John Richard Felton, "Background of the Motor Carrier Act of 1935," *Regulation and Deregulation of the Motor Carrier Industry*, ed. Felton and Dale G. Anderson (Ames: Iowa State University Press, 1989) 3–13. "Less-than-carload" refers to railroad shipments smaller than one railcar in size, similar to less-than-truckload in trucking.

17. Taff, *Commercial Motor Transportation*. See also Childs, *Trucking and the Public Interest*.

18. Dempsey and Thoms, 17–20. *Law and Economic Regulation in Transportation*; Childs, *Trucking and the Public Interest*, 49–54.

19. The use of value-of-service pricing in trucking paralleled its use in railroads. With value-of-service pricing, the value of the goods shipped determines the rate. This price structure ensures producers ship low-value raw materials by barge or rail and high-value finished goods by truck or airplane.

20. Between 1935 and 1980 the ICC and the law strongly favored collective rate-making.

21. Dorian Gerhold, *Road Transport before the Railways: Russell's London Flying Waggons* (Cambridge: Cambridge University Press, 1993).

22. Donald V. Harper and James C. Johnson, "The Potential Consequences of Deregulation of Transportation Revisited," *Land Economics* 63.2 (1987): 137–46.

23. The ICC was responsible for granting operating authority to carriers, and after the MCA of 1935 the ICC limited approval for such operating authority. A carrier that wanted to grow had to purchase the operating authority (and the attendant business) of existing carriers that wanted to sell or go out of business. In this way, the ICC was able to limit competition.

24. Dale G. Anderson and Ray C. Huttsell, "Trucking Regulation, 1935–1980," in *Regulation and Deregulation of the Motor Carrier Industry*, ed. John Richard Felton and Anderson (Ames: Iowa State University Press, 1989) 14–41.

25. Daniel J. Sweeney, Charles J. McCarthy, Steven J. Kalish, and John M. Cutler, Jr., *Transportation Deregulation: What's Deregulated and What Isn't* (Washington, D.C.: National Small Shipments Traffic Conference, 1986). See also Anderson and Huttsell, "Trucking Regulation, 1935–1980," *Regulation and Deregulation of the Motor Carrier Industry*, 22.

26. Anderson and Huttsell, "Trucking Regulation, 1935–1980," *Regulation and Deregulation of the Motor Carrier Industry*, 37–41.

27. That is, the failure to produce the "best" or optimal combination of outputs by means of the most efficient combination of inputs.

28. See Kahn, *The Economics of Regulation*. Unfortunately, while Kahn criticizes price discrimination based on "unrealistic value-of-service pricing schedules" (vol. II, 21) and favors cost-based pricing, he does not provide a convincing critique of value-of-service theory. Embroiled in a critique of regulated value-of-service pricing, he does not show why unregulated carriers ultimately would not rely on the same pricing mechanism.

29. D. Philip Locklin, *Economics of Transportation*, 7th ed. (Homewood, Ill.: Irwin, 1972) 10–11.

30. *Ibid.*, 142–70.

31. A. S. De Vany and T. R. Saving, "Product Quality, Uncertainty, and Regulation: The Trucking Industry," *American Economic Review* 67.4 (1977): 592. See also Richard Beilock, "Is Regulation Necessary for Value-of-Service Pricing?" *Rand Journal of Economics* 16.1 (1985): 93. For Marshall's Law, see Edwin Mansfield, *Applied Microeconomics* (New York: Norton, 1994) 30.

32. See Beilock, "Is Regulation Necessary for Value-of-Service Pricing?" The usefulness of value-of-service theory is best illustrated by considering freight rates intermodally. Shippers have four basic modes to choose from: water, rail, highway, and air. Obviously, the cost of transportation increases across these four modes. A ton of iron ore can be moved more economically by barge than by plane. The ore shipper's demand curve would be almost infinitely elastic at the price an air carrier would charge. Since holding costs are relatively low, this shipper likely would hold out for a price so low only a water carrier could charge it. Conversely, a computer-shipper's demand curve is relatively inelastic, as it must sell its goods quickly to keep inventory costs low. This shipper is more likely to ship a ton of computers by air to a customer who is ready to pay on delivery.

Neither shipper is terribly concerned about the carrier's costs. If an air carrier offers a price competitive with a barge, the ore shipper will take it. Myriad choices also exist within modes and between modes, reflecting market responses to an almost infinite variety of needs. Whether regulated or not, this calculus—repeated millions of times daily for millions of products—forms the basis for the logistic strategy of shippers and the business strategy of carriers.

Historically, the trucking industry settled on a synthesis of cost- and value-of-service as the basis for its tariffs. As a practical matter, cost was exceedingly difficult to determine and standardize, and shippers understood value-of-service rates well, knowing what to expect. See Childs, *Trucking and the Public Interest* 157–61.

33. George W. Bohlander and Martin T. Farris, "Collective Bargaining in Trucking—The Effects of Deregulation," *Logistics and Transportation Review* 20.3 (1984): 225. See also Derthick and Quirk, *The Politics of Deregulation* 6; Dempsey and Thoms, *Law and Economic Regulation in Transportation* 23; Pustay, "Deregulation and the U.S. Trucking Industry," *The Age of Regulatory Reform*; and M. A. Khan and Roger Reinsch, "The Deregulation Debate Continues: Is ICC Control over the Trucking Industry Necessary?" *Mid-Atlantic Journal of Business* 26.1 (1989): 67–79.

34. Derthick and Quirk, *The Politics of Deregulation* 164–74, 206, 242–44.

35. Roger C. Noll, "Regulation after Reagan," *Regulation* 11.3 (1988): 13–20. See also Thomas Gale Moore, "Transportation Policy," *Regulation* 11.3 (1988): 57–62; and Moore, "Unfinished Business in Motor Carrier Regulation," *Regulation* 14.3 (1991): 49–57.

36. Daniel J. Sweeney, "Trucking: What's Still Regulated," *Handling and Shipping Management* 27 (Aug. 1986), 11.

37. During the 1980s carriers filed rates for individual shippers using shipper codes that hid the name of the shipper and filed range tariffs that hid the actual rate. The Negotiated Rates Act of 1993 (NRA of 1993) made range tariffs illegal and required carriers to code tariffs with the name of the shipper, putting an end to that controversy (see William B. Cassidy, "Shipper Codes Must Have Names: New Law Requires Changes in Rates on File," *Transport Topics*, 17 Jan. 1994: 3). However, no sooner did that Act take effect than the application of it fell apart, as Congress eliminated tariff filings entirely in a rider to an airport funding bill, passed in August 1994.

38. Bohlander and Farris "Collective Bargaining in Trucking—The Effects of Deregulation," *Logistics and Transportation Review* 224–25. Sweeney, "Trucking: What's Still Regulated," *Handling and Shipping Management*.

39. Frank A. Smith, *Transportation in America: A Statistical Analysis of Transportation in the United States: Supplements, Updates and Corrections, December 1991* (Waldorf, Md.: Eno Transportation Foundation, 1992) 8, 10. See also Smith, *Transportation in America: A Statistical Analysis of Transportation in the United States* (Waldorf, Md.: Eno Transportation Foundation, 1991). Smith indicates "non-ICC" carriers' proportion of all intercity trucking tonnage increased nearly 3% between 1980 and 1990. In contrast, proponents of deregulation expected tonnage to shift to the regulated sector because economic deregulation would reduce incentives for private carriage.

40. During the 1980s the ICC allowed common carriers to file special tariffs for individual shippers using shipper code numbers that only the carriers could decode, rather than by company name. This allowed carriers to disguise public filings so that publicly-filed tariffs have many of the advantages of privately-negotiated contract carrier contracts, while retaining common carrier authority and protection. The NRA of 1993 made this practice illegal.

41. Taff, *Commercial Motor Transportation*, 355.

42. FedEx actually coexists as an air carrier (with its well-known air freight operations), an express carrier, and a motor freight carrier. In all cases such operations have been exempted from the laws that cover other motor carriers, such as the NLRA.

43. U.S. Congress, Office of Technology Assessment (OTA), *Gearing Up for Safety: Motor Carrier Safety in a Competitive Environment* (Washington, D.C.: U.S. Government Printing Office, 1988) 55.

44. Dempsey and Thoms, *Law and Economic Regulation in Transportation* 17.

45. Taff, *Commercial Motor Transportation* 349. The *State Motor Carrier Guide*, published by Commerce Clearing House, details current state regulations and lists state regulatory agencies.

46. OTA, *Gearing Up for Safety* 82.

47. *Ibid* 80.

48. *Ibid* 81–82.

49. Known until 1985 as the Bureau of Motor Carrier Safety; *Ibid* 148.

50. Taff, *Commercial Motor Transportation* 363–65. See also OTA, *Gearing Up for Safety* 62, 82.

51. OTA, *Gearing Up for Safety* 55–82.

52. *Ibid* 147–52.

53. Taff, *Commercial Motor Transportation* 366. See also OTA, *Gearing Up for Safety* 55–57.

54. Teamsters for a Democratic Union (TDU), "Whistle Blows on OSHA: Enforce Worker Protections," *Convoy Dispatch*, Jan./Feb. 1989: 6–7.

55. Taff, *Commercial Motor Transportation* 366–67, and OTA, *Gearing Up for Safety* 57, 60, 68, 80.

56. U.S. Code Title 49 § 521.

57. U.S. Code Title 49 § 11506.

58. CVSA is a state-based independent safety inspection system, coordinated with the FHWA. SAFETYNET is national network of carrier and driver safety records, including violations and safety citations. See OTA, *Gearing Up for Safety* 72–73, 77.

59. U.S. Code 1992 Transportation Appendix 49 App. §§ 2716–17, 2302–4, 2708.

60. William B. Cassidy, "Drug Testing: Rules Fleets Must Follow," *Fleet Owner* 85.4 (1990). See also Leon Cohan, "Hit the Mark with Random Testing," *Transportation and Distribution* 33.3 (1992): 34–36.

61. In a pilot program in cooperation with the federal government, New Jersey, Utah, Nebraska, and Minnesota all conduct roadside checks for drug and alcohol use. The rules define intoxication as a blood alcohol level of .04 percent, compared to the usual .1 percent definition of legally drunk. Drivers removed from the road under this standard can return after their blood alcohol level drops below .02 percent. See Dane Hamilton, "Troopers Begin Roadside Testing of Truckers for Alcohol Use in N.J.," *Journal of Commerce*, 29 Jan. 1993: B4, 3.

62. Dane Hamilton and Stephanie Nall, "Truckers Support New Rules for Drug and Alcohol Testing," *Journal of Commerce* 14 Dec. 1992: B2, 2. See also Bruce Ingersoll, "Rules to Test Transportation Workers for Alcohol Are Proposed by Agency," *Wall Street Journal*, 11 Dec. 1992: A2, 4; Stephanie Nall, "DOT Proposes New Drug, Alcohol Test Rules," *Journal of Commerce*, 11 Dec. 1992: A3, 1; and Martin Tolchin, "U.S. Imposes New Alcohol Test Rules," *New York Times*, 4 Feb. 1994: A15.

63. OTA, *Gearing Up for Safety* 143.

64. Transferred to the DOT in 1966. Note that DOT safety and other rules apply to many more drivers than those exempted by the FLSA.

65. In 1979 the Department of Labor estimated that the exemption applied to 1 million non-supervisory employees. See Conrad F. Fritsch, "Exemptions to the Fair Labor Standards Act, Transportation Sector," *Report of the Minimum Wage Study Commission* (Washington, D.C.: U.S. Government Print-

ing Office, 1981) 167. See also U.S. Department of Labor, Employment and Standards Administration, *Minimum Wages and Maximum Hours* (Washington, D.C.: U.S. Government Printing Office, 1979). This figure corresponds to Bureau of Labor Statistics SIC 421 nonsupervisory employment in 1979. The current figure is approximately 1.3 million.

66. The MWSC was created by the Fair Labor Standards Amendments of 1977 (Public Law 95–151) to study the FLSA of 1938 and reevaluate the notion of whether such regulation harms or benefits workers. The Commission was funded by Congress for three years, 1977 to 1980, to study this question and develop its report, which was submitted to Congress on May 24, 1981.

67. Fritsch "Exemptions to the Fair Labor Standards Act, Transportation Sector," *Report of the Minimum Wage Study Commission* 151–86.

68. Michael H. Belzer, "Collective Bargaining in the Trucking Industry: The Effects of Institutional and Economic Restructuring," diss.,Cornell University, 1993, 142–47. See also Belzer, "Collective Bargaining after Deregulation: Do the Teamsters Still Count?" *Industrial and Labor Relations Review* 48 (1995): 636–55, and "Labor Law Reform: Some Lessons from the Trucking Industry," *The 47th Annual Meeting of the Industrial Relations Research Association* (Washington, D.C.: Industrial Relations Research Association, 1995) 403–13.

69. Belzer, "Collective Bargaining in the Trucking Industry," 147–54.

70. Belzer, "Collective Bargaining after Deregulation," *Industrial and Labor Relations Review.*

71. Daniel Machalaba, "Long Haul: Trucking Firms Find It Is a Struggle to Hire and Retain Drivers," *Wall Street Journal* 28 Dec. 1993: A1, 5. See also Belzer, "Collective Bargaining after Deregulation," *Industrial and Labor Relations Review.*

Chapter 4

1. James F. Filgas and L. L. Waters, *Yellow in Motion: A History of Yellow Freight System, Incorporated* (Overland Park, Kan.: Yellow Freight System, 1987).

2. Thomas Kochan and Harry C. Katz, *Collective Bargaining and Industrial Relations* (Homewood, Ill: Irwin, 1988) 36.

3. James P. Rakowski, " Marketing Economies and the Results of Trucking Deregulation in the Less-Than-Truckload Sector," *Transportation Journal* 28 (1988): 19. Recently there has been some shift back to the use of interlines, as national carriers found that they could not efficiently deliver freight everywhere. Regional delivery of national carriers' freight has become a new niche business, and small regional carriers that have the capacity to reach remote locations and out-of-the-way cities pick up and deliver freight either in partnership with or on behalf of larger interregional and national carriers.

4. Transactions costs involve the costs of the relationship between buyer and seller and the contracting cost incurred by transactions themselves.

5. John Richard Felton, "Motor Carrier Act of 1980: An Assessment," *Regulation and Deregulation of the Motor Carrier Industry*, ed. John Richard Felton and Dale G. Anderson (Ames: Iowa State University Press, 1989) 158–61.

6. For a detailed analysis of the effects of these changes, and particularly the effects of rapid change, see Peter F. Swan, "The Effect of Changes in Operations on Less-Than-Truckload Motor Carrier Productivity and Survival," diss., University of Michigan, 1997.

7. American Trucking Associations (ATA), *Financial and Operating Statistics: Motor Carrier Annual Report* (Alexandria, Va.: ATA, 1993).

8. ATA, *American Trucking Trends* (Alexandria, Va.: Financial and Operating Statistics Service, Department of Statistical Analysis, ATA, 1979) 38; (1993) 10.

9. In 1977 Class I carriers had at least $3 million in annual gross operating revenues, while Class II carriers had at least $500,000 in revenues. Since January 1, 1980, these thresholds have been $5 million and $1 million, respectively. See ATA, *American Trucking Trends*, 1979 and 1982.

10. Charles R. Enis and Edward A. Morash, "Some Aspects of Motor Carrier Size, Concentration Tendencies, and Performance after Deregulation," *Akron Business and Economic Review* 18.1 (1987): 82–94. See also Thomas M. Corsi and Joseph R. Stowers, "Effects of a Deregulated Environment on Motor Carriers: A Systematic, Multi-Segment Analysis," *Transportation Journal* 30.3 (1991).

11. For the Airborne case, see Kristen S. Krause, "'Race to the Bottom': Contract Drivers in Airborne Trucks and Uniforms Paid Half the Wages, No Benefits for Same Work," *Traffic World* 27 July 1998.

12. Paul O. Roberts, "Comments on 'The U.S. Motor Carrier Industry Long after Deregulation,'" *Proceedings of the 34th Annual Meeting of the Transportation Research Forum*, St. Louis, Mo., 21 Oct. 1992. Roberts defines transcontinental carriers as those with an average haul of more than 1,000 ton-miles per ton. Using 1990 data, this definition included Yellow Freight System, Consolidated Freightways, Roadway Express, ABF Freight System, Watkins Motor Lines, and Northwest Transport Service (subsequently known as NW Transport and Nation's Way and now defunct). This definition excludes such arguably transcontinental carriers as Overnite Transportation (a subsidiary of Union Pacific Railroad that in 1990 operated as five regional carriers with the capacity for interregional freight movements, railing much of its transcontinental freight) and Carolina Freight Carriers (which drew back from national LTL service and later was purchased and absorbed by ABF). Roberts inexplicably excludes Miles (Herman) Trucking of Texas, a small carrier with an average haul of 1,517 miles.

13. *Ibid.*, 6–8. In 1990 the two largest carriers controlled 65% of this market. The largest, Jones Truck Lines, closed in 1991. Roadway bought the

second largest carrier, Central Freight Lines, as part of its Roadway Regional Group. The entire regional group has since been spun off into Caliber, and Caliber later was sold to Federal Express. Central was purchased by its own management in a leveraged buyout and returned to its previous status as an independent regional carrier.

14. George W. Wilson, *Economic Analysis of Intercity Freight Transportation* (Bloomington: Indiana University Press, 1980). See also James R. Frew, "The Existence of Monopoly Profits in the Motor Carrier Industry," *Journal of Law and Economics* 24.2 (1981) 289–315.

15. Richard H. Spady and Ann F. Friedlaender, "Hedonic Cost Functions for the Regulated Trucking Industry," *Bell Journal of Economics* 9.1 (1978).

16. John W. Snow, "The Problem of Motor Carrier Regulation and the Ford Administration's Proposal for Reform," *Regulation of Entry and Pricing in Truck Transportation*, ed. Paul W. MacAvoy and John W. Snow (Washington, D.C.: American Enterprise Institute for Public Policy Research, 1977), 37. See also in the same volume, Richard Klem, "Market Structure and Conduct," 119–38.

17. Theodore E. Keeler, "Deregulation and Scale Economies in the U.S. Trucking Industry: An Econometric Extension of the Survivor Principle," *Journal of Law and Economics* 32 (1989): 229–53. See also Robert W. Kling, "Deregulation and Structural Change in the LTL Motor Freight Industry," *Transportation Journal* 30.3 (1990).

18. Corsi and Stowers, "Effects of a Deregulated Environment on Motor Carriers," *Transportation Journal*. See also Curtis M. Grimm, Thomas M. Corsi, and Judith L. Jarrell, "U.S. Motor Carrier Cost Structure under Deregulation," *Logistics and Transportation Review* 25.3 (1989): 231–49. For a contrasting view, see William B. Nebesky, Starr McMullen, and Man-Keung Lee, "Market Power in the U.S. Motor Carrier Industry," Annual Meeting of the Transportation Research Forum, Daytona Beach, Fla., 3–5 Nov. 1994.

19. Thomas M. Corsi, "Motor Carrier Industry Structure and Operations, *International Symposium on Motor Carrier Transportation* (Washington, D.C.: National Academy Press, 1993), 20–23.

20. Thomas M. Corsi, Curtis M. Grimm, Ken G. Smith, and Raymond D. Smith, "Deregulation, Strategic Change, and Firm Performance among LTL Motor Carriers," *Transportation Journal* 31.1 (1991): 4–13. See also Corsi, Grimm, Smith, and Smith, "The Effects of LTL Motor Carrier Size on Strategy and Performance," *Logistics and Transportation Review* 28.2 (1992): 129–45.

21. Roberts, "Comments on 'The U.S. Motor Carrier Industry Long after Deregulation.'"

22. Mark H. Keaton, "Economies of Density and Structure of the Less-Than-Truckload Motor Carrier Industry since Deregulation," *Proceedings of the Transportation Research Forum, 36th Annual Meeting* (Arlington, Va.: Transportation Research Forum, 1994) 59–74.

23. Using the state-based Current Employment Statistics (CES) survey, the BLS samples approximately a third of a million reporting units yearly. It

reports employment, hours, and earnings data according to the 1987 *Standard Industrial Classification Manual.* Standard industrial classifications (SIC) group industries according to their primary economic activity. For the trucking industry, the BLS reports employment, hours, and earnings data for SIC 42 (Trucking and Warehousing) and SIC 421 (Trucking and Courier Services, Except Air). Using ICC data on the trucking industry, the BLS reports labor productivity according to a finer trucking industry classification: intercity trucking, Class I and II common and contract carriers (SIC 4213 part), and for intercity trucking, general freight, Class I and II common carriers of general freight (SIC 4213 part). See Executive Office of the President, Office of Management and Budget, *Standard Industrial Classification Manual, 1987* (Springfield, Va.: National Technical Information Service, 1987). See also U.S. Department of Labor, Bureau of Labor Statistics, *Productivity Measures for Selected Industries and Government Services* (Washington, D.C.: U.S. Government Printing Office, 1993); (Sept. 1992): 14–28, 78–98, 246–47. Outcomes between categories in either series are very similar. This study reports data for SIC 421 and SIC 4213, part. However, neither of these sources provides information on private carriers, which haul about half of all goods. This means that the data represent only the trucking industry and not the trucking function. If industry employment included the entire trucking function, the figures might double.

24. U.S. Department of Labor, Bureau of Labor Statistics (BLS), *Productivity Measures for Selected Industries and Government Services* (Washington, D.C.: U.S. Government Printing Office, Apr. 1993), 80.

25. For detail and analysis, see Michael H. Belzer, "Collective Bargaining after Deregulation: Do the Teamsters Still Count?" *Industrial and Labor Relations Review* 48 (1995): 636–55.

26. See Dale Belman, Kristen A. Monaco, and Taggert J. Brooks, "And Lord, Let It Be Palletized: A Portrait of Truck Drivers' Work and Life" (Ann Arbor: University of Michigan Trucking Industry Program, 1998).

27. Belzer, Michael H. "The Transformation of Labor Relations in the Trucking Industry Since Deregulation." M.S. Thesis. 1990.

28. BLS, *Productivity Measures for Selected Industries and Government Services* (1988, 1989). The BLS reports similar declines for all Class I and Class II common and contract carriers.

29. There are several reasons why the ICC granted reporting exemptions. The ICC began to grant specific reporting exemptions to many carriers who complained about the burden and reduced the reporting broadly to reduce the burden. Further, the number of carriers in the classification declined while their size increased. In addition, the ICC had insufficient staff to enforce reporting requirements of carriers that began below the threshold and grew into it. Finally, the ICC raised the thresholds broadly and in terms of specific required data (thus also reducing the *value* of the data).

30. John Duke, "Productivity Measures for Transportation Industries," Highway Related Transportation Industries Productivity Measures Symposium, Washington, D.C., 20 Nov. 1992: 11–12.

31. BLS statistics have never included intrastate carriers, Class III carriers, owner operators, and exempt haulers. This means BLS data has always been biased toward larger, interstate operations.

32. Interstate Commerce Commission (ICC), Bureau of Accounts, *Transport Statistics in the United States; Motor Carriers, Part 2* (Washington, D.C.: ICC, Bureau of Accounts, 1977–1990, individual years). Class II carriers from 1977 to 1980 were defined as $500,000 to $3 million, and Class I firms were larger than $3 million in annual gross revenue. After 1980 the Class III threshold jumped to between $1 million and $5 miliion.

33. Note that even this number excludes non-reporting carriers.

34. Duke "Productivity Measures for Transportation Industries," 31.

35. Bearth, Daniel P. "Cass Logistics Formula flaw Inflates Deregulation Savings." Transport Topics. 14 June, 1999, page 4.

36. As one researcher has noted, "In general, from the standpoint of data use in the evaluation of policy options, we would like our measure of labor productivity to appropriately account for changes in output quality which are distinguishable to the purchaser, and which command different prices in the marketplace. This is especially true if there is a general trend towards quality improvement, as anecdotal data and case studies often suggest. But the use of ton-miles as an output measure, with no further information as to quality-related characteristics, is unlikely to achieve this goal" (Stephen V. Burks, "Final Report: OTA Project on Trucking Industry Productivity" [Amherst: University of Massachusetts, Department of Economics, 1 March 1995]).

37. Ann F. Friedlaender, Richard H. Spady, and S. Judy Wang Chiang, "Regulation and the Structure of Technology in the Trucking Industry," *Productivity Measurement in Regulated Industries*, ed. Thomas G. Cowing and Rodney E. Stevenson (New York: Academic, 1981) 77–106.

38. Corsi and Stowers, "Effects of Deregulated Environment on Motor Carriers," *Transportation Journal* 19–21.

39. Nicholas A. Glaskowsky, "Effects of Deregulated Environment on Motor Carriers," 2nd ed. (Westport, Conn.: Eno Foundation, 1990) 30.

40. Donald J. Harmatuck, "Motor Carrier Cost Function Comparisons," *Transportation Journal* 31.4 (1990): 34, 45 (note 25).

41. Corsi and Stowers, "Effects of Deregulated Environment on Motor Carriers," *Transportation Journal*.

42. Donald V. Harper and James C. Johnson, "The Potential Consequences of Deregulation of Transportation Revisited," *Land Economics* 63.2 (1987): 140.

43. ATA, *American Trucking Trends* (1993) addendum.

44. Glaskowsky, "Effects of Deregulated Environment on Motor Carriers," 7–9.

45. Michael Conyngham, "I.C.C. Regulated Motor Carriers of General Freight under the National Master Freight Agreement That Terminated General Freight Operations from July 1, 1980 to May 30, 1993," Teamsters Re-

search Department Report (Washington, D.C.: International Brotherhood of Teamsters, 1993).

46. D. Philip Locklin, *Economics of Transportation*, 7th ed. (Homewood, Ill.: Irwin, 1972) 709–12.

47. See Russell B. Capelle, Jr., ed., *Quarterly Survey of General Freight Carrier Operating Results; 1967 thru 2nd Quarter 1988* (Alexandria, Va.: Economic Research Committee, Regular Common Carrier Conference, 1988). Michael W. Pustay claims that the "ICC's usage of a 95 percent operating ratio test yielded rates of return that were very generous to the carriers" (see Pustay, "Deregulation and the U.S. Trucking Industry," *The Age of Regulatory Reform*, ed. Kenneth J. Button and Dennis Swann [Oxford: Clarendon Press, 1989] 244). His use of the 95% standard is unsubstantiated, as is his claim of "generous rates of return" to the carriers. Locklin explains the difficult tension between the two standards and suggests the higher return on investment (compared to manufacturing) compensates motor carriers for the greater risk they took, long before deregulation (see Locklin, *Economics of Transportation* 709). The wide fluctuations in operating ratio since regulatory restructuring may explain the frequency of bankruptcies during periods of very high average operating ratios.

48. Glaskowsky, *Effects of Deregulation on Motor Carriers* 29.

49. Return on Equity for motor carriers is defined as Net Income (after taxes, but before extraordinary items, prior period adjustments, income from equity in affiliates, and gain or loss on disposal of discontinued segments) divided by Equity. Total Stockholders' Equity changed to Total Owners' Equity or Capital in 1988.

50. The average number of reporting carriers during this period was 1,260, but the number dropped by 50% during the last two years of the ICC's existence, as many carriers either defied the crippled agency to try to collect the data or simply ignored the ICC and thought its data-gathering responsibility had lapsed. Congress handed this responsibility to the Bureau of Transportation Statistics of the U.S. Department of Transportation, which eventually began to enforce reporting requirements. In the summer of 1999 it issued a "Rulemaking," requiring a substantially reduced reporting requirement but retaining the reporting requirement itself, along with public access to the data at the firm level.

51. Glaskowsky, *Effects of Deregulation on Motor Carriers* 41–45.

52. Paul R. Schlesinger, "Motor Carrier Industry: Traditional Small-Shipment Truckers Cope with an Uncertain Market; National Carriers Fighting Decay? Prospects for 1993 and Beyond," *Industry Viewpoint* (New York: Donaldson, Lufkin & Jenrette, 8 April 1993).

53. H. Perry Boyle, Jr., "Trucking Market Segmentation, Part III: A Look at the Trucking Industry Life Cycle" (Baltimore, Md.: Alex. Brown & Sons, Incorporated, 1993).

54. Locklin, *Economics of Transportation* 150–51, 312, 712–14.

55. Donald V. Harper and James C. Johnson, "The Potential Consequences of Deregulation of Transportation Revisited," *Land Economics* 63.2 (1987): 140–41.

Chapter 5

1. Harold M. Levinson, "Collective Bargaining and Technological Change in the Trucking Industry," *Collective Bargaining and Technological Change in American Transportation*, ed. Levinson, Charles M. Rehmus, Joseph P. Goldberg, and Mark C. Kahn (Evanston, Ill.: Northwestern University Transportation Center, 1971) 19.

2. Harold M. Levinson, "Trucking," *Collective Bargaining: Contemporary American Experience*, ed. Gerald G. Somers (Madison, Wisc.: Industrial Relations Research Association, 1980) 104–6.

3. Industry employment also declined between 1979 and 1983 and did not recover its pre-deregulation high until 1985 (see figure 4.3).

4. See Barry T. Hirsch, "Trucking Regulation, Unionization and Labor Earnings: 1973–85," *Journal of Human Resources* 23.3 (1988): 296–319.

5. In 1995 the Bureau of Labor Statistics changed the Standard Industrial Classification (SIC) Code of an undetermined number of carriers that formerly had been listed as motor carriers in Industry Group 421 ("Trucking and Courier Services, Except Air") moving them into Industry Group 451 ("Air Transportation, Scheduled, and Air Courier"), which is part of the air transportation industry. I believe this is a misclassification, since the largest of these carriers, United Parcel Service, is primarily engaged in truck transportation. The BLS argues that the fastest growing section of the business of the firms in question (they are careful not to mention UPS because the names of the firms are confidential, but obviously a $20 billion firm with hundreds of thousands of employees makes a big impact when moved from one industry to another) is overnight air service, but at this time air service represents no more than 25% of UPS's business worldwide, and less than that in the United States. They also most certainly include Federal Express in this classification, though in a FedEx tour I heard them characterize it as an LTL company. This misclassification arbitrarily cuts the size of the trucking industry dramatically and makes all data reported before the change completely incomparable with the data reported after the change. Source: personal correspondence and communication with Dominic Toto and John Murphy of the U.S. Department of Labor, Bureau of Labor Statistics, Sept. 1998.

SIC 4215 Courier Services, Except by Air :
"Establishments primarily engaged in the delivery of individually addressed letters, parcels, and packages (generally under 100 pounds), except by means of air transportation or by the United States Postal Service. Delivery is usually made by street or highway within a local area or between cities. Establishments primarily engaged in furnishing air delivery of individually addressed letters, parcels, and packages, except by the United States Postal Service, are classified in Industry 4513, and establishments of the United States Postal Service are classified in Industry 4311. Establishments primarily engaged in the delivery of advertising and other unaddressed letters, par-

cels, and packages are classified in Industry 7319. Establishments primarily engaged in undertaking the transportation of goods from shippers to receivers for a charge covering the entire transportation, but making use of other transportation establishments to effect the entire delivery, are classified in Industry 4731. Establishments primarily engaged in furnishing armored car services are classified in Services, Industry 7381."

SIC 4513 Air Courier Services:
"Establishments primarily engaged in furnishing air delivery of individually addressed letters, parcels, and packages (generally under 100 pounds), except by the U.S. Postal Service. While these establishments deliver letters, parcels, and packages by air, the initial pickup and the final delivery are often made by other modes of transportation, such as by truck, bicycle, or motorcycle. Separate establishments of air courier companies engaged in providing pickup and delivery only; "drop-off points"; or distribution centers are all classified in this industry. Establishments of the U.S. Postal Service are classified in Industry 4311; and establishments furnishing delivery of individually addressed letters, parcels, or packages (generally under 100 pounds) other than by air are classified in Industry 4215. Establishments primarily engaged in undertaking the transportation of goods from shippers to receivers for charges covering the entire transportation, but making use of other transportation establishments to effect the entire delivery, are classified in Industry 4731."

6. The Teamsters Union represents most unionized trucking employees, with a very small fraction of the industry represented by a handful of other unions, most notably the United Transportation Employees and the International Association of Machinists.

7. The ATA did not report the number of drivers at each company before 1990. Using ATA data for 1990, I estimate that 50% of all carrier employees were drivers and assumed the same proportion applied to previous years. This is a conservative generalization because BLS data show the proportion of supervisory to production employees was constant or rose slightly between 1977 and 1990. I multiplied the number of drivers by the union density at each carrier. Since the latter data were obtained from my 1991 survey and current research, and the survey population was based on carriers existing in ATA tapes from previous years (as discussed in chapter 3), information on union representation is limited to carriers listed as Class I general freight during those years. Thus, the same data discontinuity discussed in chapter 3 affects these results. Finally, I assume failed carriers were union shops, as probably most were.

In sum, while CPS data include all truck drivers, from DOT-regulated intercity truck drivers to unregulated local couriers, ICC-based data are limited to the interstate general freight market. This approach avoids confounding broad changes in delivery markets with changes in the general freight trucking industry.

8. The largest U.S. union is the National Education Association, with 2 million members. A handful of unions have more than 1 million members, including the United Food and Commercial Workers International Union, the American Federation of State, County, and Municipal Employees, and the Service Employees International Union.

9. Eugene H. Methvin, "Additional Views of Commissioner Eugene Hilburn Methvin," *The Edge: Organized Crime, Business, and Labor Unions Appendix* (Washington, D.C.: U.S. Government Printing Office, 1985) 2. See also Bureau of National Affairs, "Teamsters, Employer Groups Begin National Master Freight Bargaining," *Daily Labor Report* 16 Jan. 1985: A-8.

10. For more on the decentralization of U.S. industrial relations, see Harry C. Katz, "The Decentralization of Collective Bargaining: A Literature Review and Comparative Analysis," *Industrial and Labor Relations Review* 47 (1993): 3–22.

11. Levinson, "Trucking," *Collective Bargaining* 104–6.

12. *Ibid* 124, 140.

13. *Ibid* 139–44.

14. Bureau of National Affairs, "Teamsters, Employer Groups Begin National Master Freight Bargaining," *Daily Labor Report* 16 Jan. 1985: A-8.

15. See Grant M. Davis, Norman A. Weintraub, and William Holey, Jr., "Employee Stock Ownership Programs and Their Use in Trucking: Capital Formation, Employee Participation or Survival," *Logistics and Transportation Review*, 23 (1987). See also Davis and Weintraub, "Labor-Management Relations: ESOPs in the Trucking Industry," *Profit Sharing and Gainsharing* (1990; Metuchen, N.J. IMLR Press/Rutgers University; London: Scarecrow Press).

16. Bureau of National Affairs, "Teamsters, Employer Groups Begin National Master Freight Bargaining," A-8.

17. The number of carriers represented by various associations, and the number of employees they represent, is kept secret as a matter of bargaining strategy. Therefore, estimates vary between sources and citation dates.

18. Charles R. Perry, *Deregulation and the Decline of the Unionized Trucking Industry* (Philadelphia: Wharton Industrial Research Unit, 1986) 105–10.

19. Bureau of National Affairs, "Teamsters, Employer Groups Begin National Master Freight Bargaining," A-8.

20. Bureau of National Affairs, "Trucking Industry Talks Get Underway," *Daily Labor Report* 15 Jan. 1988: A-5.

21. Bureau of National Affairs, "Teamsters and Freight Carrier Group Begin Talks on Master Trucking Accord," *Daily Labor Report* 27 Nov. 1990: A-6.

22. Teamsters for a Democratic Union, *Convoy Dispatch*, Dec. 1993/Jan. 1994: 3.

23. Teamster contracts traditionally have established grievance committees with even representation from management and the union (four, six, or eight representatives total). If the grievance was "deadlocked," either party had the right to all lawful economic recourse, meaning a strike or lockout. In

practice, this structure allowed the union great bargaining leverage, as any unresolved grievance might result in an expensive and disruptive work stoppage. This possibility had recently been made quite real, as trucking management had the opportunity to observe a national strike of UPS early in 1994, following UPS's unilateral doubling of its package weight limit from 75 to 150 pounds.

24. Michael Wickham, "CEO's Perspective on the Trucking Industry," Eighth Annual Conference of the National Trucking Industrial Relations Association, St. Petersburg Beach, Fla., 7 Nov. 1994.

25. Michael H. Belzer, "Collective Bargaining after Deregulation: Do the Teamsters Still Count?" *Industrial and Labor Relations Review* 48 (1995): 644–45. In 1991 I conducted a telephone survey of 223 of the 250 Class I general freight carriers I could locate. I asked executives of these carriers to approximate the proportion of their unionized drivers. This survey suffered from the obvious survivor bias; only carriers operating a decade after deregulation could be surveyed. Nonetheless, little change in union representation occurred among surviving carriers during an obviously turbulent era.

26. My survey results do not show the large number of carriers, many of them union shops, that went out of business during the period. A large percentage of the union's losses occurred as a direct result of bankruptcies caused by the new regulatory regime. The Teamsters Union's research department reports that carriers employing 48% of all Class I and II general freight workers have gone out of business since the passage of the Motor Carrier Act of 1980. See Michael Conyngham, "I.C.C. Regulated Motor Carriers of General Freight under the National Master Freight Agreement That Terminated General Freight Operations from July 1, 1980 to May 30, 1993," Teamsters Research Department Report (Washington, D.C.: International Brotherhood of Teamsters, 1993).

27. This practice became the subject of the President's Commission on Organized Crime in the mid-1980s, as the involvement of labor racketeers in labor leasing became public.

28. See Dale Belman, Kristen A. Monaco, and Taggert J. Brooks, "And Lord, Let It Be Palletized: A Portrait of Truck Drivers' Work and Life" (Ann Arbor: University of Michigan Trucking Industry Program, 1998).

29. See Thomas Gale Moore, "The Beneficiaries of Trucking Regulation," *Journal of Law and Economics* 21.2 (1978): 327–43.

30. Nancy L. Rose, "The Incidence of Regulatory Rents in the Motor Carrier Industry," *Rand Journal of Economics* 16.3 (1985): 299–318. See also Rose, "Labor Rent Sharing and Regulation: Evidence from the Trucking Industry," *Journal of Political Economy* 95.6 (1987): 1146–78. See also Hirsch, "Trucking Regulation, Unionization and Labor Earnings: 1973–85." According to Michael Pustay, the remainder of the rents allegedly were captured by carrier stockholders in the form of inflated values of operating rights. See Pustay, "Regulatory Reform and the Allocation of Wealth: An Empirical Analysis," *Quarterly Review of Economics and Business* 23 (Mar. 1983), and also his, "De-

regulation and the U.S. Trucking Industry," *The Age of Regulatory Reform*, ed. Kenneth J. Button and Dennis Swann (Oxford: Clarendon Press, 1989).

31. For a detailed comparison and analysis, see Michael H. Belzer, *The Motor Carrier Industry: Truckers and Teamsters under Siege* (Madison, Wisc.: Industrial Relations Research Association, 1994).

32. Samuel R. Friedman, *Teamsters Rank and File: Power, Bureaucracy, and Rebellion at Work and in a Union* (New York: Columbia University Press, 1982).

33. Clifford Winston, Thomas M. Corsi, Curtis M. Grimm, and Carol A. Evans, *The Economic Effects of Surface Freight Deregulation* (Washington, D.C.: Brookings Institution, 1990). Paul Roberts considers these estimates excessively high and "completely unbelievable." However, he agrees with Winston et al. that organized labor has been the biggest loser from economic deregulation. See Roberts, "Comments on 'The U.S. Motor Carrier Industry Long after Deregulation," Transportation Research Forum, St. Louis, Mo., 21 Oct. 1992. See also Corsi, "Motor Carrier Industry Structure and Operations," *International Symposium on Motor Carrier Transportation* (Washington: National Academy Press, 1993).

34. Methodology:

Conversion factor from 1977 to 1982–1984 dollars: 1.642036125
    {100/60.9 (1982–1984 index / 1977 index)}
Avg. average welfare gain, 1982–1984 dollars * 12 years: $94,384,236,453
    {([$4.79 billion * inflator] * 12) * 1,000,000,000}
Unadjusted cumulative earnings loss: $77,348,498,764.22
Adjusted cumulative earnings loss: $55,799,391,406
Proportion of adjusted earnings loss to total welfare gain: 59.12%
    {(cumulative loss per trucking worker minus cumulative loss per manufacturing worker) / total welfare gain}
Proportion of unadjusted earnings loss to total welfare gain: 81.95%
    {unadjusted cumulative earnings loss / total welfare gain}

35. Belzer, "Collective Bargaining after Deregulation," *Industrial and Labor Relations Review*.

36. In this survey, 101 carriers are organized by the Teamsters and five are organized by other unions. Teamsters average slightly higher pay, although the difference is not statistically significant.

37. Belzer, "Collective Bargaining after Deregulation," *Industrial and Labor Relations Review*.

38. Belman, Monaco, and Brooks, "And Lord, Let It Be Palletized."

39. For a full analysis, see Michael H. Belzer "Collective Bargaining in the Trucking Industry: The Effects of Institutional and Economic Restructuring," diss., Cornell University, 1993; and see also Belzer, "Collective Bargaining after Deregulation," *Industrial and Labor Relations Review*.

40. For a detailed explanation of the methods used to develop this analysis, see Belzer, "Collective Bargaining in the Trucking Industry," chapters 5 and 6.

41. Leonard W. Weiss, "Concentration and Labor Earnings," *American Economic Review* 56. 1, (Mar. 1966): 96–117.

42. See Appendix.

43. See chapter 6 for more information.

44. Michael J. Arendes, "Tonnage Index Plunged in April," *Transport Topics* 14 June 1994: 27.

45. Barry T. Hirsch, "Trucking Deregulation and Labor Earnings: Is the Union Premium a Compensating Differential?" *Journal of Labor Economics* 11.2 (1993): 279–301.

46. Hirsch, "Trucking Regulation, Unionization and Labor Earnings: 1973–85," *Journal of Human Resources*.

47. Pustay, "Deregulation and the U.S. Trucking Industry," *The Age of Regulatory Reform* 252.

48. These data reflect average earnings of all employees of trucking companies, including drivers and other production employees, clerical employees, and management.

49. The adjusted partial R^2 measures the relative influence of all predictors on the dependent variable, wages. For example, it supplies a measure of the effect of the Teamsters Union on wages, with all possible relationships between the Teamsters and other independent variables taken out. The dramatic increase in the adjusted R^2 for the union and the market share of the firm shows the most important influences on wages.

50. These figures are based on data available to the author for years prior to 1990. In 1990 the American Trucking Associations reclassified carriers according to their own understanding of the type of operations in which they were engaged. Thus, while the ICC classified 191 carriers as "Class I General Freight Carriers Engaged in Intercity Service," the ATA classified 500 carriers in that category. While the ATA's reclassification may have been justified (as the ICC had not made such a reclassification since deregulation, despite massive industrial restructuring), the reclassification introduced tremendous discontinuities in the data. However, the general trend is consistent. Non-union earnings were 76.3% of union earnings in 1987, and 75.7% of union earnings in 1990. Earnings data also understate the gap, as union members consciously accepted lower wages in trade for higher benefits during this period.

51. Winston, Corsi, Grimm, and Evans, *The Economic Effects of Surface Freight Deregulation* 5.

52. Wage data do not include benefits. In terms of total compensation, union wage declines may overstate their losses. The Teamsters elected to freeze wages during the early and mid-1980s and shift revenue increases to their Health and Welfare Funds. The wage data reported here do not reflect increases in health and welfare payments, except that lower wages may be compensated by retention of higher benefits.

Chapter 6

1. Harold M. Levinson, "Trucking," *Collective Bargaining: Contemporary American Experience*, ed. Gerald G. Somers (Madison, Wisc.: Industrial Relations Research Association, 1980) 111–19.

2. Some operations, especially in LTL, pay either by the number of miles actually driven, or by an agreed standard mileage that has been verified as the actual mileage between two points according to an agreed routing. Other operations, especially irregular route TL carriers, pay drivers according to some standard, such as the *Rand McNally Road Atlas* or *Household Movers Guide*. These systems calculate mileage according to the absolute shortest distance, regardless of highway, which usually is much shorter than the true mileage driven.

3. Since all Master Freight carriers pay a reduced rate for new employees with an 18-month catch-up, I treat them as single-rate payers.

4. Layovers are periods of off-duty time required between "shifts." Layovers are normal between shifts of work approaching the maximum allowed by law. They are abnormal when forced mid-shift by circumstances out of the driver's control or when they are substantially longer than the statutory eight-hour break. Drivers may be forced to layover waiting for freight, to load or unload, for extended repairs, or otherwise waiting for a dispatch. The union contract defines as abnormal any layover exceeding some standard length, such as 11 hours, and union carriers pay excess layovers. Most non-union carriers do not.

5. Michael H. Belzer, "Collective Bargaining in the Trucking Industry: The Effects of Institutional and Economic Restructuring," diss., Cornell University, 1993, and Belzer, "Collective Bargaining after Deregulation: Do the Teamsters Still Count?" *Industrial and Labor Relations* Review 48 (1995).

6. The mean risk-shifting index for all surveyed carriers with valid data is 1.88, with a standard deviation of .84 (n = 201).

7. The standard economic argument, largely theoretical and recently disproven empirically by David E. Card and Alan B, Krueger, is that raising the minimum wage reduces employment, particularly of people the policy is supposed to help. See Card and Krueger, *Myth and Measurement: The New Economics of the Minimum Wage* (Princeton: Princeton University Press, 1995).

8. Conrad F. Fritsch, "Exemptions to the Fair Labor Standards Act, Transportation Sector," *Report of the Minimum Wage Study Commission*, ed. Minimum Wage Study Commission (Washington, D.C.: U.S. Government Printing Office, 1981) 151.

9. *Ibid* 154.

10. Michael H. Belzer, "Labor Law Reform: Some Lessons from the Trucking Industry," *The 47th Annual Meeting of the Industrial Relations Research* Association (Washington, D.C.: Industrial Relations Research Association, 1995) 403–13. Also see Dale Belman, Kristen A. Monaco, and Taggert J. Brooks, "And Lord, Let It Be Palletized: A Portrait of Truck Drivers' Work and Life" (Ann Arbor: University of Michigan Trucking Industry Program, 1998).

11. Chicago's powerful Local 705 agreed to implement a 45-hour workweek (that is, 45 hours before being paid overtime) in the 1982 tank contract, replacing a contract term providing overtime after eight hours daily. The contract further provided for the elimination of dedicated city boards, so city

drivers with 45 hours of local work could be sent on the road, where overtime does not apply, depriving them of overtime pay for any of their work.

12. Charles R. Perry, *Deregulation and the Decline of the Unionized Trucking Industry* (Philadelphia: Wharton Industrial Research Unit, 1986). See also Barry T. Hirsch, "Trucking Deregulation and Labor Earnings: Is the Union Premium a Compensating Differential?" *Journal of Labor Economics* 11.2 (1993): 287. See also Michael H. Belzer, *Paying the Toll: Economic Deregulation of the Trucking Industry* (Washington, D.C.: Economic Policy Institute, 1994) 43.

13. A worker seeking a job usually sets a minimum wage standard for jobs he finds acceptable. This reservation wage—the level below which a worker will not go to accept a job—is often based on previous wages and wage offers. Since drivers leaving the unionized sector can expect wage offers from 20% to 50% lower, they frequently resist and simply leave the trucking labor market.

14. These particular data come from *Financial and Operating Statistics*, an annual publication of the American Trucking Associations.

15. As indicated elsewhere, the University of Michigan Trucking Industry Program's driver survey finds that the average non-union driver works 70 hours per week. For this purpose, I am assuming a paid vacation (if included in earnings) is paid 40 hours for a vacation week. However, the driver survey also showed that 40% of all drivers get no paid vacation, so this caveat may be irrelevant.

16. It is very difficult to estimate real earnings for real labor time using the crude data available. In these calculations I have used average annual earnings of full-time-equivalent employees of Class I intercity general freight trucking carriers. I multiplied the average hours per week for non-union drivers reported by the University of Michigan driver survey by 52.25 weeks per year and divided average gross earnings by the number of hours worked. To arrive at hourly wage estimates corrected for overtime, as if these employees were covered by the FLSA, I changed 70 actual hours to 85 paid hours (40 hours straight time plus 30 hours at time-and-one-half). The exceedingly long hours worked by truck drivers magnifies the effect of the overtime exemption.

17. This calculation is based on a declining number of carriers, emblematic of the declining data quality and transformation in the industry. In 1977 870 carriers out of a possible 3,402 reported (a 27% ratio), but in 1992 only 103 carriers out of 1,493 reported (a 7% ratio), reflecting declining coverage of the data as a result of regulatory change and the change in the industry itself. The increase could be an artifact of the change in "who reports" or it could be a systematic change.

18. Elisa R. Braver, Carol W. Preusser, David F. Preusser, Herbert M. Baum, Richard Beilock, and Robert Ulmer, *Who Violates Work Hour Rules? A Survey of Tractor-Trailer Drivers* (Arlington, Va:. Insurance Institute for Highway Safety, 1992).

19. Belman, Monaco, and Brooks, "And Lord, Let It Be Palletized."

20. For another account of long driver hours, see also Lawrence J. Ouellet, *Pedal to the Metal: The Work Lives of Truckers* (Philadelphia: Temple University Press, 1994) 28.

21. Belman, Monaco, and Brooks, "And Lord, Let It Be Palletized."

22. Belzer, "Collective Bargaining after Deregulation," *Industrial and Labor Relations Review*, and Belzer, "*Labor Law Reform.*"

23. See Belzer, "Collective Bargaining after Deregulation," *Industrial and Labor Relations Review*.

24. Again, see the University of Michigan truck driver survey for data to support this contention.

25. Daniel Machalaba, "Long Haul: Trucking Firms Find It Is a Struggle to Hire and Retain Drivers," *Wall Street Journal* 28 Dec. 1993: A1, 5.

26. Machalaba, "Long Haul," *Wall Street Journal*. See also Jim McNamara, "Lorry Drivers Wanted for Long Haul: M.S. Carriers Looks to Britain for Qualified Hands," *Transport Topics*, (17 Jan. 1994): 12.

27. See C. D. Wylie, T. Shultz, James C. Miller, Merrill M. Mitler, and R. R. Mackie, *Commercial Motor Vehicle Driver Fatigue and Alertness Study* (Washington, D.C., and Ottawa: Federal Highway Administration of the U.S. Department of Transportation and Transport Canada, 1996), and see also University of Michigan Transportation Research Institute, "Potential Hours-of-Service Regulations for Commercial Drivers: Report of the Expert Panel on Review of the Federal Highway Administration Candidate Options for Hours of Service Regulations" (Ann Arbor: University of Michigan Transportation Research Institute, 1998).

28. See Belzer, "Collective Bargaining in the Trucking Industry," chapter 6; some data from 1991 trucking industry survey by author remain unpublished.

29. At least not at current rates within the current structure. Valuable freight that is worth moving at a higher price will shift to LTL carriers, large TL firms that move their long-distance freight by rail, or premium TL firms that are large enough to create hub-and-spoke or relay systems. Less valuable freight will wait. See Machalaba, "Long Haul," *Wall Street Journal* A5.

30. Machalaba, "Long Haul," *Wall Street Journal*. McNamara, "Lorry Drivers Wanted for Long Haul," *Transport Topics*.

31. Hirsch, "Trucking Deregulation and Labor Earnings," 294–95. The study covered the years 1983 through 1990.

32. Belzer, "Collective Bargaining after Deregulation," *Industrial and Labor Relations Review* 161–63.

Chapter 7

1. See Robert H. Frank and Philip J. Cook, *The Winner-Take-All Society: How More and More Americans Compete for Ever Fewer and Bigger Prizes, Encouraging Economic Waste, Income Inequality, and an Impoverished Cultural Life* (New York: Free Press, 1995).

2. Frank A. Smith, *Transportation in America: A Statistical Analysis of Transportation in the United States: Supplements, Updates and Corrections* (Waldorf, Md.: Eno Transportation Foundation, 1992).

3. Daniel Machalaba, "Long Haul: Trucking Firms Find It Is a Struggle to Hire and Retain Drivers," *Wall Street Journal* 28 Dec. 1993. See also John Larkin, "The Truckload Outlook Is Very Bullish. For LTL, We Are Optimistic Short-Term but Less Optimistic Long-Term," *Transport Topics* (24 Jan. 1994): 8.

4. See Michael H. Belzer, "Collective Bargaining after Deregulation: Do the Teamsters Still Count?" *Industrial and Labor Relations Review* 48 (1995).

5. Michael H. Belzer, "Collective Bargaining in the Trucking Industry: The Effects of Institutional and Economic Restructuring," diss., Cornell University, 1993; Machalaba, "Long Haul," *Wall Street Journal*.

6. Elisa R. Braver, Carol W. Preusser, Daniel F. Preusser, Herbert M. Baum, Richard Beilock, and Robert Ulmer, *Who Violates Work Hour Rules? A Survey of Tractor-Trailer Drivers* (Arlington, Va.: Insurance Institute for Highway Safety, 1992).

7. U.S. Congress, Office of Technology Assessment (OTA), *Gearing Up for Safety: Motor Carrier Safety in a Competitive Environment* (Washington, D.C.: U.S. Government Printing Office, 1988) 147–52. See also C. D. Wylie, T. Shultz, James C. Miller, Merrill M. Mitler, and R. R. Mackie, "Commercial Motor Vehicle Driver Fatigue and Alertness Study" (Washington, D.C., and Ottawa: Federal Highway Administration of the U.S. Department of Transportation and Transport Canada, 1996).

8. Monte Williams, "Faked Driver Logs Cited in Propane Truck Crash," *New York Times* 20 Aug. 1996, Section 1:28.

9. "Propane Carrier Pleads Guilty to Log Falsification," *Journal of Commerce* 1 Nov. 1996: 2B. See also "Propane Hauler Pleads Guilty to Falsifying Driver Logs," *HazMat Transport News* 29 Oct. 1996, and "Company Kept False Logs on Driver's Hours," *New York Times* 13 Oct., 1996, Section 1:44.

10. For a further discussion, see Gene C. Griffin, Julene M. Rodriguez, and Brenda K. Lantz, *Job Satisfaction of U.S. Commercial Drivers* (Fargo: North Dakota State University, Upper Great Plains Transportation Institute, 1993), Report #90.

11. There is little trucker-specific research on these problems. Certainly, from the perspective of public health policy and industrial hygiene, such a study would be valuable. See also Gregory A. Belenky, J. McKnight, Merrill M. Mitler, Alison Smiley, Louis Tijerina, Patricia F. Waller, Walter W. Wierwille, and David K. Willis, "Potential Hours-of-Service Regulations for Commercial Drivers: Report of the Expert Panel on Review of the Federal Highway Administration Candidate Options for Hours of Service Regulations" (Ann Arbor: University of Michigan Transportation Research Institute, 1998).

12. This section reads: "Nothing in this Act shall be construed as authorizing the execution or application of agreements requiring membership in a labor organization as a condition of employment in any State or Terri-

tory in which execution or application is prohibited by State or Territorial law."

13. Recent research suggests the presence of another factor in the LTL industry: reciprocal gift exchange. Reciprocal gift exchange, in trucking, is the exchange of higher than market wages in exchange for effort. Although the presence of reciprocal gift exchange has not been proven, it suggests that wages in LTL may remain higher than those in TL even in long-term equilibrium, absent collective bargaining. The amount of such premium is undetermined. See Stephen V. Burks, "The Origins of Parallel Segmented Labor and Product Markets: A Reciprocity-Based Agency Model with an Application to Motor Freight," diss., University of Massachusetts, 1999.

14. See Dale Belman, Kristen A. Monaco, and Taggert J. Brooks, "And Lord, Let It Be Palletized: A Portrait of Truck Drivers' Work and Life" (Ann Arbor: University of Michigan Trucking Industry Program, 1998).

15. For this purpose I divide average annual earnings by actual work hours less 10 days of paid holiday and vacation at the median; 40% of non-union drivers take no vacation days.

16. Method: 70 hours per week times 50.25 weeks gives 3,517.5 hours per year, plus 10 days of vacations and holidays gives 3,597.5 actual work hours. Dividing the average non-union earnings of $35,551 by 3,597.5 hours gives us $9.88 per hour. Assuming the application of FLSA rules, the average driver would be paid for 4,351.25 hours, and dividing the average annual earnings by 4,351.25 hours comes to $8.17 per hour.

17. To the ICC, Instruction 27 applied to Class I intercity motor carriers earning at least 75% of their revenue from the movement of intercity freight. Ironically, that definition disqualifies UPS, because of the amount of intra-city work.

Chapter 8

1. James A. Gross, *Broken Promise: The Subversion of the U.S. Labor Relations Policy, 1947–1994* (Philadelphia: Temple University Press, 1995).

2. Hamid Azari-Rad, Anne Yeagle, and Peter Philips, "The Effects of the Repeal of Utah's Prevailing Wage Law on the Labor Market in Construction," *Restoring the Promise of American Labor Law*, ed. Sheldon Friedman, Richard W. Hurd, Rudolph A. Oswald, and Ronald L. Seeber (Ithaca, N.Y.: ILR Press, 1995). See also Peter Philips, Garth Mangum, Norm Waitzman, and Anne Yeagle, "Losing Ground: Lessons from the Repeal of Nine 'Little Davis-Bacon' Acts," Unpublished article (Salt Lake City: University of Utah, 1995).

3. Norman J. Waitzman, "Worker Beware: The Relationship between the Strength of State Prevailing Wage Laws and Injuries in Construction, 1976–1991," unpublished report (Washington, D.C.: Center to Protect Workers' Rights, Feb. 1996).

4. U.S. Department of Housing and Urban Development, Office of the Inspector General, *HUD Audit Report on Monitoring and Enforcing Labor Standards* (Washington, D.C.: HUD, 1985).

5. This issue is addressed monthly in Peter Cockshaw's *Construction Labor News + Opinion*, a monthly construction labor newsletter. See, most recently, Rick Haglund, "Booming Building Industry Can't Fill Construction Jobs," *Ann Arbor News* 22 Nov. 1998: E1. Again, ironically the individuals and organizations cited in the article as complaining about the skilled labor shortage represent the non-union, anti-union forces within the construction industry, the forces that created the problem in the first place.

6. John S. Heywood and James H. Peoples, "Deregulation and the Prevalence of Black Truck Drivers," *Journal of Law and Economics* 37 (Apr. 1994): 133–55. See also Barry T. Hirsch and David A. Macpherson, "Earnings and Employment in Trucking: Deregulating a Naturally Competitive Industry," *Regulatory Reform and Labor Markets*, ed. James H. Peoples (Norwell, Mass.: Kluwer, 1997).

7. See Glossary for definitions.

8. Mark Harvey, *Towards the Insecurity Society: The Tax Trap of Self-Employment* (London: Institute of Employment Rights, 1995).

Glossary

For brief definitions of labor relations terms, see Robert E. Doherty, *Industrial and Labor Relations Terms: A Glossary* (Ithaca, N.Y.: ILR Press, 1979 [1989 edition]).

1. For detailed information on this complex area of law, see the following sources, Doherty, Robert E. *Industrial and Labor Relations Terms: A Glossary*. Ithaca: ILR / Cornell University Press, 1989, page 5; Leslie, Douglas L. *Labor Law in a Nutshell*. 2nd ed. St. Paul, MN: West Publishing, 19867, pages 122–5 ff.

Bibliography

American Trucking Associations. *American Trucking Trends*. Alexandria, Va.: Financial and Operating Statistics Service, Department of Statistical Analysis, American Trucking Associations, 1979 and 1982.

———. *1992 Financial and Operating Statistics; Motor Carrier Annual Report*. Alexandria, Va.: American Trucking Associations, 1993. Data used also from 1977, 1982, 1987, and 1990.

Anderson, Dale G., and Ray C. Huttsell. "Trucking Regulation, 1935–1980." *Regulation and Deregulation of the Motor Carrier Industry*. Ed. John Richard Felton and Anderson. Ames: Iowa State University Press, 1989.

Arendes, Michael J. "Tonnage Index Plunged in April." *Transport Topics* June 1994:27.

Azari-Rad, Hamid, Anne Yeagle, and Peter Philips. "The Effects of the Repeal of Utah's Prevailing Wage Law on the Labor Market in Construction." *Restoring the Promise of American Labor Law*. Ed. Sheldon Friedman, Richard W. Hurd, Rudolph A. Oswald, and Ronald L. Seeber. Ithaca, N.Y.: ILR Press, 1995.

Bearth, Daniel P. "Cass Logistics Formula Flaw Inflates Deregulation Savings." *Transport Topics*. 14 June 1999, page 4.

Beilock, Richard. "Is Regulation Necessary for Value-of-Service Pricing?" *Rand Journal of Economics* 16.1 (1985): 93–102.

Belenky, Gregory A., J. McKnight, Merrill M. Mitler, Alison Smiley, Louis Tijerina, Patricia F. Waller, Walter W. Wierwille, and David K. Willis. "Potential Hours-of-Service Regulations for Commercial Drivers: Report of the Expert Panel on Review of the Federal Highway Administration Candidate Options for Hours of Service Regulations." Ann Arbor: University of Michigan Transportation Research Institute, 1998.

Belman, Dale, Kristen A. Monaco, and Taggert J. Brooks. "And Lord, Let It Be Palletized: A Portrait of Truck Drivers' Work and Life." Ann Arbor: University of Michigan Trucking Industry Program, 1998.

Belzer, Michael H. "The Transformation of Labor Relations in the Trucking Industry since Deregulation." M.S. Thesis. Cornell University, 1990.

———. "Collective Bargaining in the Trucking Industry: The Effects of Institutional and Economic Restructuring." Diss. Cornell University, 1993.

———. "The Motor Carrier Industry: Truckers and Teamsters under Siege."

Contemporary Collective Bargaining in the Private Sector. Ed. Paula B. Voos. Madison, Wisc.: Industrial Relations Research Association, 1994.

———. *Paying the Toll: Economic Deregulation of the Trucking Industry.* Washington, D.C.: Economic Policy Institute, 1994.

———. "Collective Bargaining after Deregulation: Do the Teamsters Still Count?" *Industrial and Labor Relations Review* 48 (1995): 636–55.

———. "Labor Law Reform: Some Lessons from the Trucking Industry." *The 47th Annual Meeting of the Industrial Relations Research Association.* Ed. Paula B. Voos. Washington, D.C.: Industrial Relations Research Association, 1995.

Belzer, Michael H., and Richard W. Hurd. "Government Oversight, Union Democracy, and Labor Racketeering: Lessons from the Teamsters Experience." *Journal of Labor Research* 20.3 (1999): 343–65.

Benson, Herman. "Union Democracy Triumphs over Organized Crime." *Dissent* (1992): 138–42.

Black, Clementina. *Sweated Industry and the Minimum Wage.* London: Duckworth & Company, 1907.

Bohlander, George W., and Martin T. Farris. "Collective Bargaining in Trucking—The Effects of Deregulation." *Logistics and Transportation Review* 20.3 (1984): 223–38.

Boyle, H. Perry, Jr. "Trucking Market Segmentation, Part III: A Look at the Trucking Industry Life Cycle." Baltimore, Md.: Alex. Brown & Sons, Incorporated, 1993.

Braver, Elisa R., Carol W. Preusser, David F. Preusser, Herbert M. Baum, Richard Beilock, and Robert Ulmer. *Who Violates Work Hour Rules? A Survey of Tractor-Trailer Drivers.* Arlington, Va.: Insurance Institute for Highway Safety, 1992.

Breyer, Stephen G. *Regulation and Its Reform.* Cambridge: Harvard University Press, 1982.

Brill, Steven. *The Teamsters.* New York: Simon, 1978.

Bureau of National Affairs. "Teamsters, Employer Groups Begin National Master Freight Bargaining." *Daily Labor Report* 16 Jan. 1985: A-8.

———. "Teamsters Modify Voting Eligibility Policy to Settle Challenge to Master Freight Vote." *Daily Labor Report* 13 June 1985: A-2.

———. "Teamsters Locals Ratify New Contract Raising Pay and Benefits for UPS Employees." *Daily Labor Report* 24 Aug. 1987: A-9.

———. "Trucking Industry Talks Get Underway." *Daily Labor Report* 15 Jan. 1988: A-5.

———. "Teamsters Announce Ratification of National Master Freight Agreement." *Daily Labor Report* 20 May 1988: A-9.

———. "Teamsters and Freight Carrier Group Begin Talks on Master Trucking Accord." *Daily Labor Report* 27 Nov. 1990: A-6.

Burks, Stephen V. "Final Report: OTA Project on Trucking Industry Productivity." Washington: Office of Technology Assessment, 1995.

———. "The Origins of Parallel Segmented Labor and Product Markets: A Reciprocity-Based Agency Model with an Application to Motor Freight." Ph.D. Diss. University of Massachusetts, 1999.

Cadbury, Edward, and George Shann. *Sweating*. Social Service Handbooks No. 5. Ed. Percy Alden. London: Headley Brothers, 1907.

Capelle, Russell B., Jr. "Quarterly Survey of General Freight Carrier Operating Results; 1967 thru 2nd Quarter 1988." Alexandria, Va.: Economic Research Committee, Regular Common Carrier Conference, 1988.

Card, David E., and Alan B. Krueger. *Myth and Measurement: The New Economics of the Minimum Wage*. Princeton, N.J.: Princeton University Press, 1995.

Cassidy, William B. "Drug Testing: Rules Fleets Must Follow." *Fleet Owner* 85.4 (1990): 83–86.

———. "Shipper Codes Must Have Names: New Law Requires Changes in Rates on File." *Transport Topics* 17 Jan. 1994: 3.

Childs, William R. *Trucking and the Public Interest: The Emergence of Federal Regulation 1914–1940*. Knoxville: University of Tennessee Press, 1985.

Cohan, Leon. "Hit the Mark with Random Testing." *Transportation and Distribution* 33.3 (1992): 34–36.

Commons, John R. "Introduction." *History of Labour in the United States*. Ed. John R. Commons. New York: Macmillan, 1918. 2 vols.

"Company Kept False Logs on Driver's Hours." *New York Times*. 13 Oct. 1996, sec. 1: 44.

Conyngham, Michael. "I.C.C. Regulated Motor Carriers of General Freight under the National Master Freight Agreement That Terminated General Freight Operations from July 1, 1980 to May 30, 1993." Teamsters Research Department Report. Washington, D.C.: International Brotherhood of Teamsters, 1993.

Corsi, Thomas M. "Motor Carrier Industry Structure and Operations." *International Symposium on Motor Carrier Transportation*. Washington, DC: National Academy Press, 1993.

Corsi, Thomas M., Curtis M. Grimm, Ken G. Smith, and Raymond D. Smith. "Deregulation, Strategic Change, and Firm Performance among LTL Motor Carriers." *Transportation Journal* 31.1 (1991): 4–13.

Corsi, Thomas M., Curtis M. Grimm, Ken G. Smith, and Raymond D. Smith. "The Effects of LTL Motor Carrier Size on Strategy and Performance." *Logistics and Transportation Review* 28.2 (1992): 129–45.

Corsi, Thomas M., and Joseph R. Stowers. "Effects of a Deregulated Environment on Motor Carriers: A Systematic, Multi-Segment Analysis." *Transportation Journal* 30.3 (1991): 4–28.

Davis, Grant M., and Norman A. Weintraub. "Labor-Management Relations: ESOPs in the Trucking Industry." *Profit Sharing and Gain Sharing*. Ed. Myron J. Roomkin. Metuchen, N.J.: IMLR Press / Rutgers University and

The Scarecrow Press, 1990. 97–108 of *Institute of Management and Labor Relations Series*. Ed. James Chelius.

De Vany, A. S., and T. R. Saving. "Product Quality, Uncertainty, and Regulation: The Trucking Industry." *American Economic Review* 67.4 (1977): 583–94.

Dempsey, Paul Stephen, and William E. Thoms. *Law and Economic Regulation in Transportation*. Westport, Conn.: Quorum, 1986.

Derthick, Martha, and Paul J. Quirk. *The Politics of Deregulation*. Washington, DC: Brookings Institution, 1985.

Dobbs, Farrell. *Teamster Rebellion*. New York: Monad, 1972.

Doherty, Robert E. *Industrial and Labor Relations Terms: A Glossary*. Ithaca: ILR/Cornell University Press, 1989.

Duke, John. "Productivity Measures for Transportation Industries." *Highway Related Transportation Industries Productivity Measures Symposium*. Washington, D.C. 20 Nov. 1992.

Dulles, Foster Rhea. *Labor in America: A History*. New York: Thomas Y. Crowell, 1949.

Engel, Cynthia. "Competition Drives the Trucking Industry." *Monthly Labor Review* 121.4 (Apr. 1988): 34–41.

Enis, Charles R., and Edward A. Morash. "Some Aspects of Motor Carrier Size, Concentration Tendencies, and Performance after Deregulation." *Akron Business and Economic Review* 18.1 (1987): 82–94.

Felton, John Richard. "Background of the Motor Carrier Act of 1935." *Regulation and Deregulation of the Motor Carrier Industry*. Ed. Felton and Dale G. Anderson. Ames: Iowa State University Press, 1989.

———. "Motor Carrier Act of 1980: An Assessment." *Regulation and Deregulation of the Motor Carrier Industry*. Ed. Felton and Dale G. Anderson. Ames: Iowa State University Press, 1989.

Filgas, James F., and L. L. Waters. *Yellow in Motion: A History of Yellow Freight System, Incorporated*. Overland Park, Kan: Yellow Freight System, 1987.

Frank, Robert H., and Philip J. Cook. *The Winner-Take-All Society: How More and More Americans Compete for Ever Fewer and Bigger Prizes, Encouraging Economic Waste, Income Inequality, and an Impoverished Cultural Life*. New York: Free Press, 1995.

Frew, James R. "The Existence of Monopoly Profits in the Motor Carrier Industry." *Journal of Law and Economics* 24.2 (1981): 289–315.

Friedlaender, Ann F. *The Dilemma of Freight Transport Regulation*. Washington, D.C.: Brookings Institution, 1969.

Friedlaender, Ann F., Richard H. Spady, and S. Judy Wang Chiang. "Regulation and the Structure of Technology in the Trucking Industry." *Productivity Measurement in Regulated Industries*. Ed. Thomas G. Cowing and Rodney E. Stevenson. New York: Academic, 1981. 77–106.

Friedman, Samuel R. *Teamsters Rank and File: Power, Bureaucracy, and Rebellion at Work and in a Union*. New York: Columbia University Press, 1982.

Fritsch, Conrad F. "Exemptions to the Fair Labor Standards Act, Transportation Sector." *Report of the Minimum Wage Study Commission.* Ed. Minimum Wage Study Commission. Washington, D.C.: U.S. Government Printing Office, 1981. 151–86.

Furlong, Tom. "Gasoline Tankers Seen as 'Rolling Bombs' of the Road." *Los Angeles Times* 21 Sept. 1992: A1.

Garnel, Donald. *The Rise of Teamster Power in the West.* Berkeley: University of California Press, 1972.

Gerhold, Dorian. *Road Transport before the Railways: Russell's London Flying Waggons.* Cambridge: Cambridge University Press, 1993.

Glaskowsky, Nicholas A. *Effects of Deregulation on Motor Carriers.* 2nd ed. Westport, Conn.: Eno Foundation, 1990.

Griffin, Gene C., Julene M. Rodriguez, and Brenda K. Lantz. *Job Satisfaction of U.S. Commercial Drivers.* Fargo: North Dakota State University, Upper Great Plains Transportation Institute, 1993, Report #90.

Grimm, Curtis M., Thomas M. Corsi, and Judith L. Jarrell. "U.S. Motor Carrier Cost Structure under Deregulation." *Logistics and Transportation Review* 25.3 (1989): 231–49.

Gross, James A. "The Demise of the National Labor Policy: A Question of Social Justice." *Restoring the Promise of American Labor Law.* Ed. Sheldon Friedman, Richard W. Hurd, Rudolph A. Oswald, and Ronald L. Seeber. Ithaca, N.Y.: ILR Press, 1994.

———. *Broken Promise: The Subversion of U.S. Labor Relations Policy, 1947–1994.* Philadelphia: Temple University Press, 1995.

Haglund, Rick. "Booming Building Industry Can't Fill Construction Jobs." *Ann Arbor News* 22 Nov. 1998: E1.

Hamilton, Dane. "Troopers Begin Roadside Testing of Truckers for Alcohol Use in N.J." *Journal of Commerce* 29 Jan. 1993: B4, 3.

Hamilton, Dane, and Stephanie Nall. "Truckers Support New Rules for Drug and Alcohol Testing." *Journal of Commerce* 14 Dec. 1992: B2, 2.

Harmatuck, Donald J. "Motor Carrier Cost Function Comparisons." *Transportation Journal* 31.4 (1990): 31–46.

Harper, Donald V., and James C. Johnson. "The Potential Consequences of Deregulation of Transportation Revisited." *Land Economics* 63.2 (1987): 137–46.

Harvey, Mark. *Towards the Insecurity Society: The Tax Trap of Self-Employment.* London: Institute of Employment Rights, 1995.

Heywood, John S., and James H. Peoples. "Deregulation and the Prevalence of Black Truck Drivers." *Journal of Law and Economics* 37 (1994): 133–55.

Hirsch, Barry T. "Trucking Regulation, Unionization and Labor Earnings: 1973–85." *Journal of Human Resources* 23.3 (1988): 296–319.

———. "Trucking Deregulation and Labor Earnings: Is the Union Premium a Compensating Differential?" *Journal of Labor Economics* 11.2 (1993): 279–301.

Hirsch, Barry T., and David A. Macpherson. "Earnings and Employment in Trucking: Deregulating a Naturally Competitive Industry." *Regulatory Reform and Labor Markets*. Ed. James H. Peoples. Norwell, Mass.: Kluwer, 1997.

Hobson, John A. *Problems of Poverty: An Inquiry into the Industrial Condition of the Poor*. 8th ed. London: Methuen & Company, 1913.

Ingersoll, Bruce. "Rules to Test Transportation Workers for Alcohol Are Proposed by Agency." *Wall Street Journal* 11 Dec. 1992: A2, 4.

Interstate Commerce Commission, Bureau of Accounts. *Transport Statistics in the United States; Motor Carriers, Part 2*. Washington, D.C.: Interstate Commerce Commission, Bureau of Accounts, 1977–1990.

Interstate Commerce Commission. *The U.S. Motor Carrier Industry Long After Deregulation*. Washington, D.C.: The Interstate Commerce Commission, 1992.

James, Ralph, and Estelle Dinerstein James. *Hoffa and the Teamsters: A Study of Union Power*. Princeton, N.J.: Van Nostrand, 1965.

Kahn, Alfred E. *The Economics of Regulation*. Cambridge, Mass.: MIT Press, 1988.

Kane, Edward J. "Interaction of Financial and Regulatory Innovation." *American Economics Association Papers and Proceedings* 78.2 (1988): 328–34.

Katz, Harry C. "The Decentralization of Collective Bargaining: A Literature Review and Comparative Analysis." *Industrial and Labor Relations Review* 47 (1993): 3–22.

Keaton, Mark H. "Economies of Density and Structure of the Less-Than-Truckload Motor Carrier Industry since Deregulation." *Proceedings of the Transportation Research Forum, 36th Annual Meeting*. Arlington, Va.: Transportation Research Forum, 1994. 59–74.

Keeler, Theodore E. "Deregulation and Scale Economies in the U.S. Trucking Industry: An Econometric Extension of the Survivor Principle." *Journal of Law and Economics* 32 (1989): 229–53.

Kerr, Clark. "The Balkanization of Labor Markets." *Labor Mobility and Economic Opportunity*. Ed. E. Wight Bakke. New York: Technology Press of the Massachusetts Institute of Technology, and John Wiley and Sons, 1954. 92–110.

Kerr, Clark, and Abraham Siegel. "The Inter-Industry Propensity to Strike." *Industrial Conflict*. Ed. Arthur Kornhauser, Robert Dubin, and Arthur M. Ross. New York: McGraw Hill, 1954.

Khan, M. A., and Roger Reinsch. "The Deregulation Debate Continues: Is ICC Control over the Trucking Industry Necessary?" *Mid-Atlantic Journal of Business* 26.1 (1989): 67–79.

Klem, Richard. "Market Structure and Conduct." *Regulation of Entry and Pricing in Truck Transportation*. Ed. Paul W. MacAvoy and John W. Snow. Washington, D.C.: American Enterprise Institute for Public Policy Research, 1977. 119–38.

Kling, Robert W. "Deregulation and Structural Change in the LTL Motor Freight Industry." *Transportation Journal* 30.3 (1990): 47–53.

Kochan, Thomas A., Harry C. Katz, and Robert B. McKersie. *The Transformation of American Industrial Relations*. New York: Basic Books, 1986.

Kochan, Thomas, A., and Harry C. Katz. *Collective Bargaining and Industrial Relations*. Homewood, Ill.: Irwin, 1988.

Krantz, Les. *The National Business Employment Weekly Jobs Rated Almanac*. New York: J. Wiley, 1995.

Krause, Kristen S. "'Race to the Bottom': Contract Drivers in Airborne Trucks and Uniforms Paid Half the Wages, No Benefits for Same Work." *Traffic World* 27 July, 1998.

La Botz, Dan. *Rank-and-File Rebellion*. New York: Verso, 1990.

Larkin, John. "The Truckload Outlook Is Very Bullish. For LTL, We Are Optimistic Short-Term but Less Optimistic Long-Term." *Transport Topics* 24 Jan. 1994: 8.

Leiter, Robert D. *The Teamsters Union: A Study of Its Economic Impact*. New York: Bookman, 1957.

Leslie, Douglas L. *Labor Law in a Nutshell*. 2nd ed. St. Paul, MN: West Publishing, 1986.

Levinson, Harold M. "Collective Bargaining and Technological Change in the Trucking Industry." *Collective Bargaining and Technological Change in American Transportation*. Ed. Levinson, Charles M. Rehmus, Joseph P. Goldberg, and Mark C. Kahn. Evanston, Ill.: Northwestern University Transportation Center, 1971.

———. "Trucking." *Collective Bargaining: Contemporary American Experience*. Ed. Gerald G. Somers. Madison, Wisc.: Industrial Relations Research Association, 1980.

Locklin, D. Philip. *Economics of Transportation*. 7th ed. Homewood, Ill.: Irwin, 1972.

Machalaba, Daniel. "Long Haul: Trucking Firms Find It Is a Struggle to Hire and Retain Drivers." *Wall Street Journal* 28 Dec. 1993: A1, 5.

Mansfield, Edwin. *Applied Microeconomics*. New York: Norton, 1994.

McNamara, Jim. "Lorry Drivers Wanted for Long Haul: M.S. Carriers Looks to Britain for Qualified Hands." *Transport Topics* 17 Jan. 1994: 12.

Methvin, Eugene H. "Additional Views of Commissioner Eugene Hilburn Methvin." *The Edge: Organized Crime, Business, and Labor Unions Appendix*. Washington, D.C.: U.S. Government Printing Office, 1985.

Moore, Thomas Gale. "The Beneficiaries of Trucking Regulation." *Journal of Law and Economics* 21.2 (1978): 327–43.

———. "Transportation Policy." *Regulation* 11.3 (1988): 57–62.

———. "Unfinished Business in Motor Carrier Deregulation." *Regulation* 14.3 (1991): 49–57.

Nall, Stephanie. "DOT Proposes New Drug, Alcohol Test Rules." *Journal of Commerce* 11 Dec. 1992: A3, 1.

Nebesky, William, B. Starr McMullen, and Man-Keung Lee. "Market Power in the U.S. Motor Carrier Industry." Annual Meeting of the Transportation Research Forum. Daytona Beach, Fla. 3–5 Nov. 1994.

Noll, Roger G. "Regulation after Reagan." *Regulation* 11.3 (1988): 13–20.

Ouellet, Lawrence J. *Pedal to the Metal: The Work Lives of Truckers*. Philadelphia: Temple University Press, 1994.

Perry, Charles R. *Deregulation and the Decline of the Unionized Trucking Industry*. Philadelphia: Wharton Industrial Research Unit, 1986.

Philips, Peter, and Cihan Bilginsoi. "Prevailing Wage Regulations and School Construction Costs: Evidence from British Columbia." *Journal of Education Finance* (forthcoming).

Philips, Peter, Garth L. Mangum, Norman J. Waitzman, and Anne Yeagle "Construction Safety Put at Risk." *New Solutions* 6.1 (1995): 77–83.

Philips, Peter, Garth L. Mangum, Norm Waitzman, and Anne Yeagle. "Losing Ground: Lessons from the Repeal of Nine 'Little Davis-Bacon' Acts." Salt Lake City: University of Utah, 1995. Unpublished article.

Philips, Peter, Hamid Azari-Rad, and Anne Yeagle. "The Effect of the Repeal of Utah's Prevailing Wage Law on the Construction Labor Market." *Restoring the Promise of American Labor Law*. Ed. Sheldon Friedman, Richard W. Hurd, Rudolph A. Oswald, and Ronald L. Seeber. Ithaca, NY: ILR Press, 1994. 207–21.

Philips, Peter, and Norman Waitzman. "The Effects of Unionization and State Prevailing Wage Laws on Injuries in Construction, 1976 to 1991." *Abstracts* of the American Public Health Association, 124th Annual Meeting, November 17–21, 1996. New York City, entitled: *Empowering the Disadvantaged, Social Justice in Public Health*, p. 407.

"Propane Carrier Pleads Guilty to Log Falsification." *Journal of Commerce* 1 Nov. 1996: 2B.

"Propane Hauler Pleads Guilty to Falsifying Driver Logs." *HazMat Transport News* 29 Oct. 1996.

Pustay, Michael W. "Regulatory Reform and the Allocation of Wealth: An Empirical Analysis." *Quarterly Review of Economics and Business* 23.1 (1983): 19–28.

———. "Deregulation and the U.S. Trucking Industry." *The Age of Regulatory Reform*. Ed. Kenneth J. Button and Dennis Swann. Oxford: Clarendon Press, 1989.

Rakowski, James P. "Marketing Economies and the Results of Trucking Deregulation in the Less-Than-Truckload Sector." *Transportation Journal* 28 (1988): 11–28.

Reagan, Michael D. *Regulation: The Politics of Policy*. Boston: Little, 1987.

Roberts, Paul O. "Comments on 'The U.S. Motor Carrier Industry Long after Deregulation.'" *Proceedings of the 34th Annual Meeting of the Transportation Research Forum* 21–23 Oct. 1992. [Pre-meeting proceedings]

Robyn, Dorothy. *Braking the Special Interests*. Chicago: University of Chicago Press, 1987.

Rose, Nancy L. "The Incidence of Regulatory Rents in the Motor Carrier Industry." *Rand Journal of Economics* 16.3 (1985): 299–318.

———. "Labor Rent Sharing and Regulation: Evidence from the Trucking Industry." *Journal of Political Economy* 95.6 (1987): 1146–78.

Sachs, Jeffrey D., and Howard J. Shatz. "Trade and Jobs in U.S. Manufacturing." *Brookings Papers on Economic Activity* 1 (1994): 1–84.

Saposs, David J. "Colonial and Federal Beginnings (to 1827)." *History of Labour in the United States*. Ed. John R. Commons. New York: Macmillan, 1918. 25–165. Vol. 1.

Schlesinger, Paul R. "Motor Carrier Industry: Traditional Small-Shipment Truckers Cope with an Uncertain Market; National Carriers Fighting Decay? Prospects for 1993 and Beyond." *Industry Viewpoint*. New York: Donaldson, Lufkin & Jenrette, 8 April 1993.

Schmiechen, James A. *Sweated Industries and Sweated Labor: The London Clothing Trades, 1860–1914*. Urbana: University of Illinois Press, 1984.

Shepherd, William G. *The Economics of Industrial Organization*. Englewood Cliffs: Prentice-Hall, 1979.

Simons, Henry C. *Economic Policy for a Free Society*. Chicago: University of Chicago Press, 1948.

Sloane, Arthur A. *Hoffa*. Cambridge, Mass.: MIT Press, 1991.

Smith, Frank A. *Transportation in America: A Statistical Analysis of Transportation in the United States*. Waldorf, Md.: Eno Transportation Foundation, 1991.

———. *Transportation in America: A Statistical Analysis of Transportation in the United States: Supplements, Updates and Corrections, December 1991*. Waldforf, Md.: Eno Transportation Foundation, 1992.

Snow, John W. "The Problem of Motor Carrier Regulation and the Ford Administration's Proposal for Reform." *Regulation of Entry and Pricing in Truck Transportation*. Ed. Paul W. MacAvoy and Snow. Washington, D.C.: American Enterprise Institute for Public Policy Research, 1977.

Snow, John W., and Stephen Sobotka. "Certificate Values." *Regulation of Entry and Pricing in Truck Transportation*. Ed. Paul W. MacAvoy and Snow. Washington, D.C.: American Enterprise Institute for Public Policy Research, 1977. 153–56.

Spady, Richard H., and Ann F. Friedlaender. "Hedonic Cost Functions for the Regulated Trucking Industry." *Bell Journal of Economics* 9.1 (1978): 159–79.

Swan, Peter F. "The Effect of Changes in Operations on Less-Than-Truckload Motor Carrier Productivity and Survival." Diss. University of Michigan, 1997. 192.

Swann, Dennis. "The Regulatory Scene." *The Age of Regulatory Reform*. Ed. Kenneth J. Button and Swann. Oxford: Clarendon Press, 1989.

Sweeney, Daniel J. "Trucking: What's Still Regulated." *Handling and Shipping Management* (Aug. 1986): 11.

Sweeney, Daniel J., Charles J. McCarthy, Steven J. Kalish, and John M. Cutler, Jr. *Transportation Deregulation: What's Deregulated and What Isn't.* Washington, D.C.: National Small Shipments Traffic Conference, 1986.

Taff, Charles A. *Commercial Motor Transportation.* Centreville, Md.: Cornell Maritime, 1986.

Teamsters for a Democratic Union. "We Are the Majority: UPS Members Reject, IBT Imposes Contract." *Convoy Dispatch* Oct. 1987: 1.

———. "Members Contest NMFA Ratification: Mathis Says 36% Yes Is Good Enough for Him." *Convoy Dispatch* July 1988: 1.

———. "Whistle Blows on OSHA: Enforce Worker Protections." *Convoy Dispatch* Jan./Feb. 1989: 6–7.

———. "Teamsters Target Issues, Plan Strategy." *Convoy Dispatch* Dec. 1993/Jan. 1994: 3.

Tolchin, Martin. "U.S. Imposes New Alcohol Test Rules." *New York Times* 4 Feb. 1994: A15.

U.S. Congress, Office of Technology Assessment. *Gearing Up for Safety: Motor Carrier Safety in a Competitive Environment.* Washington, D.C.: U.S. Government Printing Office, 1988.

U.S. Department of Labor, Bureau of Labor Statistics. *Productivity Measures for Selected Industries and Government Services.* Washington, D.C.: U.S. Government Printing Office, 1988 and 1989.

———. *Employment, Hours, and Earnings, United States, 1909–90.* Washington, D.C.: U.S. Government Printing Office, 1991.

———. *Supplement to Employment and Earnings.* Washington, D.C.: U.S. Government Printing Office, 1991.

———. *BLS Handbook of Methods.* Bulletin 2414; September 1992 ed. Washington, D.C.: U.S. Government Printing Office, 1992.

U.S. Department of Labor, Employment and Standards Administration. *Minimum Wages and Maximum Hours.* Washington, D.C.: U.S. Government Printing Office, 1979.

Waitzman, Norman J. "Worker Beware: The Relationship between the Strength of State Prevailing Wage Laws and Injuries in Construction, 1976–1991." Unpublished report. Washington, D.C.: Center to Protect Workers' Rights, Feb. 1996.

Walton, Richard E., Joel Cutcher-Gershenfeld, and Robert B. McKersie. *Strategic Negotiations: A Theory of Change in Labor-Management Relations.* Boston: Harvard Business School Press, 1994.

Weiss, Leonard W. "Concentration and Labor Earnings." *American Economic Review* 56.1 (Mar. 1966): 96–117.

Williams, Monte. "Faked Driver Logs Cited in Propane Truck Crash." *New York Times* 20 Aug. 1996, Sect. 1: 28.

Wilson, George W. *Economic Analysis of Intercity Freight Transportation.* Bloomington: Indiana University Press, 1980.

Winston, Clifford, Thomas M. Corsi, Curtis M. Grimm, and Carol A. Evans. *The Economic Effects of Surface Freight Deregulation*. Washington, D.C.: Brookings Institution, 1990.

Wylie, C. D., T. Shultz, James C. Miller, Merrill M. Mitler, and R. R. Mackie. *Commercial Motor Vehicle Driver Fatigue and Alertness Study*. Washington, D.C., and Ottawa: Federal Highway Administration of the U.S. Department of Transportation and Transport Canada, 1996.

Index